IMAGES
of America

CORTEZ

I0807108

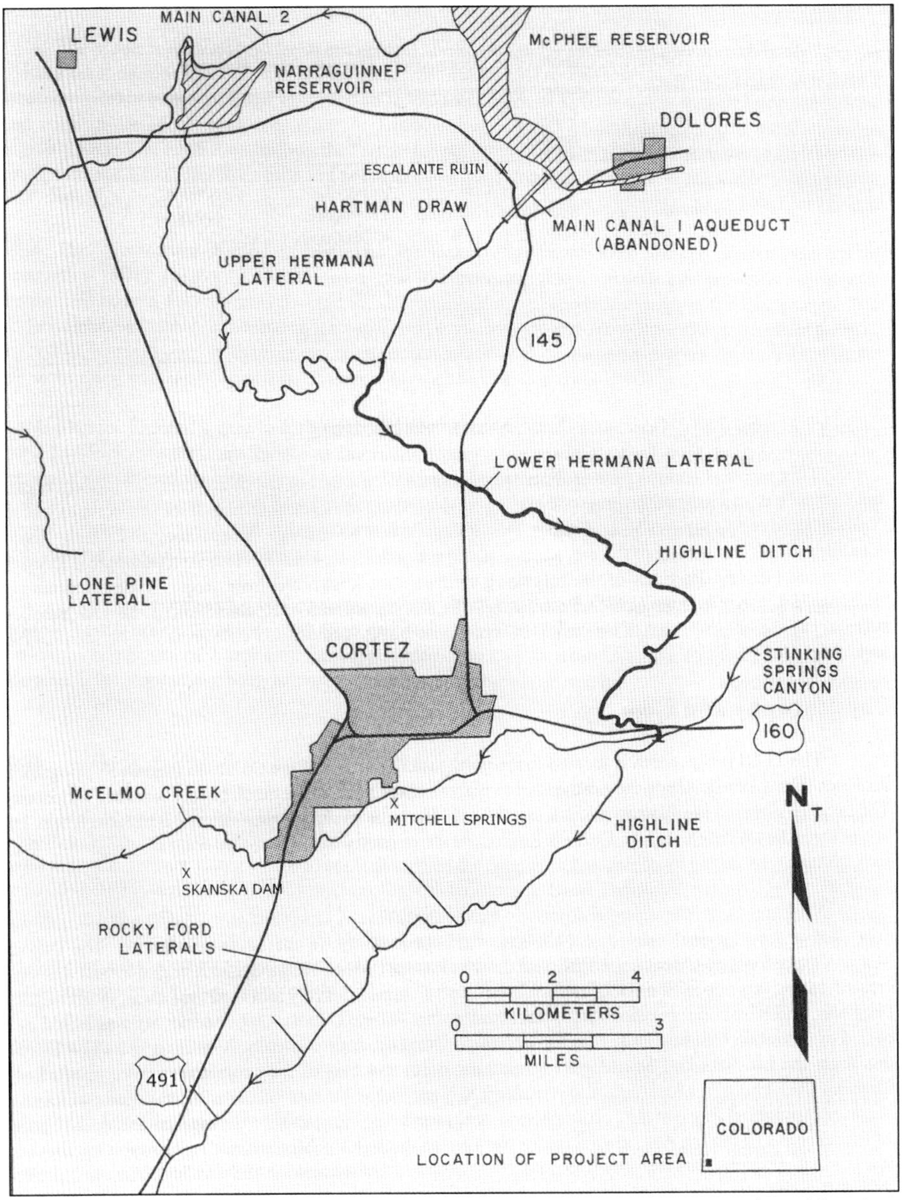

This map shows prehistoric and early sites of water resources, an essential and hard-to-find commodity in the high deserts of the San Juan River basin. Prehistoric water sites, springs, and reservoirs used by the Anasazi, incoming Spanish explorers, and white settlers are marked by an X. Early canals and ditches are included, as is the 1986 McPhee Reservoir project. (Courtesy of Anasazi Heritage Center and modified by the authors.)

On the Cover: Men and mules work together to dig the Main No. 1 Canal at Big Bend on the Dolores River, with financing secured from Boston investors by Maj. James W. Hanna. Begun in November 1885, water was diverted from the river on May 17, 1888. The month before, the *Montezuma Journal* reported that the one-mile tunnel connected to the No. 1, which would carry the water into Montezuma Valley, was "one of the greatest irrigation enterprises, not only in the state, but in the West." (Courtesy of Anasazi Heritage Center.)

IMAGES
of America

CORTEZ

Vila Schwindt, Janet Weeth,
and Dale Davidson

ARCADIA
PUBLISHING

ISBN 978-0-7385-7474-5

Published by Arcadia Publishing
Charleston, South Carolina

Printed in the United States of America

Library of Congress Control Number: 2010939493

For all general information, please contact Arcadia Publishing:
Telephone 843-853-2070
Fax 843-853-0044
E-mail sales@arcadiapublishing.com
For customer service and orders:
Toll-Free 1-888-313-2665

Visit us on the Internet at www.arcadiapublishing.com

To the people of Cortez, the enduring little city that could

Contents

ACKNOWLEDGMENTS

Captivated by the little city that sits on the edge of all that is beautiful in the American Southwest, the authors came together with a mutual respect for a town that has struggled mightily to establish itself in a valley with very little water but a full circle of fabulous views. Those who settle in Cortez either develop a fierce self-reliance and independence, or they come to fully appreciate the inhabitants who do. The authors would like to honor and thank all those who contributed to this book, hoping that we have not missed too many whom we contacted directly, knowing that others have contributed indirectly. Especially, we would like to mention Roy Paul, history aficionado; Fred Blackburn, historian and author; Carolyn Landis, Victoria Atkins, and others with Anasazi Heritage Center; Byron Maynes, president, First National Bank of Cortez; Larry McGee, president, Citizens State Bank of Cortez; Barbara Grist Photography; Barbara Breternitz; Larry Hauser; Mesa Verde National Park Service, especially Tara Travis and Lauren Finn at the Research Center; publisher Suzy Meyer and photographer Sam Green, *Cortez Journal*; Bobbe Jones, Empire Electric Association; Joanie Howland and staff, Cortez Public Library; Dawn Lightenburger, City of Cortez; Chris Eastin, vice president of RMD at Skanska; Ken Wright, Wright Water Engineers; First United Methodist Church of Cortez; St. Margaret Mary Catholic Church; Dotty Wayt; Helen McClellan; John Porter; Patsy Brown; Jack Winbourn; Bill Fraser; David Fraley; Lucy Hadley; Joyce Lawrence, Vivienne Kenyon, Tommy Johnson, June Head, and others with Montezuma County Historical Society; Troy Lichliter; the Henry Wilson family; the Basil Slavens family; Sue Patterson, Lorraine Vogel; Herma Watson; Saralynn Risenhoover; the Dr. Emil E. Johnson family; Keenan and Beverlee Ertel; William R. Hartley; Bill Finley; Steve Hinton; Richard Lindsay; Kent and Sharon Lindsay; Vince Conti; and Deb Avery and Brenda Hindmarsh, Cortez Cultural Center. A percentage of the authors' royalties from the sale of this book will benefit the Cortez Cultural Center. We absolutely must add our warm thanks to the editors and publishers at Arcadia for their excellent skills of patience, prodding, and occasional threats to ensure the success of this title.

Briefly, we would like to explain how the authors divided the responsibilities. Not one of us could have finished this book without the other two. Vila Schwindt wrote the manuscript. Janet Weeth made a huge effort in compiling an accurate timeline of events from roughly 1886 to 1986. Dale Davidson scanned and organized well over 200 photographs—beyond what appears here. We each used our best talents and supported the whole project by filling in any lack of information or photographs.

INTRODUCTION

For all its numerous streams . . . Colorado is a dry country.
—Hubert Howe Bancroft, 1890

Cortez is an unlikely little city. It lacks many of the amenities that support the development of a small urban area. It does not abut a railroad. It is not perched next to a dependable water supply such as a lake or river. Yet, Cortez perseveres despite these missing advantages. One has to ask why.

In the 1800s, people who came to the San Juan River basin had to want to come to the San Juan basin. The area was and still is remote. Travel was arduous across the rugged landscape that we admire today for its stark beauty. There were no wagon roads or trails. Immigrants traveled by horse—when they could afford one. Otherwise, they journeyed by foot. No comforts of civilization greeted them.

Why was this area desirable despite its remoteness? The valley is full of rich aeolian loams that are very productive with the addition of a little water. Sodbusters and ranchers saw this valley as a cornucopia of wealth awaiting their use. These farmlands were convenient to the western Ute Indian Agency and to the mines of the La Plata Mountains and Telluride. The farmers and ranchers needed supplies, as did the Ute Agency and the miners. And so Cortez endured.

The shortage of water was a more pressing problem. Prehistoric peoples of the area acknowledged water scarcity by their water conservation practices. Water continued to be an essential commodity, as illustrated by the high prices the Mitchell brothers charged for water at the turn of the century. James W. Hanna and M.J. Mack, early water entrepreneurs, employed extraordinary engineering efforts to move water to Cortez, a town they designed and for which they built cornerstone structures.

Although Cortez had very early rights on the Dolores River, if a drought dried up the river, Cortez would be waterless, too. Decades of political maneuvering brought a new solution. The Ute Mountain Utes were first promised water in 1899. The McPhee Reservoir project in the 1980s finally brought dependable water to them and to Cortez.

As the years pass, Cortez continues to support energy and mining booms tied to oil and uranium. It enjoys increasing trade with the Ute and Navajo American Indian peoples. The little city in southwest Colorado supports area tourism. It has outlasted economic downturns from the decline of extractive resources to competition from corporate agriculture. It has survived. Cortez is indeed "the little city that could."

—Janet Weeth, December 2010

One

Centuries Without Water

Cortez is a little city that stands on a low hill at the edges of the Colorado Rockies, the sentinel escarpment of Mesa Verde—a portion of which is known to the world as Mesa Verde National Park, the canyonlands of southeastern Utah, and the high deserts of New Mexico and Arizona. The area's climate receives a mean annual precipitation of about 13 inches. This varies because of differences in elevation and geography within the San Juan River basin.

All peoples who have called the Four Corners region their home over the past 14 centuries have had to concern themselves with regular water shortages. The Anasazi people used reservoirs, stone terraces, and check dams to irrigate fields of corn, beans, and squash. One theory holds that drought caused these people to migrate elsewhere by the 1300s, but archaeologists are still finding evidence and developing theories as to why the Anasazi abandoned their villages. They had established a resident population exceeding the number of people here now.

The first recorded European intrusion into the Cortez area was in 1761, when Don Juan Maria de Rivera explored the La Plata Mountains looking for wealth. A more well-known expedition was led by the Franciscan fathers Francisco Atanasio Dominguez and Silvestre Velez de Escalante in 1776. The Spaniards were well established in the American Southwest—in 1852, a little over 200 miles to the east in San Luis, settlers built the oldest continuously used irrigation system in Colorado.

Settlers arrived to stay in Montezuma Valley as early as 1871 as cattlemen, sodbusters, and American Indian traders. The US Congress–sponsored Hayden Survey in the early 1870s included William Henry Jackson. Jackson's photographs of the terrain and peoples helped demystify the American West after the Civil War. About the same time, the Ute Indian tribe ceded the San Juan Mountains to the government. This opened the area to development. Colorado joined the Union in 1876, and in its southwest corner a Ute tepee harbored a baby boy born to Reese Richards and his wife—the area's first white child.

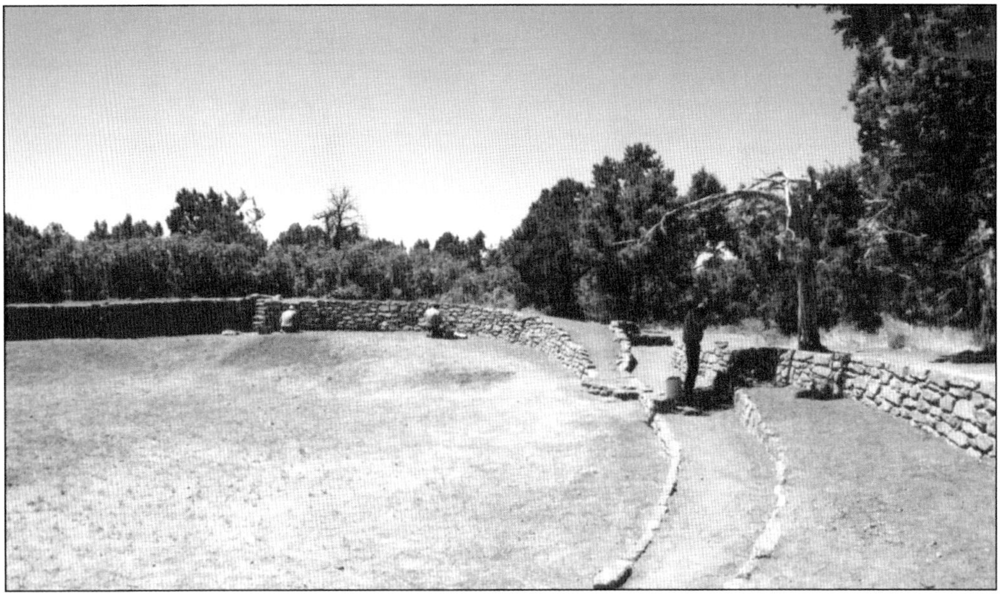

This photograph is of Mummy Lake on Mesa Verde. Archaeologists estimate that several thousand people lived in the area and that much of the top of Mesa Verde was cultivated. In 1969, a team of archaeologists led by Dr. David Breternitz excavated this man-made reservoir and a remarkable water supply system that irrigated crops of corn, beans, and squash for the Anasazi. Given the region's aridity, saving precipitation for year-round use was essential. (Courtesy of Mesa Verde National Park Research Center.)

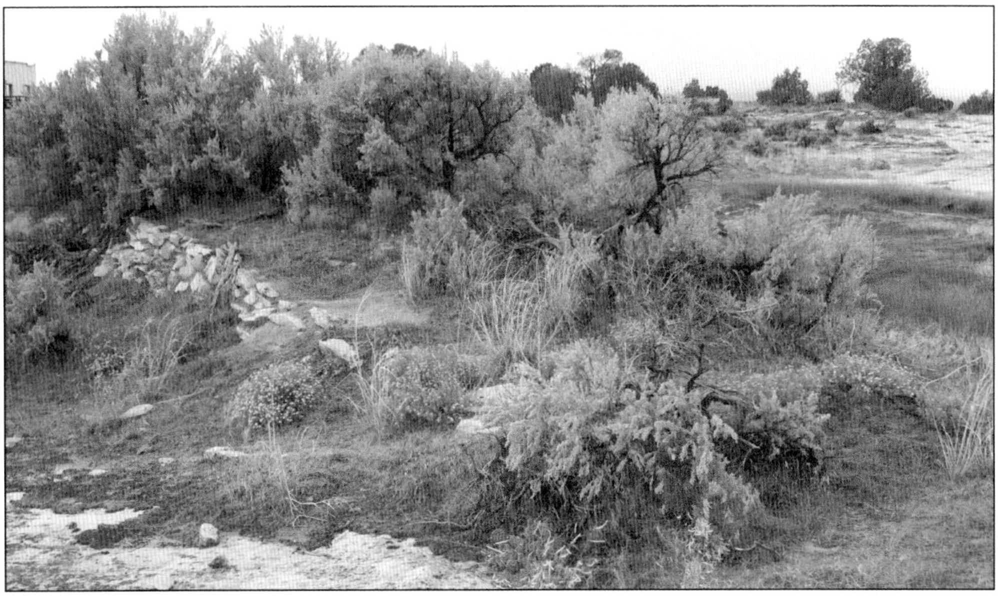

An Anasazi reservoir can be found southwest of Cortez near the Skanska headquarters that overlook McElmo Canyon. In this photograph, the remaining rock dam sits to the left, and the filled-in area that was the lake is to the right. Other smaller dams and reservoirs were built nearby. Anasazi farmers built reservoirs, canals, and stone terraces to conserve water and to settle the silt for domestic water use. The reservoir is recorded as noteworthy and estimated to be similar in capacity to Mummy Lake. (Photograph by Barbara Grist Photography.)

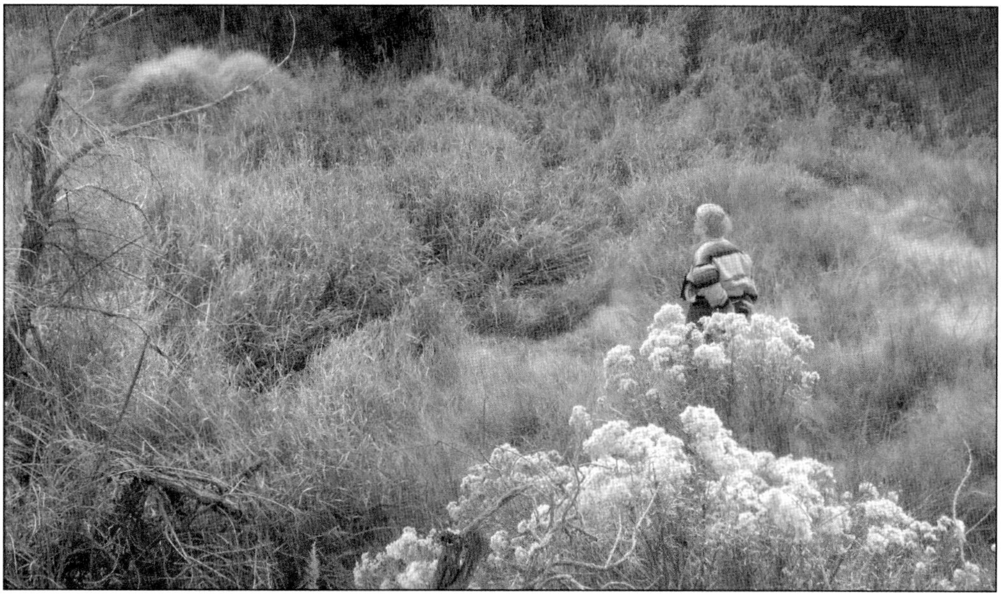

Author Janet Weeth explores the abandoned water source site of Mitchell Springs. The Mitchell brothers were friends of the Wetherill family. The brothers developed two springs, carved out of a settling pond next to the creek, and sold water to area residents for 25¢ a bucket, 50¢ a barrel, or 5¢ a glass. Henry later worked cattle for the Wetherills. Stanley traded goods up and down the valley. Herndon co-staked the Mitchell-Merrick Mine. Porter may have run a store at the springs. (Courtesy of Dale Davidson.)

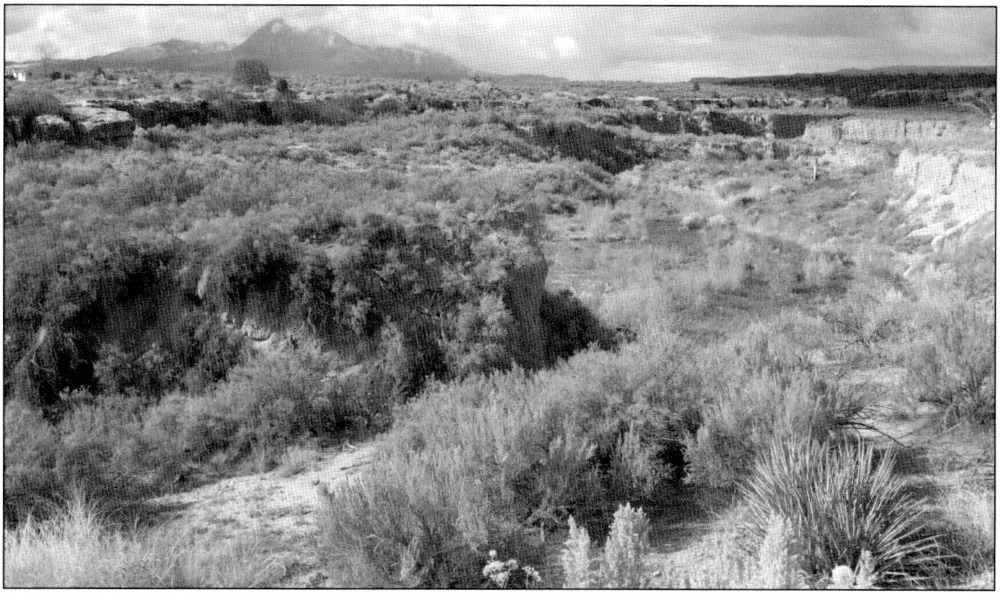

McElmo Canyon snakes toward the head of Sleeping Ute Mountain. This view is typical of what pioneers saw when they arrived in Montezuma Valley. The Mitchell Springs Anasazi ruins are on the rim in front of the Ute's "head" and halfway between the juniper and cottonwood in the canyon. Good spring water was available nearby when the site was occupied. The double cut of the canyon is due to the 1911 floods. The creek water is too alkaline to be potable. (Photograph by Barbara Grist Photography.)

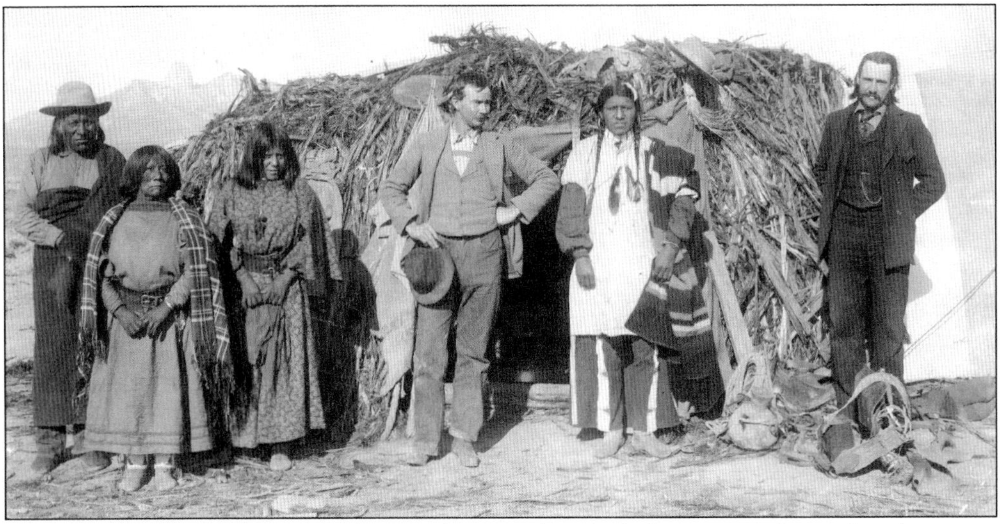

George Day photographed Ute Indians and two unidentified white men in front of a wikiup near Towaoc, Colorado, between 1880 and 1900. Trouble between Utes and whites was limited until May 1881, when Utes killed three white men. One of the men had whipped two Utes for stealing horses. Posses went out that summer to no effect. In June 1885, a group of cowboys attacked a Ute camp at Beaver Creek, north of Cortez, and killed 11. (Courtesy of Denver Public Library, Western History Collection, X-30348.)

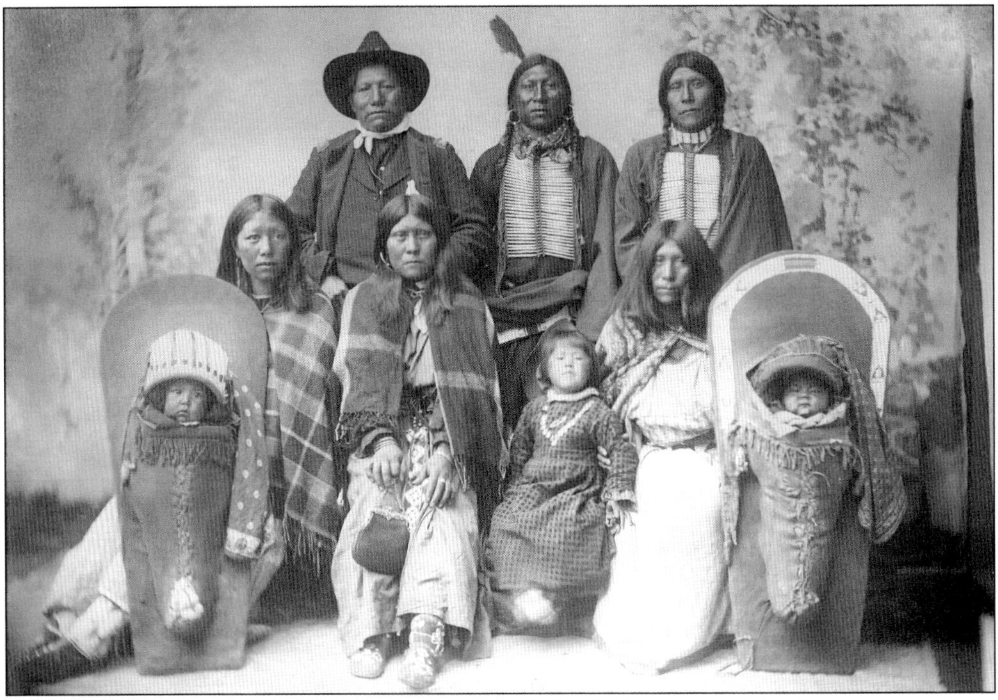

Ute chief Severo and his family pose for William Henry Jackson, a prolific photographer of the West and its peoples. The Utes exhibit the blending of cultures, as evidenced by the cradleboards for the babies, braids, blankets, and bone breastplates for the men, compared with the plaid dress for the young girl and the wool hat, vest, and coat on Severo. (Courtesy of History Colorado, William Henry Jackson Collection, Scan No. 20103577.)

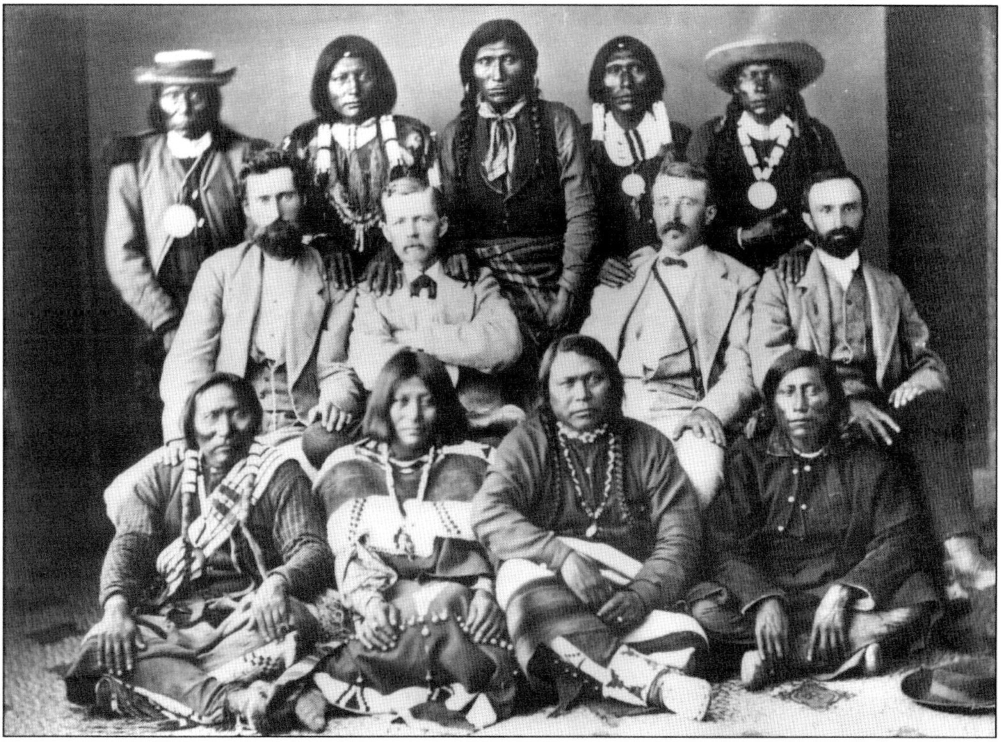

Ute tribal leaders pose in a formal portrait with US officials in Washington, DC, after they had negotiated the Brunot Treaty in 1873. This second land treaty with Utes removed four million acres from their reservation so Anglo mining ventures could be pursued. Pictured are, from left to right, (first row) Guerro, Chipeta, Chief Ouray, and Piah; (second row) Uriah M. Curtis, Maj. J.B. Thompson, Gen. Charles Adams, and Otto Mears; (third row) Washington, Susan, Johnson No. 2, Captain Jack, and John. (Courtesy of Denver Public Library, Western History Collection, X-30679.)

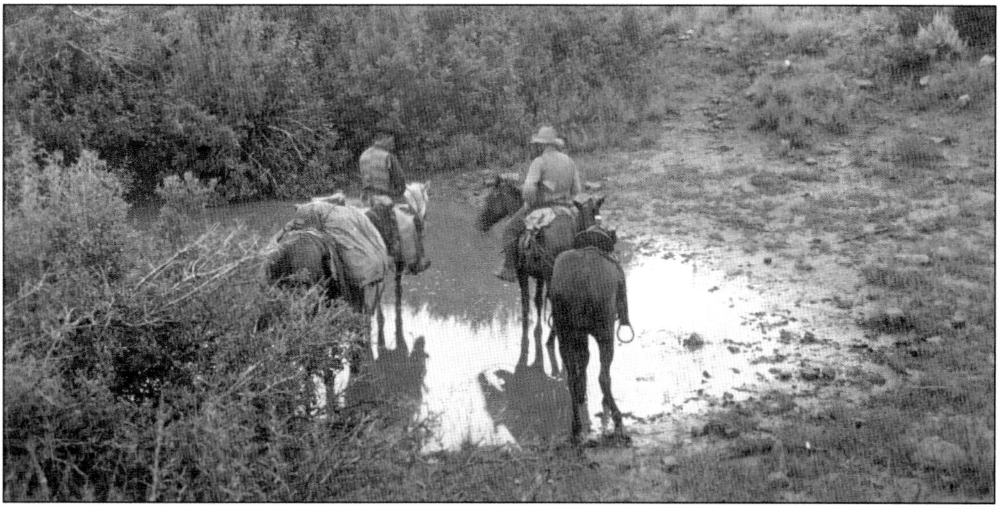

In arid country, no one takes water for granted. These cowboys and their horses use an ancient reservoir built by the Anasazi in Morefield Canyon. This photograph was taken atop Mesa Verde between 1873 and 1906, after the lands were ceded to the US government but before they became a national park. (Courtesy of Wright Water Engineers, Inc.)

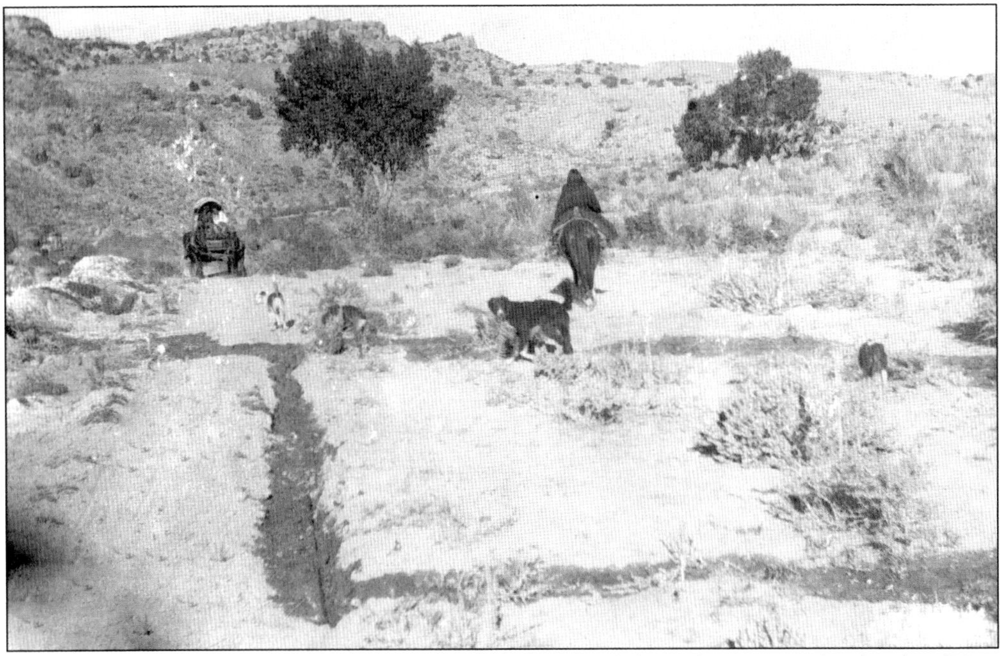

Winters were wet and roads were few. Just before the turn of the 20th century, this family of Utes was lucky to find a road through the sagebrush. White settlers had similar problems getting a wagon or car from one place to another, winter or summer, well into the 20th century. (Courtesy of Denver Public Library, Western History Collection, X-21032.)

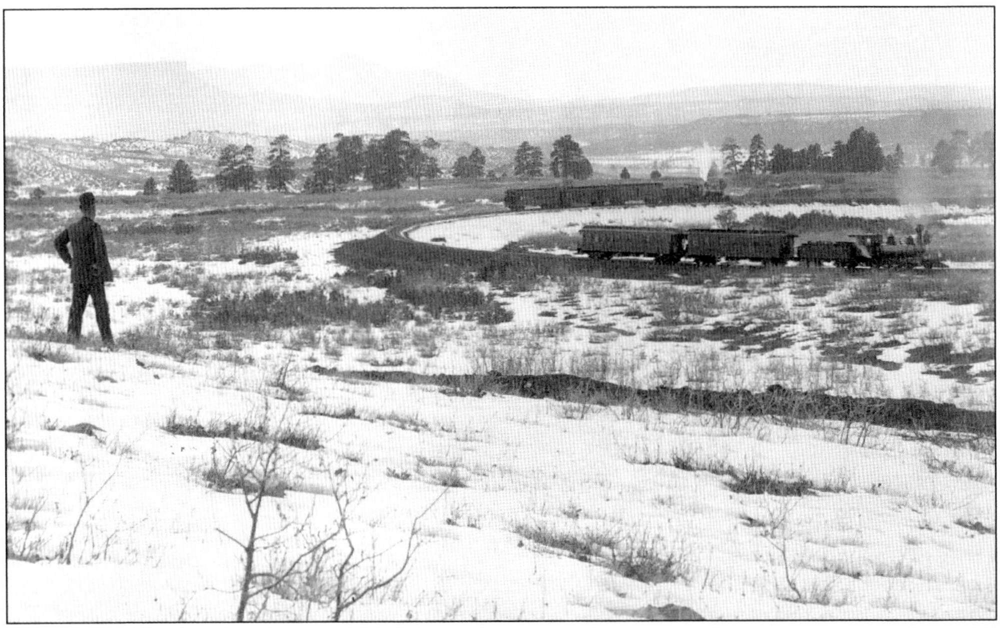

Two Denver and Rio Grande Southern Railroad trains traverse a railroad loop between Dolores and Mancos. As much as citizens of Cortez lobbied to get the railroad through their town, including attempts to host a station between Gallup, New Mexico, and Salt Lake City, this loop was as close as any railroad got. Railroad companies found too little commerce to justify the expense. (Courtesy of Denver Public Library, Western History Collection, William Henry Jackson WHJ-1246.)

Maj. James W. Hanna, who homesteaded the original townsite, had a vision for Cortez. Hanna could see Dolores River water coming to the valley and a railroad extending from Gallup, New Mexico, through Cortez to Salt Lake City. He incorporated Montezuma Valley Water Supply Co. in 1885 with $200,000 capital stock raised mostly from investors in Boston. The completed ditch would extend from the Dolores River to Hartman Draw and include 11 laterals. The system would serve 50,000 people and irrigate 200,000 acres. Started in November 1885, a full head of water did not reach Montezuma Valley until 1889. The silver panic of 1893 ended any plans for a north-south railroad. (Courtesy of Denver Public Library, Western History Collection, Charles A. Nast Z-2026.)

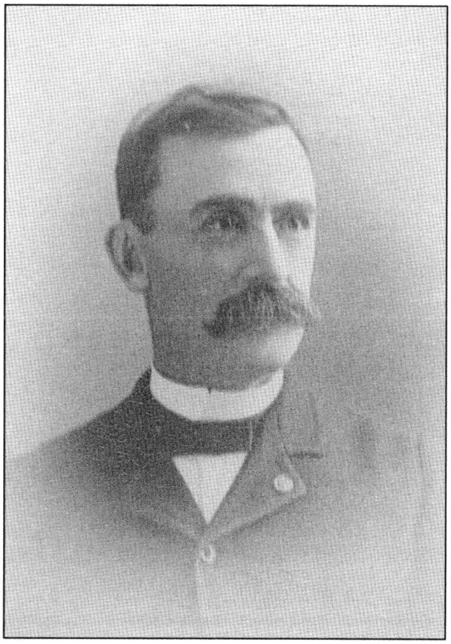

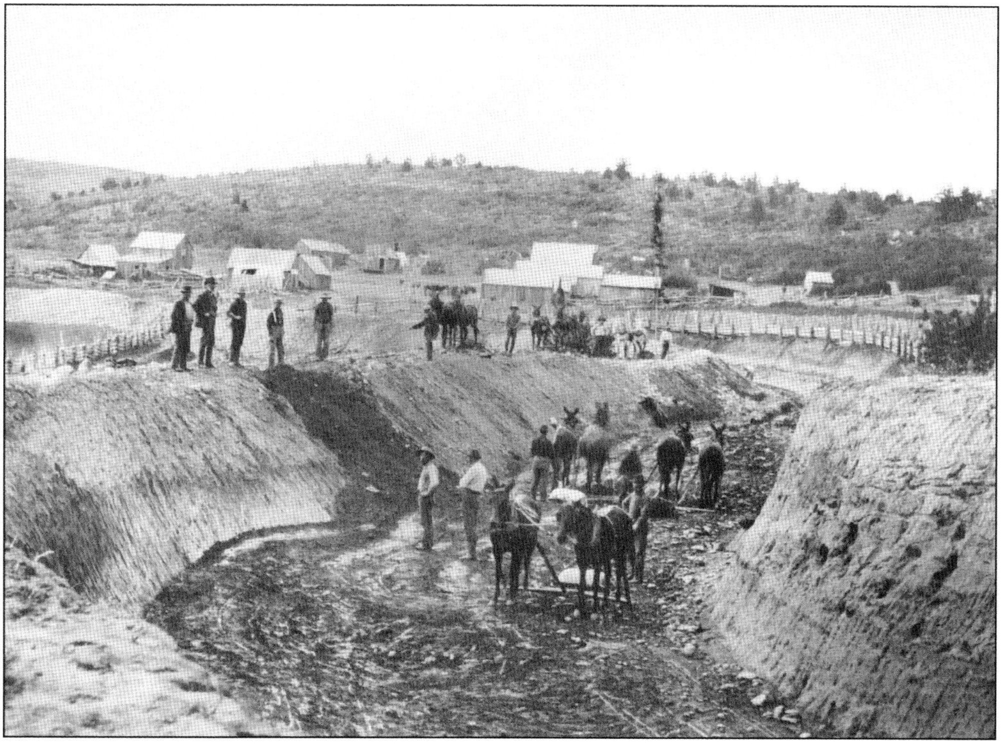

Considered "one of the greatest irrigation enterprises, not only in the state, but in the West" by the *Montezuma Journal*, the Main No. 1 Canal began at Big Bend. Men and materials had to be hauled through undeveloped territory. Men worked 12-hour shifts for $1 a day and often camped nearby. Ironically, the farmers who contracted to work had not prepared their fields and could not pay for the newly available water. This caused Montezuma Valley Water Supply Co. to fold. (Courtesy of Anasazi Heritage Center.)

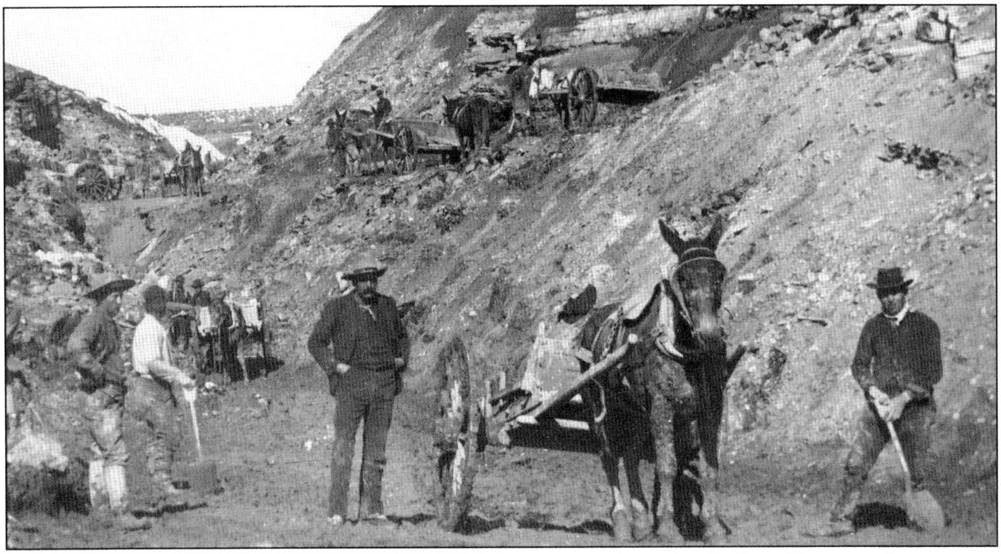

Men and mules hauled tons of dirt and rocks to move water from the Dolores River to the western half of Montezuma Valley. The Great Cut was 4,000 feet long and 40 feet deep through the Dolores Divide and connected to the No. 2 Canal. B.S. LaGrange, from Greeley, arranged that financing. When construction of the one-mile tunnel began under James Hanna's company, a group of citizens petitioned for a new county to be created from the west end of La Plata County. The new Montezuma County chose Cortez as its county seat. (Courtesy of Montezuma County Historical Society.)

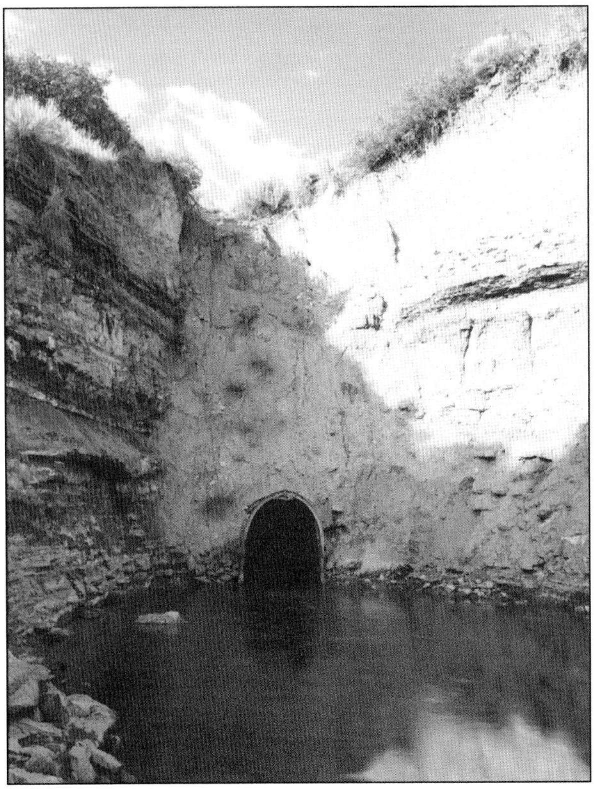

A Mancos Valley settler, Almarion Root, first attempted to construct a water diversion tunnel in 1874. In 1885, M.J. Mack surveyed the tunnel for Montezuma Valley Water Supply Co. and work began anew. Although construction of train tunnels was common throughout the 19th century, tunnels for irrigation water presented new engineering problems. Originally designed to be four feet in diameter, the Montezuma tunnel was soon expanded to seven-by-nine feet. Brothers George and Chris Wilkerson contracted to assist with construction and hauled drilling equipment from Denver. (Courtesy of Anasazi Heritage Center.)

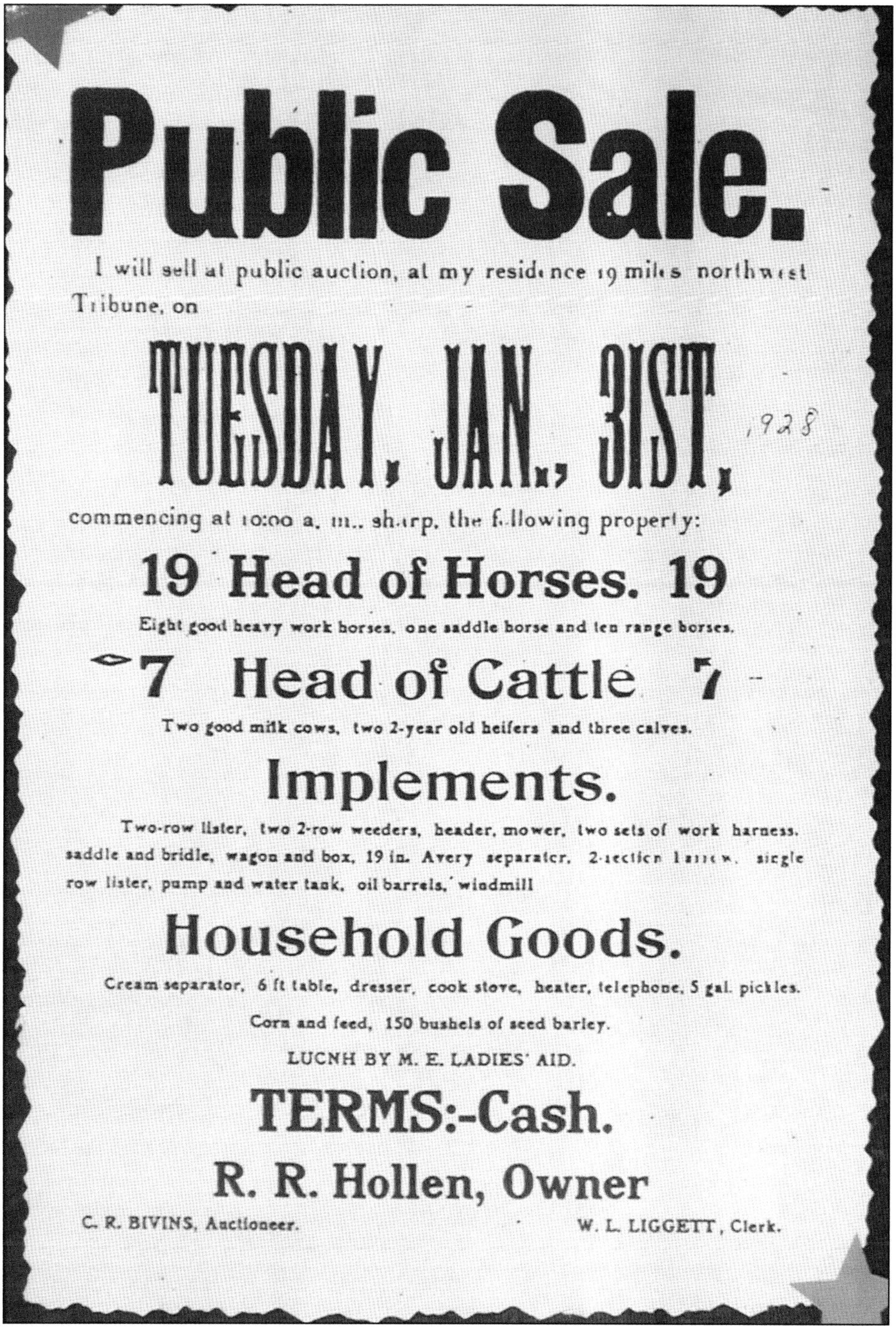

This poster advertises the sale of property belonging to the R.R. Hollen family of Tribune, Kansas, who resettled north of Cortez in the dryland area. In 1888, speculators moved into Cortez and Montezuma Valley. H. Brigham was the first land agent, followed by Stephen J. Smith and C.M. Rauh. B.L. Arbecam and James Hanna eased out of water and into land. The Denver & Rio Grande and the D&RG Southern railroad companies also promoted land sales around Cortez. (Courtesy of Anasazi Heritage Center.)

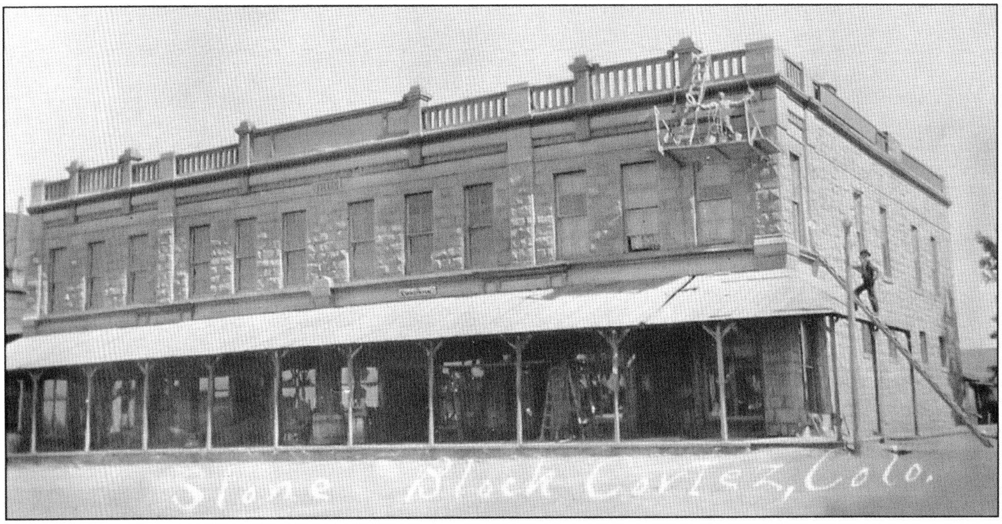

The Stone Block housed James Hanna's Montezuma Valley Water Supply Co. and Cortez Land and Investment Co. The building is 75 by 100 feet, stands two stories high, and cost $20,000. The stonework was done by Peter Baxstrom. An immigrant from Sweden and then Kansas, Baxstrom arrived by foot in Cortez in 1885 with three young sons, ages 10, 8 and 5. Peter, and later his son Harry, completed many stone buildings in Montezuma Valley. (Courtesy of First National Bank of Cortez.)

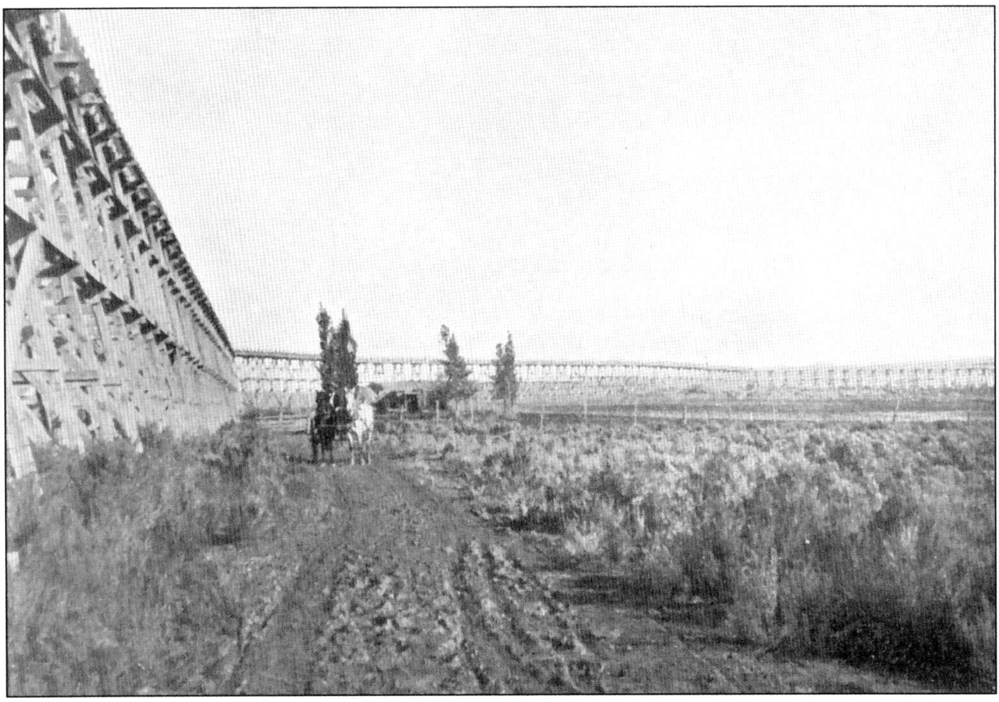

James Hanna supervised the building of a three-mile elevated flume to carry good water to Cortez for domestic use. The flume began at what was later known as Smithville, where the Cortez lateral crosses State Highway 145. David H. Lemmon contracted for the construction of the flume and predicted completion on March 1, 1888. However, the flume was not completed until July 4, 1890. (Courtesy of USGS.)

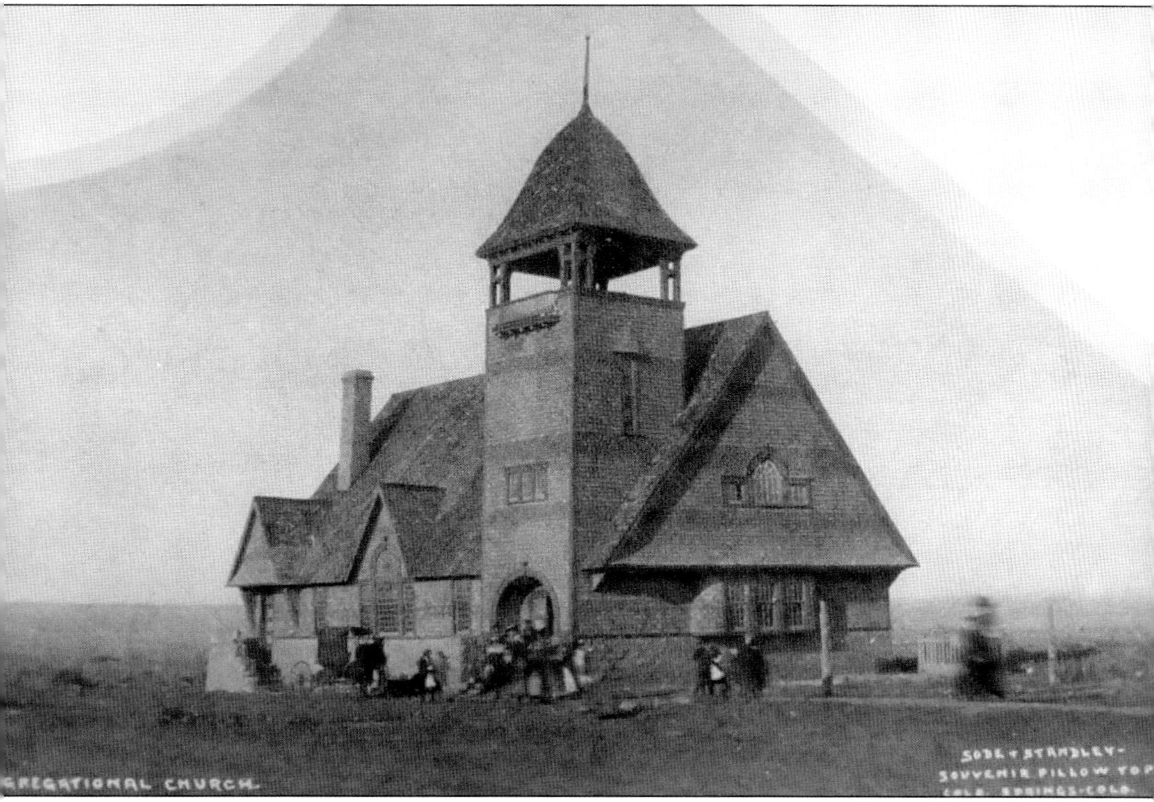

The Congregational Church was built in 1889 at the northeast corner of Montezuma Avenue and Market Street. The first pastor was Rev. Joel P. Harper, who died in December 1890 and was buried at the corner of the church (his remains were later moved to the Cortez Cemetery). Before the building burned in 1930, the church served as a community center and hosted socials, box suppers, and fun events for youth. The Christian Science Church was also built in 1889, at Market and North Streets. The town needed churches, since the Tom McCarty gang marked that year by riding its horses into the saloon, the Clifton Hotel, Mrs. Lamb's millinery, and other businesses, and shooting at dogs and lights. Town marshal Dick Flunkett apparently did nothing, but Frank Clyde Thompson Sr. successfully kept the leader from entering the A.L. Thompson Mercantile. At least 300 people lived in Cortez, including 50 to 60 women and more than 60 school-age children. (Courtesy of First National Bank of Cortez.)

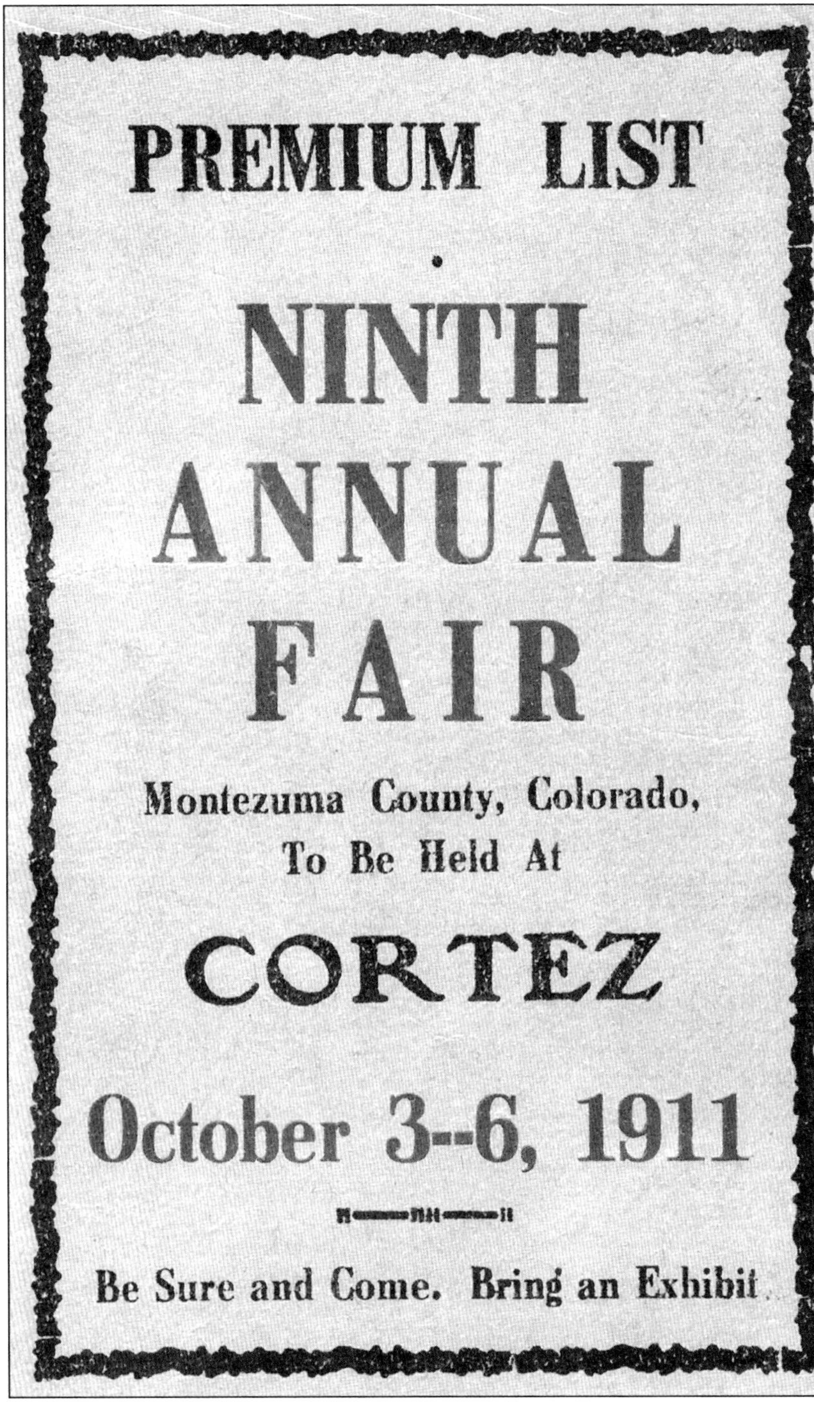

PREMIUM LIST

NINTH ANNUAL FAIR

Montezuma County, Colorado,
To Be Held At

CORTEZ

October 3--6, 1911

Be Sure and Come. Bring an Exhibit

Montezuma held its first county fair in 1902. Raising a family on an 80- to 160-acre homestead was more than a dawn-to-dark enterprise. Clearing the land, building a barn—often first—and then a cabin, plowing, planting crops and a garden, milking cows, and tending livestock was backbreaking work but promised ownership of one's own place. When they could, the new settlers got together for a dance or the annual county fair. (Courtesy of Cortez Public Library.)

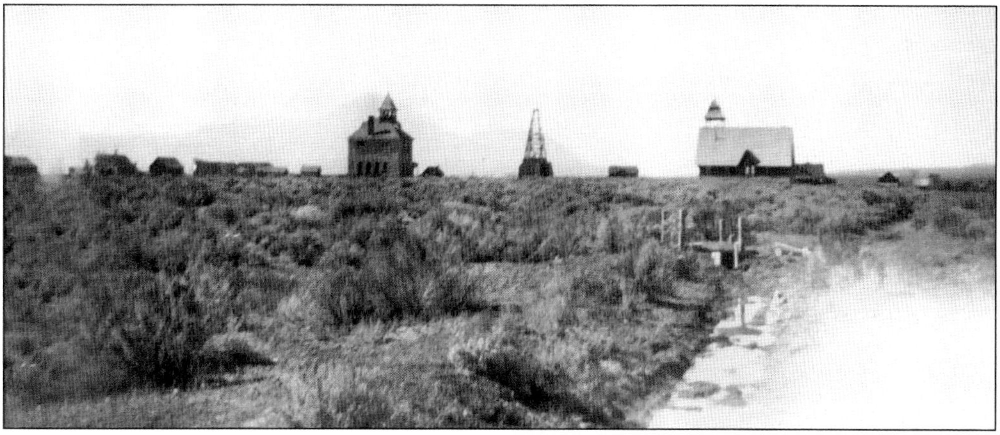

This c. 1892–1900 photograph includes the Montezuma Avenue school, water well rigging, the Congregational Church, and Sleeping Ute Mountain. The well dug at the intersection of Main and Market Streets produced no potable water. Water was hauled by horse and wagon from Mitchell Springs and stored in at least one cistern that was set up at the intersection for use at no charge. (Courtesy of Denver Public Library, Western History Collection, X-21407.)

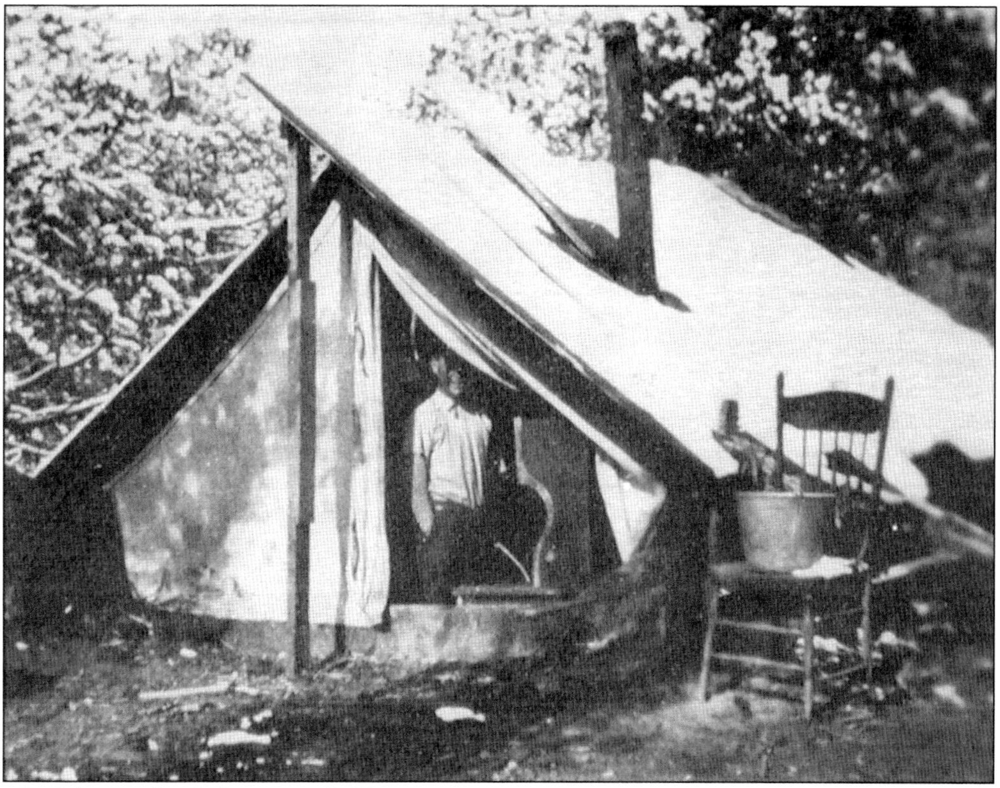

The Johnson family homesteaded land atop a mesa due west of Cortez. By lowering the floor level of his tent, Johnson incorporated a house-heating technology similar to that used by early Anasazi in their pit houses. Goodman Point residents struggled for more than a century to obtain domestic water. In 2009, Montezuma Water Company, which provides domestic water to rural areas, announced a financially solid project. Hauling water from in-town commercial spigots is still common for many county residents. (Courtesy of Anasazi Heritage Center.)

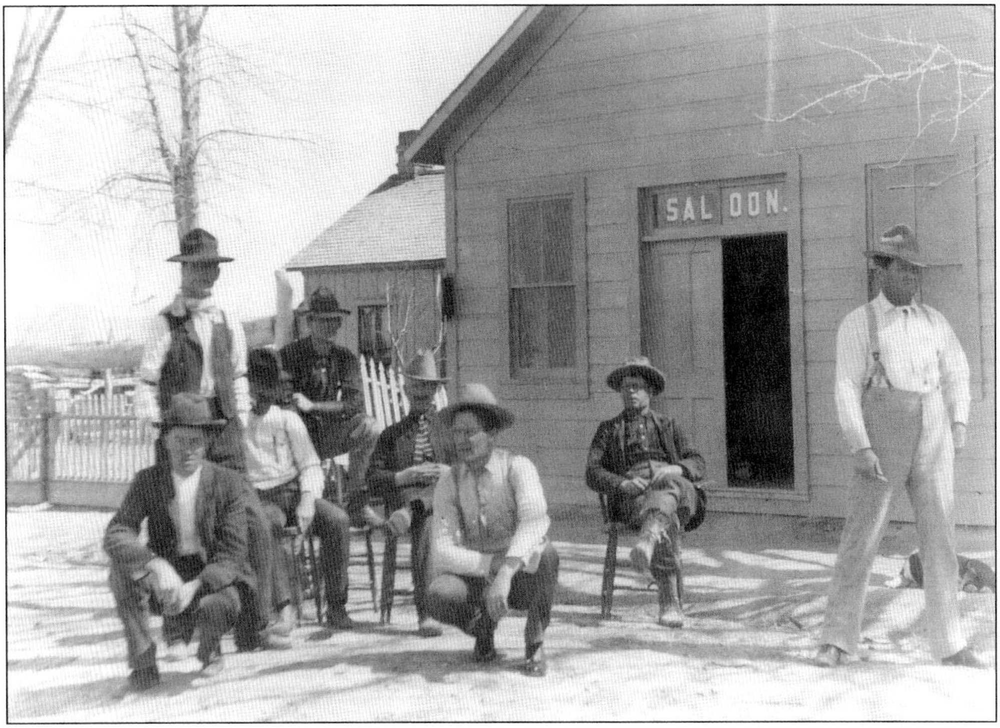

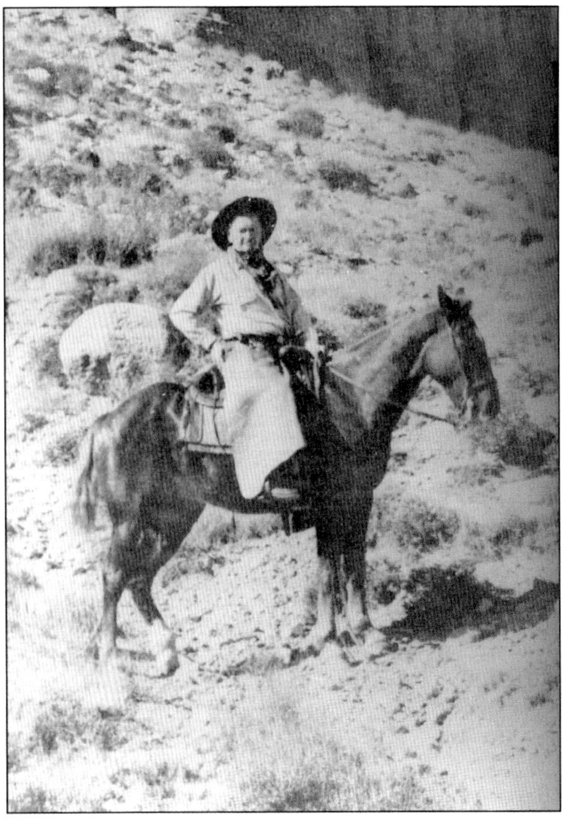

Robert "Butch Cassidy" Parker (seated with striped tie) and Harry Longabaugh, otherwise known as the Sundance Kid (standing by tree), take a break from robbing banks and hunker in the shade. This Green River, Utah, saloon was a hangout of the Wild Bunch in 1889. Cortez ranchers Jim and Bob Nash, who summered their stock at Groundhog Mountain, met and admired Butch while he was horse wrangling for the Adsit outfit on Lone Cone. (Used by permission, Utah State Historical Society. All rights reserved.)

Native Utahan Matt Warner sits on a fast horse in rough terrain. Warner was a member of the McCarty gang, the Younger gang, and the Wild Bunch. Robber's Roost in southeastern Utah harbored the Wild Bunch and their remuda of fine horses. This photograph was taken in Warner's later years, after he chose to work on the right side of the law. (Used by permission, Utah State Historical Society. All rights reserved.)

Taken in the 1870s, this photograph of Harry Longabaugh (the Sundance Kid) and his common-law wife, Etta Place, was taken in Buffalo, Wyoming, before the outlaws headed for Bolivia. Rumors suggested Longabaugh was related to the respectable Longenbaugh family that lived near Cortez. (Used by permission, Utah State Historical Society. All rights reserved.)

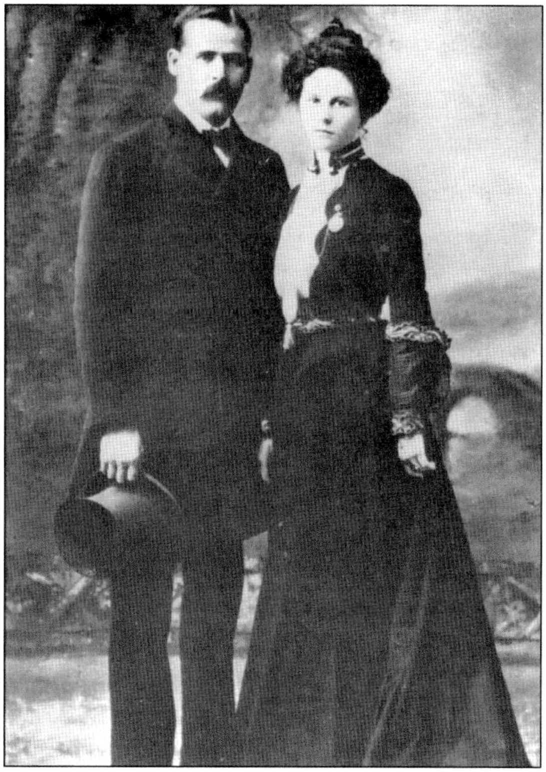

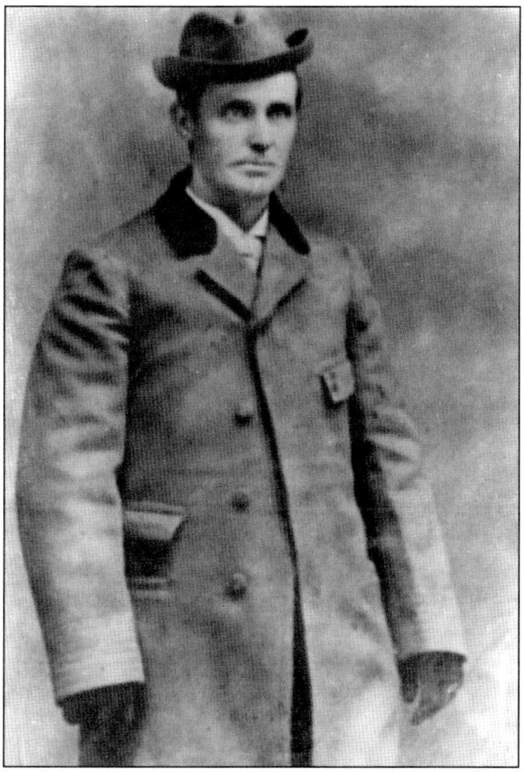

Tom McCarty was one of a few western outlaws who later lived a peaceful life. Appreciative of fast horses and easy money, he was known to accompany Butch Cassidy in robbing the San Miguel Bank of Telluride of $21,000. The McCarty gang operated from Grand Junction to Telluride, Colorado, and south, and stayed at Robber's Roost on occasion. (Used by permission, Utah State Historical Society. All rights reserved.)

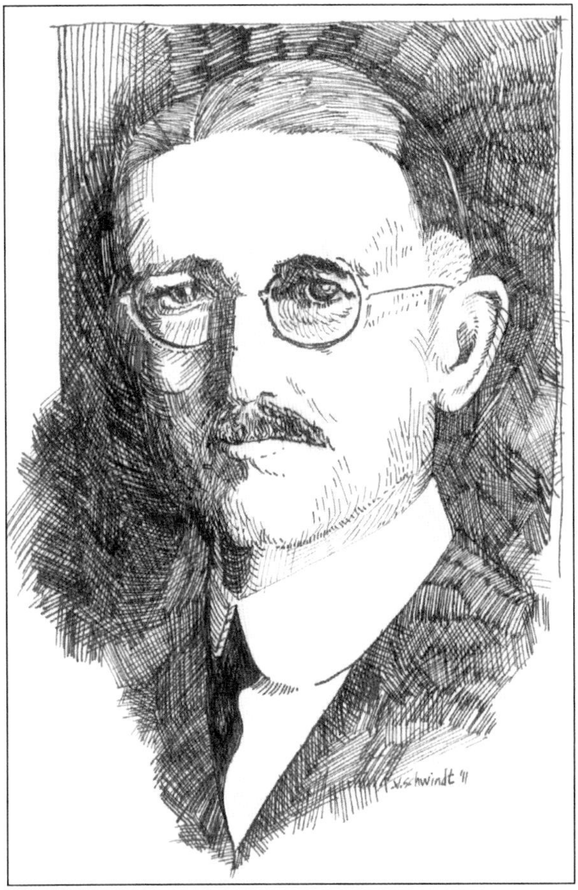

Stephen J. Smith came to Cortez as secretary and bookkeeper for E.S. Turner, a Boston investor in James Hanna's water company. Turner, H.B. Chamberlain, and others started Cortez's first bank, Montezuma Valley Bank, in 1887 with cash capital of $30,000. Smith managed the bank until 1891 when it closed. He continued to serve the community as county clerk and recorder, as manager of the water and town companies, as secretary of the irrigation district, and as a church official. (Illustration courtesy of Vila Schwindt.)

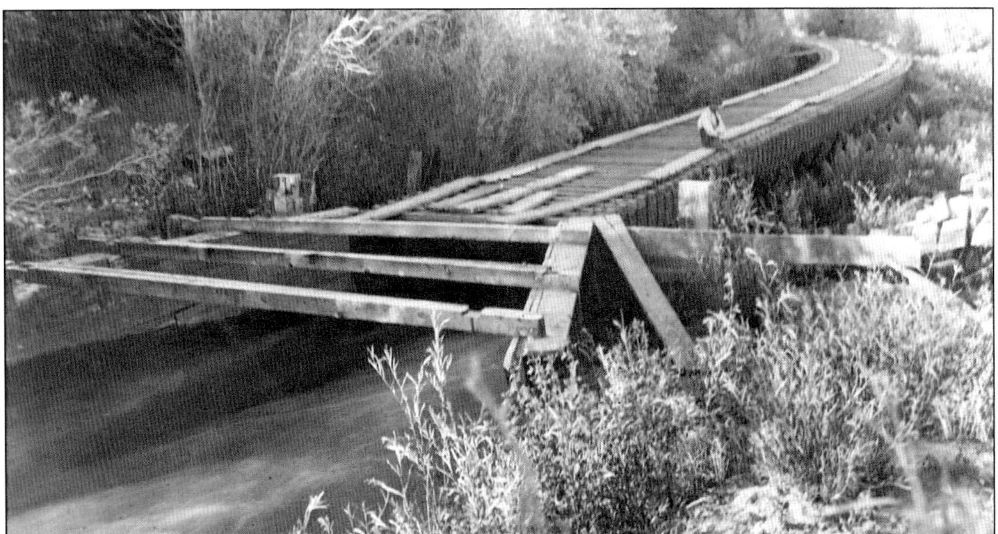

Wooden flumes were built to move water when the terrain was not cooperative. An unidentified man gives perspective to the size of the intake flume that moves water in the No. 1 Canal. (Courtesy of Anasazi Heritage Center.)

Two

Fires Cannot Quench Growth

The year 1888 dawned on a population of 300 in Cortez, including 60 women and 60 school-age children. In the next ten years, seventeen buildings arose above boardwalks and tends. The Hotel Clifton, a Woodmen of the World Hall, two restaurants, a general mercantile, a leather goods shop, a grocery, a meat market, a dairy, three drugstores, a liquor store, a tobacconist, a barber, a watchmaker and jeweler, two millineries and dressmakers, two painters and paperhangers, four attorneys, a photographer, two architects, a Chinese washee and two other laundries, a contractor, two masons, a lumberyard, four blacksmiths and wagon makers, a wheelwright, a freighter, two liveries and feed stores, a coal dealer, a water company, and a sawmill comprised 40-some businesses. Owners wore different hats, as they do today, to provide services and products that fit the season and current developments.

Two water companies merged to become the Colorado Consolidated Land and Water Company, blending liabilities and irregular progress on ditch construction. Montezuma Valley's landscape had changed from one of primarily grasslands to sagebrush due to winter overgrazing.

Montezuma split from La Plata County in 1889. Cortez, the new county seat, built a courthouse at First and Chestnut Streets so that the governor-appointed officials could manage the 2,640 square miles. The first election was held in 1891.

Domestic water arrived in Cortez in 1890 via a wooden flume. Eleven major canals were being built to serve the county with water from the Dolores River. Water companies struggled with residents, investors, and state agencies for money and solutions. By 1900, the population of Cortez had decreased to 125. Water was essential to its survival. Annual precipitation alternated between drought and floods. The Ute tribe laid legal claim to available waters. Two fires, one in 1898 and another in 1908, destroyed multiple downtown businesses.

Still, companies formed and promoted telephones and electricity. Mesa Verde National Park was established in 1906. Two banks opened. Industry and faith built more reservoirs, canals, ditches, and pipelines, and improved water delivery and reliability.

The first automobiles arrived. A new school with six classrooms was built on First Street. Drilling for oil began, mostly west of town. Cortez formed a fire protection district. In 1917, Dr. Emil E. Johnson established a hospital in Cortez. The town grew with resolute determination.

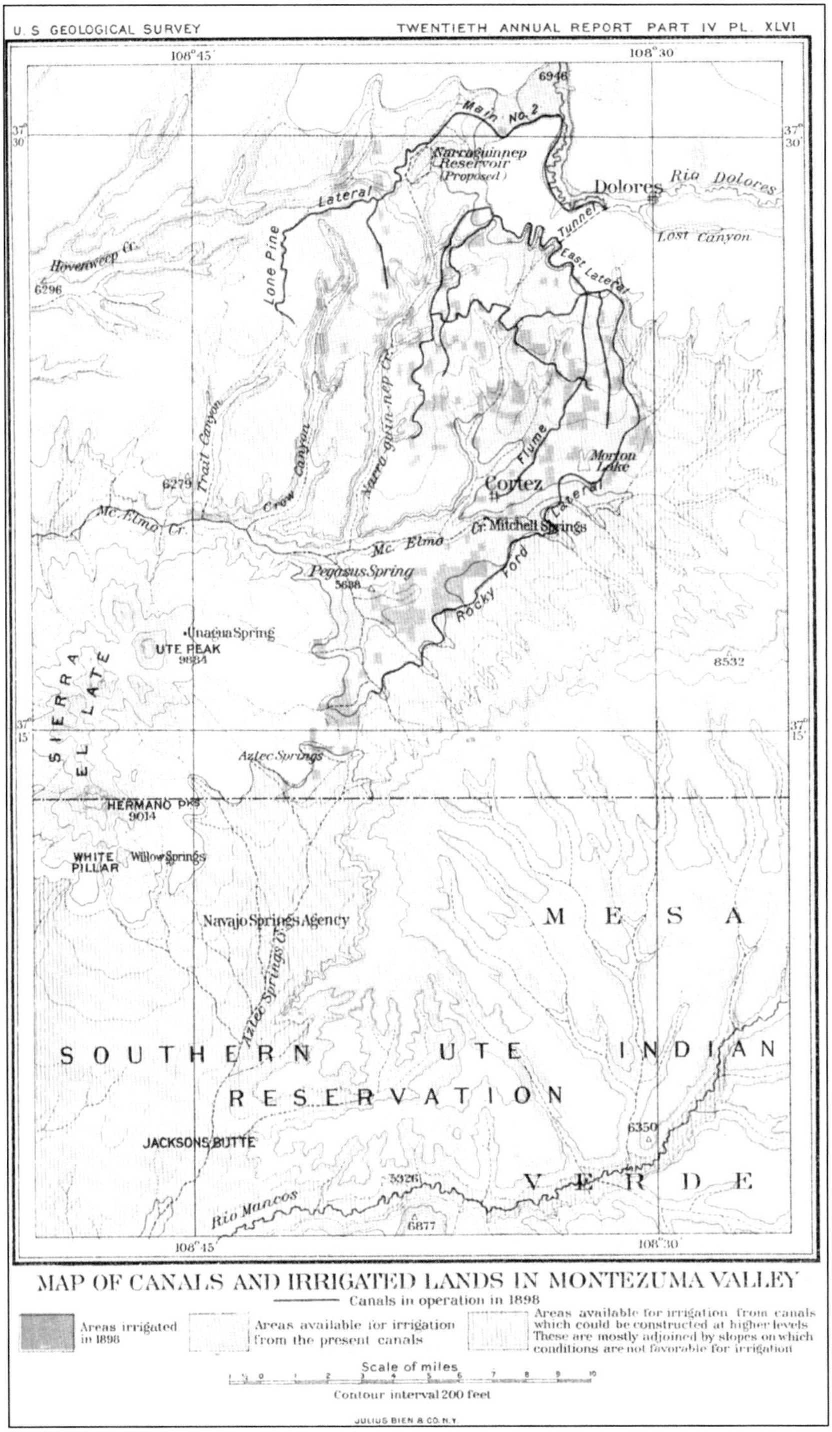

This US Geological Survey map shows Montezuma Valley, from Dolores in the north to Jackson Butte (now known as Chimney Rock) in the south. Areas are marked that were being irrigated in 1898, with other areas indicated as being available for irrigation or potentially irrigated with additional canal construction. (Courtesy of USGS.)

Ute Mountain Utes elected Jack House, age 33, to the tribal council in 1937. He served the Weeminuche group until his death in 1971. Named by Chief John Miller as his successor in 1935, Chief House spoke little English, ran cattle on the reservation in nomadic fashion, and had substantial influence on how his people dealt with the ever-changing Indian policies of Washington. Politically adept, Chief House worked to gain facility improvements, to regain land and water for his people, to develop Anasazi ruins on the reservation for tourism, and to increase the Utes' rights to self-determination. (Courtesy of Cortez Public Library.)

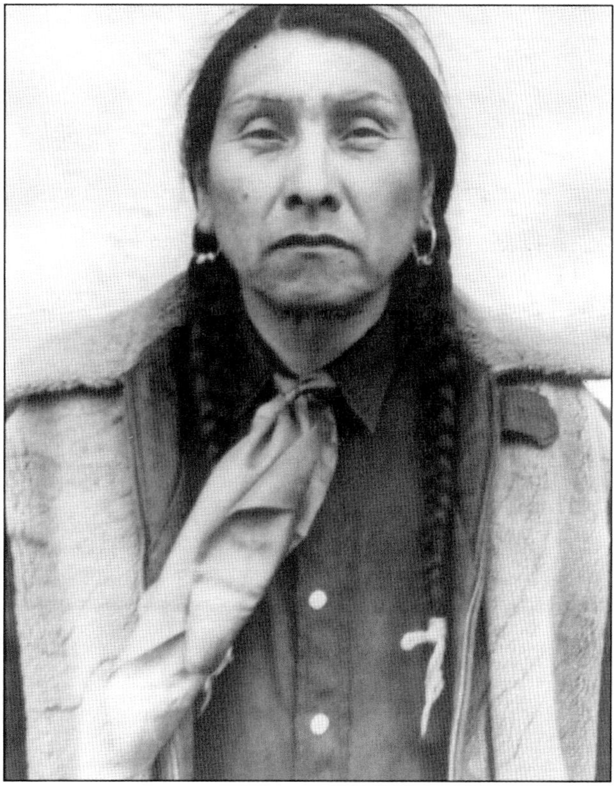

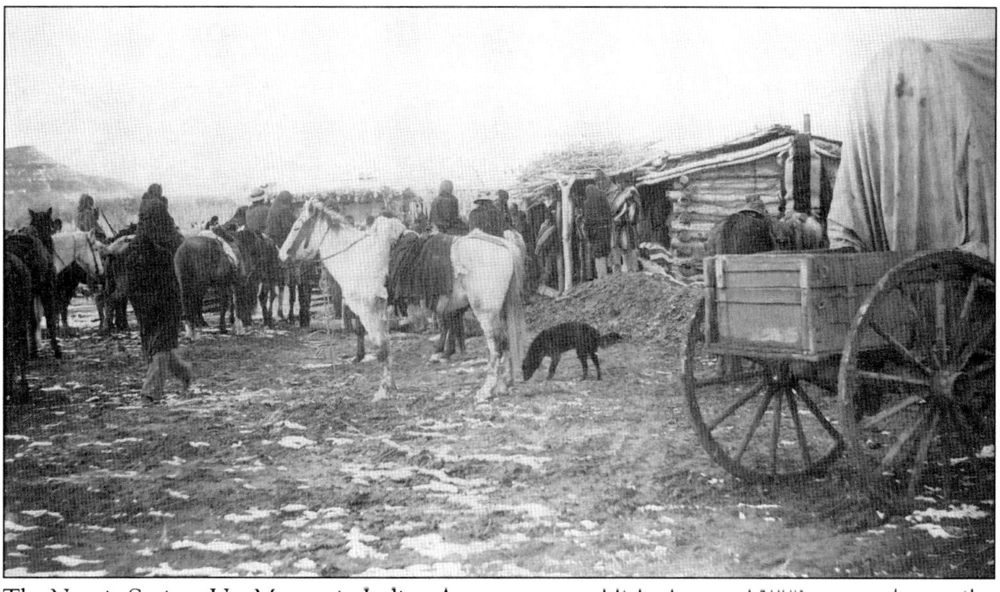

The Navajo Springs Ute Mountain Indian Agency was established around 1870, two to three miles south of the current tribal headquarters. Originally built of logs, framed stucco buildings were added later. The government's goal was to "educate all Indians to become useful and industrious citizens." Negotiations began with the Montezuma Valley irrigation company. In 1898, the US Senate recommended an appropriation for the purchase of water so that Utes could farm their land. (Courtesy of Denver Public Library, Western History Collection, X-30357.)

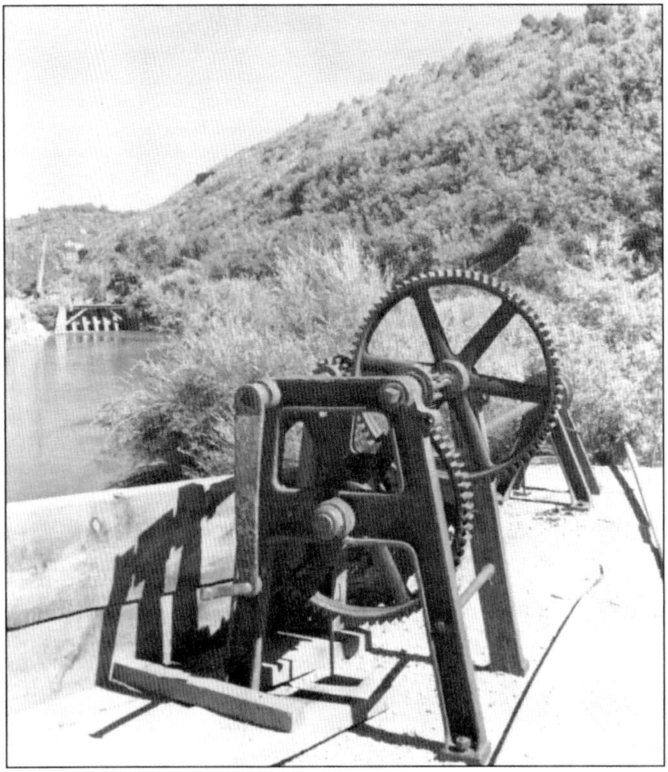

Crude by today's standards, this headgate mechanism controlled the intake of Dolores River waters to the mile-long tunnel that delivered irrigation water to Montezuma Valley farmers and ranchers. (Courtesy of Anasazi Heritage Center.)

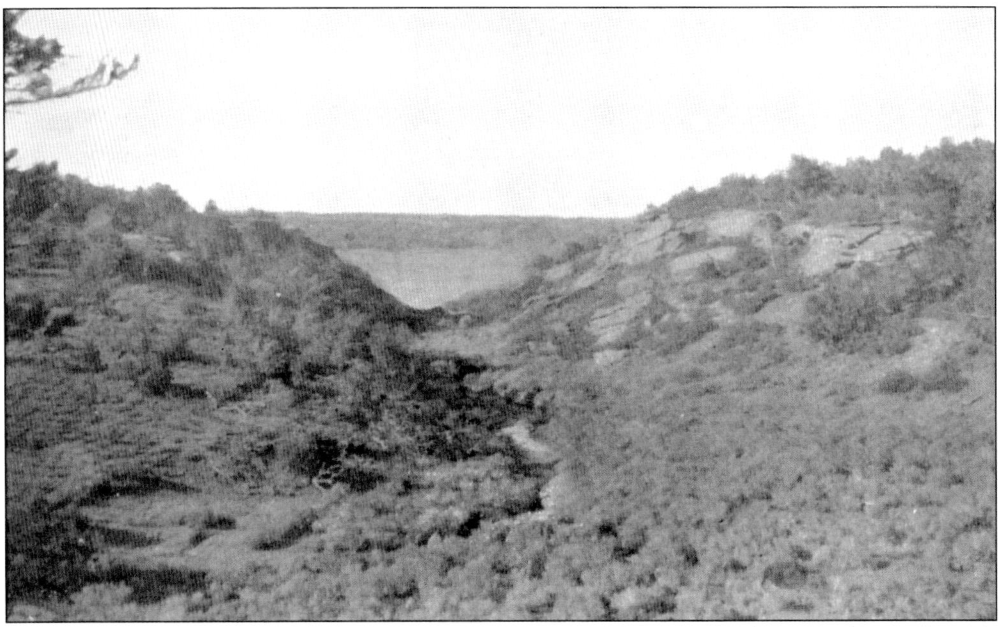

This early photograph was likely taken near Narraguinnep Springs, looking southwest through the canyon into the reservoir site. About 1885, the J.H. Spalding family emigrated from Silverton to Narraguinnep Springs, which was one of the year-round sources for water in the valley. The terrain mostly was Mancos shale covered by sage and grass lowlands, with piñon-juniper forest above sandstone ridges. (Courtesy of USGS.)

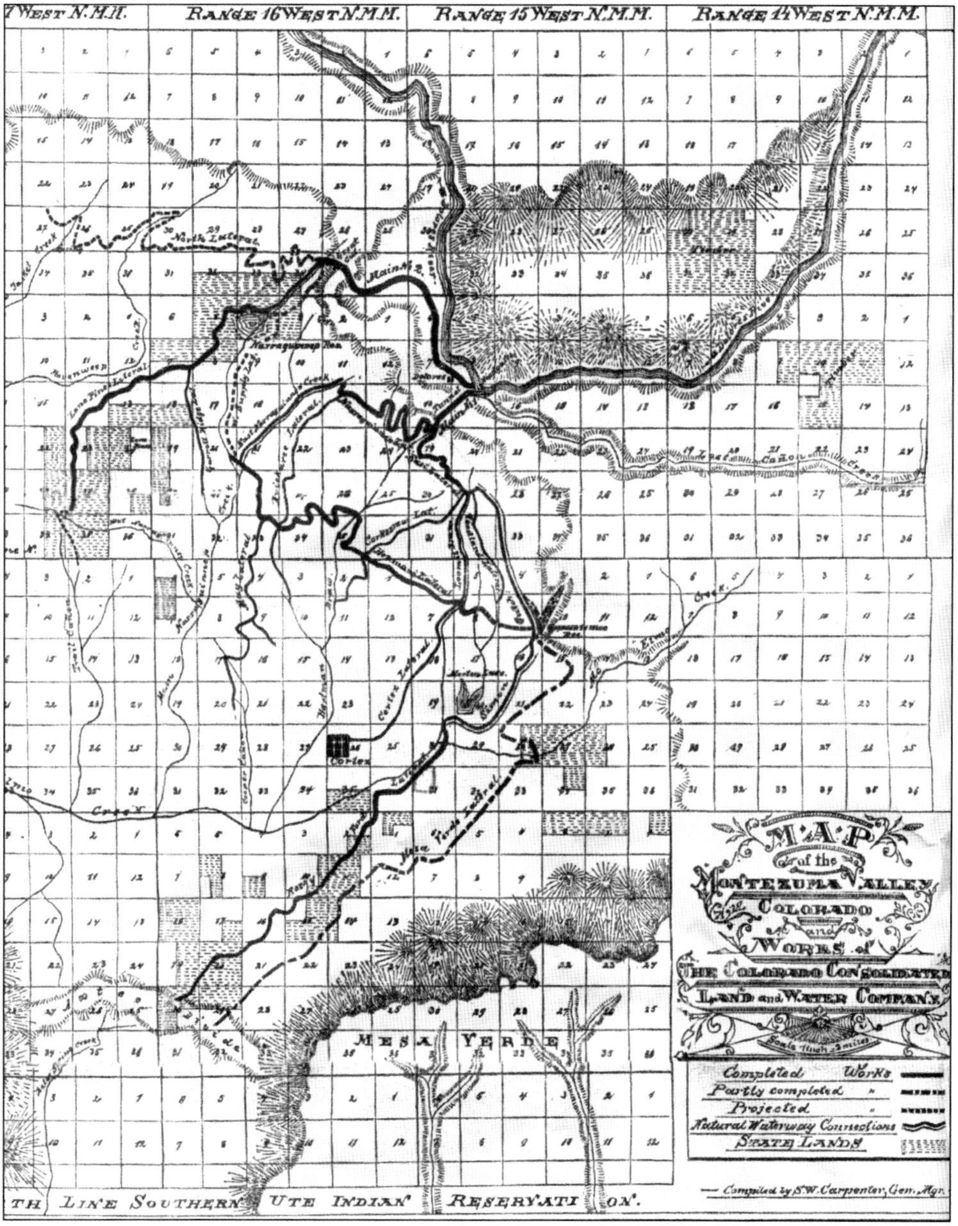

This 1890 map illustrating completed, partly completed, and projected canals, along with natural waterway connections and state lands, was compiled in 1898 by S.W. Carpenter, general manager for the Colorado Consolidated Land and Water Company, and published in a real estate brochure. Construction on the Narraguinnep Reservoir began in the spring of 1888. Rights for its 6,000-acre-feet of water were filed by the Dolores No. 2 Land and Canal Company. The No. 2 Ditch, owned by B.S. LaGrange, diverged from the No. 1 tunnel intake and included the Great Cut and the Morton Flume. The canal was designed to fill Narraguinnep Reservoir and carry water through an elaborate ditch and canal system to irrigate the Yellow Jacket, Hovenweep, Trail, Alkali, and part of McElmo Canyons. The Dolores No. 2 Land and Canal Company merged with Montezuma Water Supply Co. in 1890 to become the Colorado Consolidated Land and Water Company. (Courtesy of Cortez Public Library.)

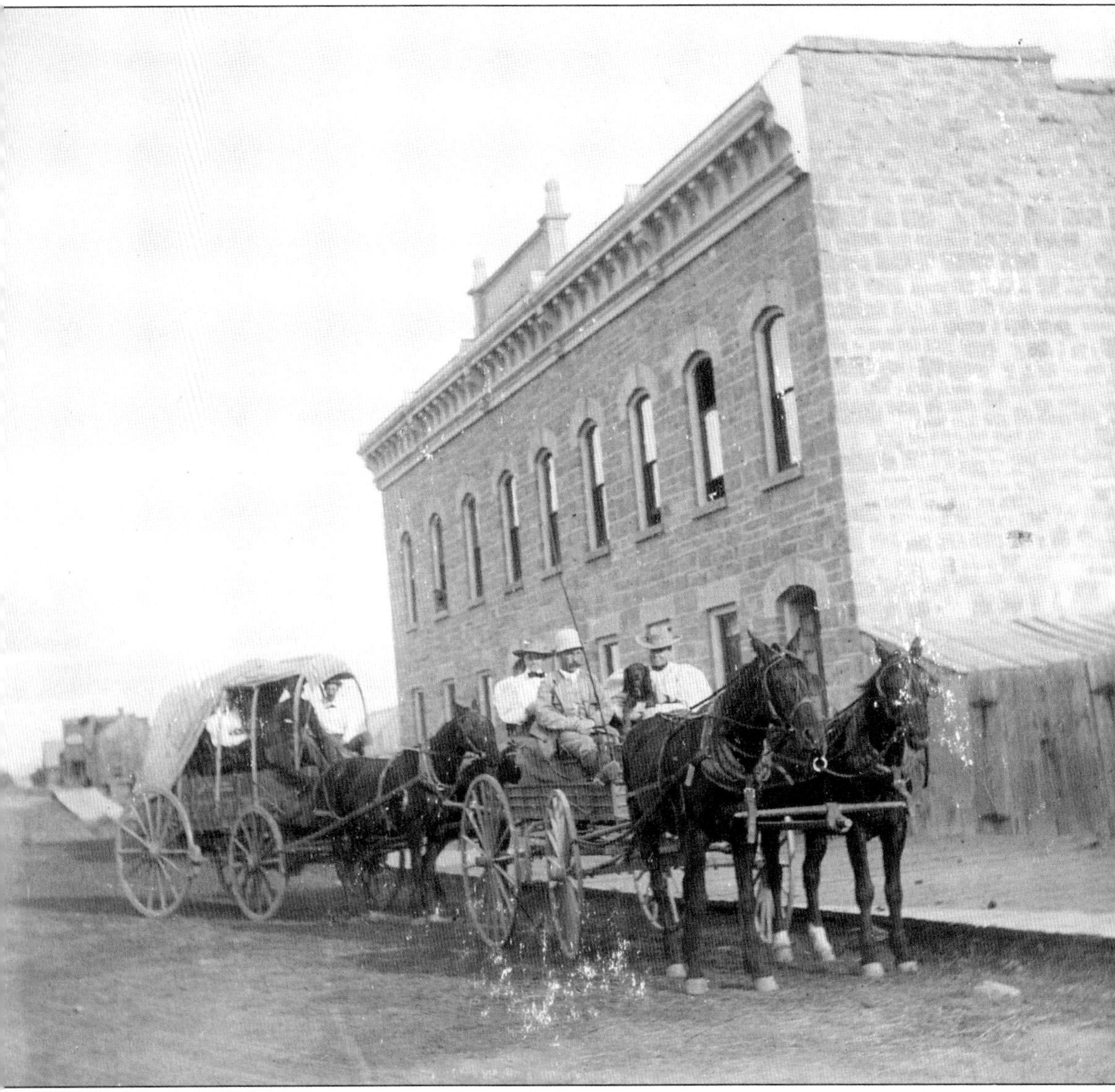

Two wagonloads of tourists gather in front of Montezuma County's courthouse on West First Street for a day's outing to the Anasazi ruins on Mesa Verde. The ground floor of the courthouse rented office space to Dr. Bernard J. Byrnes, who also ran Cortez's post office. Harry B. Harrison had a bank there. The county paid rent on the upper story for $600 per year. Montezuma split from La Plata County on April 18, 1889, by an act of the Colorado General Assembly. Montezuma County was placed in the 21st Senatorial District, the La Plata–Montezuma Representative District, and the 6th Judicial District. James Hanna was Montezuma's first representative to the legislature. Gov. Charles S. Thomas appointed the first set of county officials, with William Franklin Ordway for Dolores, Frank W. Thomas for Cortez, and George Bauer for Mancos, as commissioners. He appointed Thomas Payson as treasurer, William M. Smith as clerk and recorder, R. Pearly Wasson as sheriff, Dr. George Williams as coroner, George N. Morton as judge, T.J. Wattles as assessor, I.O. Miller as superintendent of schools, and Walter Pearl as surveyor. (Courtesy of Denver Public Library, Western History Collection, X-21029.)

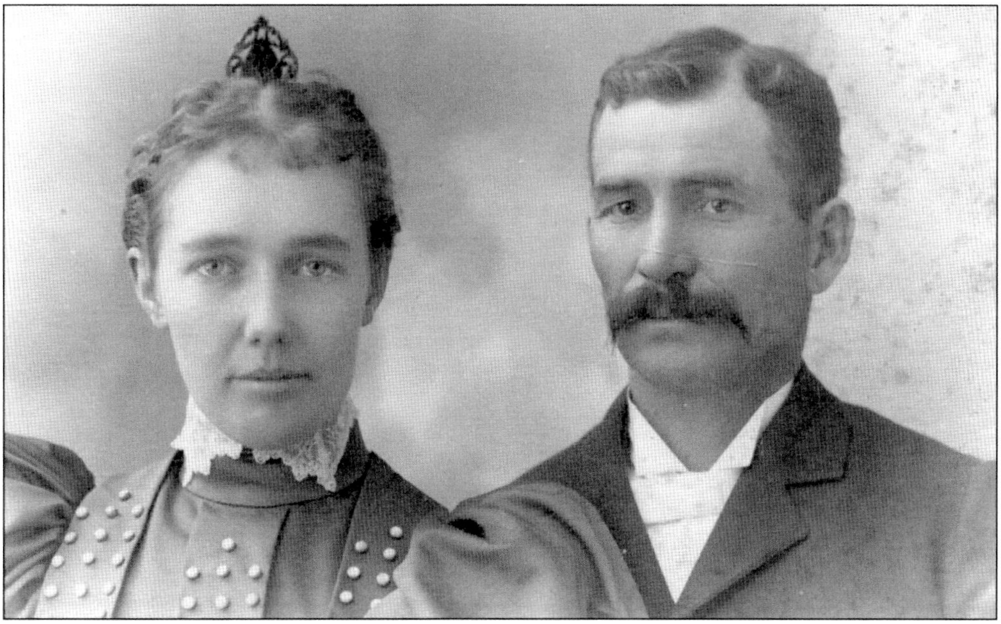

Anna Lida Fuller and Herman M. Guillet pose for their wedding photograph. The couple was married in Waterman, Illinois, on February 19, 1896. The Guillet brothers, Pete and Herm, had established their general merchandise store in Cortez in 1893 or 1894, so Herm had returned to Illinois to marry. Herm served as Cortez's first mayor, as county commissioner, on the school board, and on the town board. (Courtesy of Herma Jean Watson.)

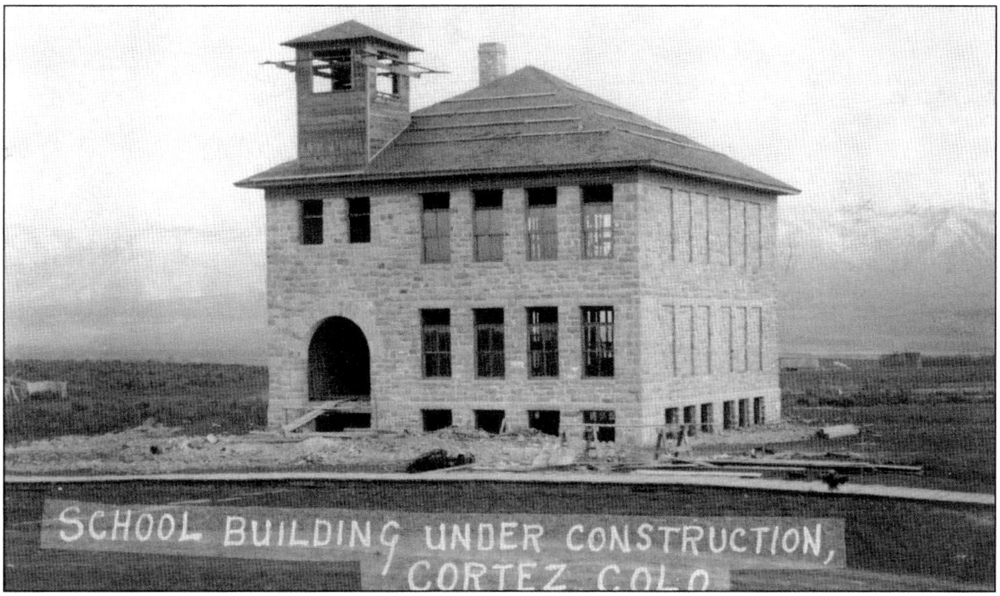

J.W. Denny was county superintendent of schools in 1907 when residents pushed for a new, larger school building to serve grades one through 12. School District 17 bought lots on First Street for $500. School board members were Will Bozman, R.R. "Bob" Smith, and Harry Sprague. Peter Baxtrom built it. I. Edward Levy was its first superintendent and principal. Max Schertel taught German and mathematics. Gertrude Foster taught grammar and English. Anna P. Smith taught primary grades. Mrs. Royal Calkins taught vocal music. (Courtesy of Cortez Area Chamber of Commerce.)

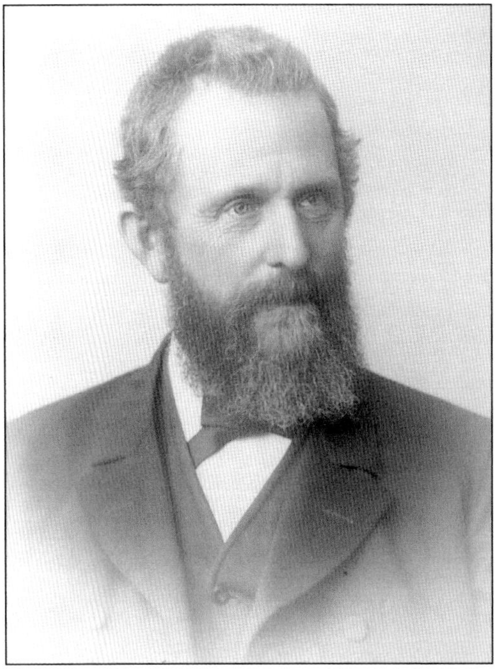

Dave M. Longenbaugh was a founder of the Cortez Methodist Church and was the first teacher in Cortez. He gave of his time in many ways to ensure that Cortez had schools and churches, the foundations for a more civilized existence. (Courtesy of First United Methodist Church of Cortez.)

In 1890, the new county had a population of 1,529, including 549 school-age children. The school district purchased two lots on East Montezuma Avenue from the city for $1, and Peter Baxstrom built a two-story schoolhouse for $13,374. The older grades attended school there. The first and second grades were taught in a frame building on the northwest corner of Main and Chestnut Streets. The third and fourth grades were taught at the back of Doctor Quinn's building across Chestnut Street. (Courtesy of First National Bank of Cortez.)

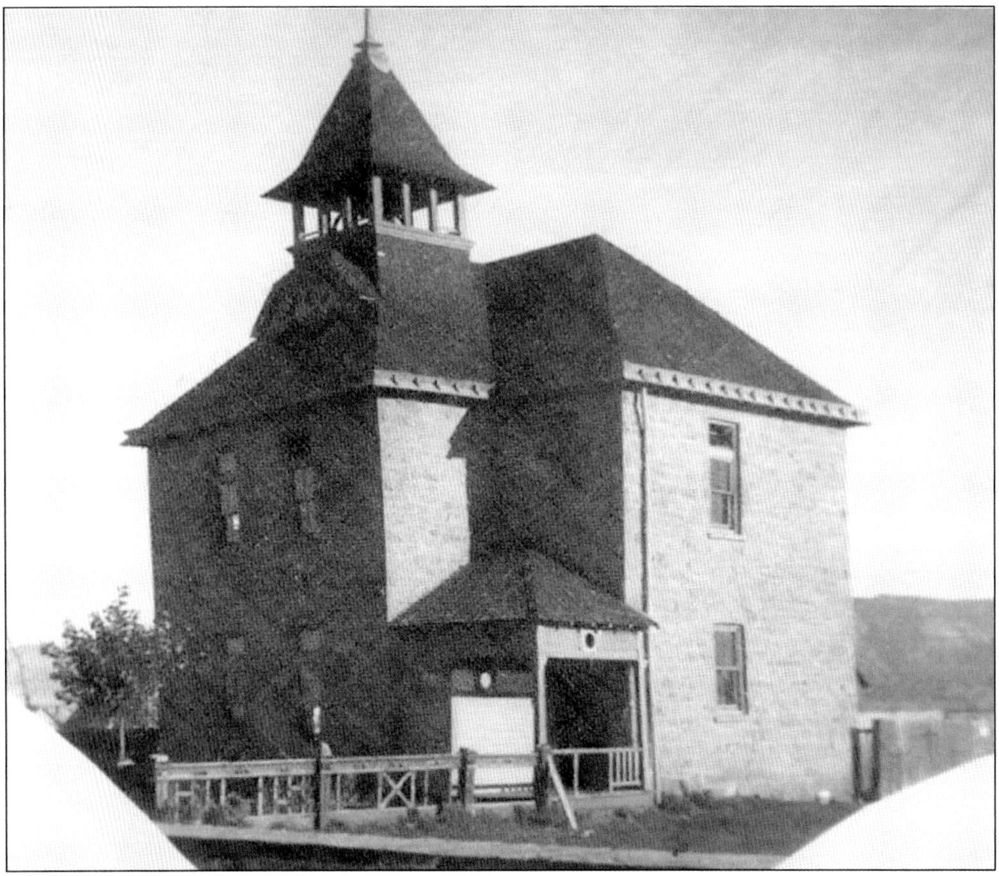

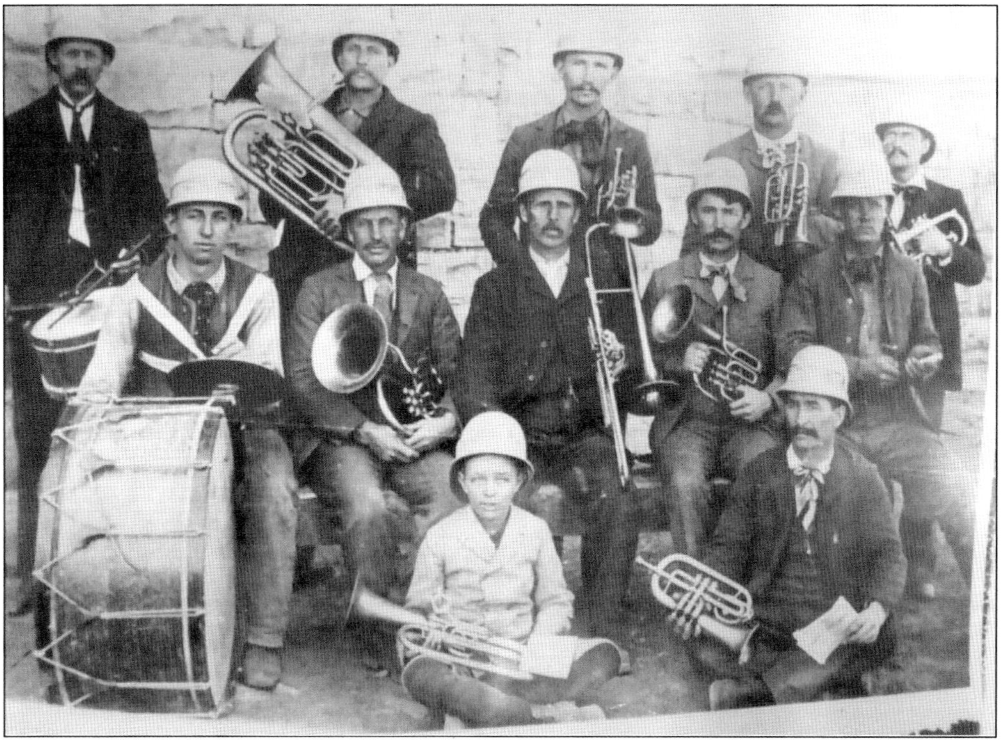

Members of the Cortez Band pose before playing. Included in this image are, from left to right, (first row) Frank Thomas and Herm Guillet; (second row) Mr. Briley, Mr. Winship (or Bob Smith), unidentified, Pete Guillet, and unidentified; (third row) Bob Smith (or Mr. Lamb), unidentified, Ern Guillet, Sterl Thomas, and Mr. Lamb (or Doc Sperry). The Guillet brothers kept the band's instruments in the back of their store in the Stone Block. (Courtesy of Grace Thomas Swenk and Cortez Public Library.)

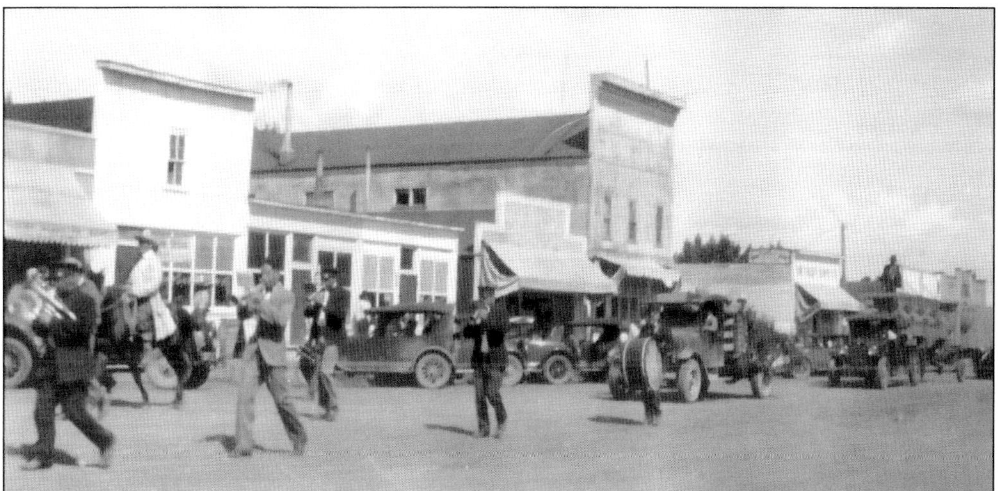

The Cortez Band was well known in the area and played for parades and concerts beyond Montezuma County. The band, and later the high school band, played a major part in the rural community's activities. With no video or MP3 players, early pioneers appreciated the live music provided by local and touring talent. (Courtesy of Larry Hauser.)

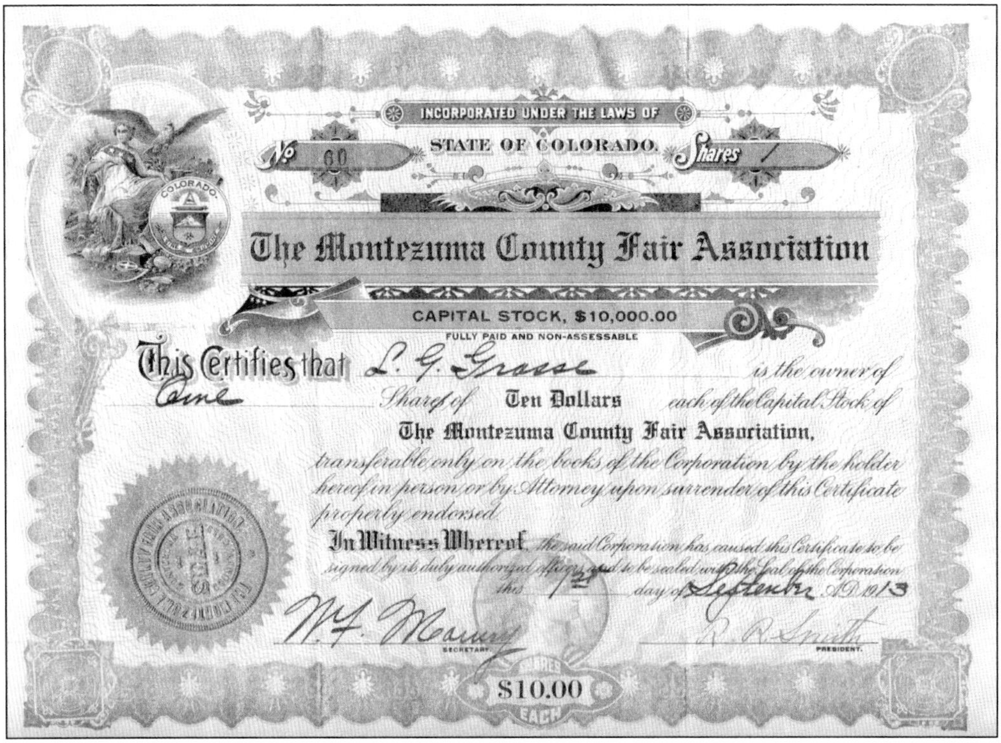

INCORPORATED UNDER THE LAWS OF STATE OF COLORADO.

No 60 Shares 1

The Montezuma County Fair Association

CAPITAL STOCK, $10,000.00

FULLY PAID AND NON-ASSESSABLE

This Certifies that L. G. Grasse is the owner of One Share of Ten Dollars each of the Capital Stock of The Montezuma County Fair Association, transferable only on the books of the Corporation by the holder hereof in person or by Attorney upon surrender of this Certificate properly endorsed.

In Witness Whereof, the said Corporation has caused this Certificate to be signed by its duly authorized officers and to be sealed with the Seal of the Corporation this 1st day of September A.D. 1913

W. F. Mowry SECRETARY. R. R. Smith PRESIDENT.

SHARES $10.00 EACH

Leopold Grasse, who owned a boot, saddle, and harness store on Main Street, supported the fair by purchasing initial stock in the association and received this certificate of investment. J.W. Bozman, Guy Harrison, G.H. Rudy, William F. Mowry, R.R. "Bob" Smith, H. Brigham Jr., and George Reed incorporated the County Fair Association in 1909 with capital stock of $10,000. (Courtesy of Montezuma County Extension.)

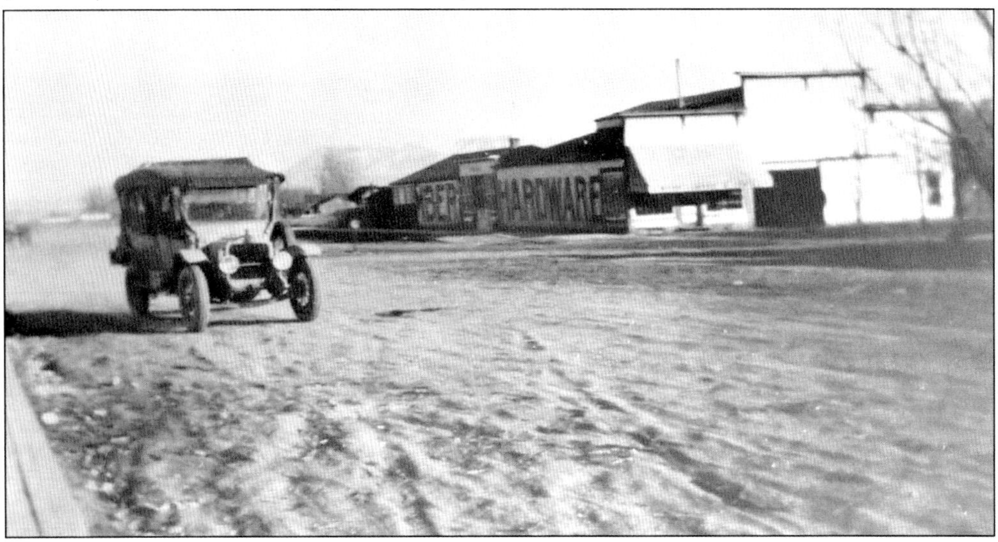

The Mead-Hengstler Lumber Co. on South Beech and Main Streets reported income of nearly $30,000 in 1909—from lumber, hardware, and John Deere tractor sales. Cortez was home for at least one other lumber company, Cortez Lumber, managed by Harry Beall. (Courtesy of First National Bank of Cortez.)

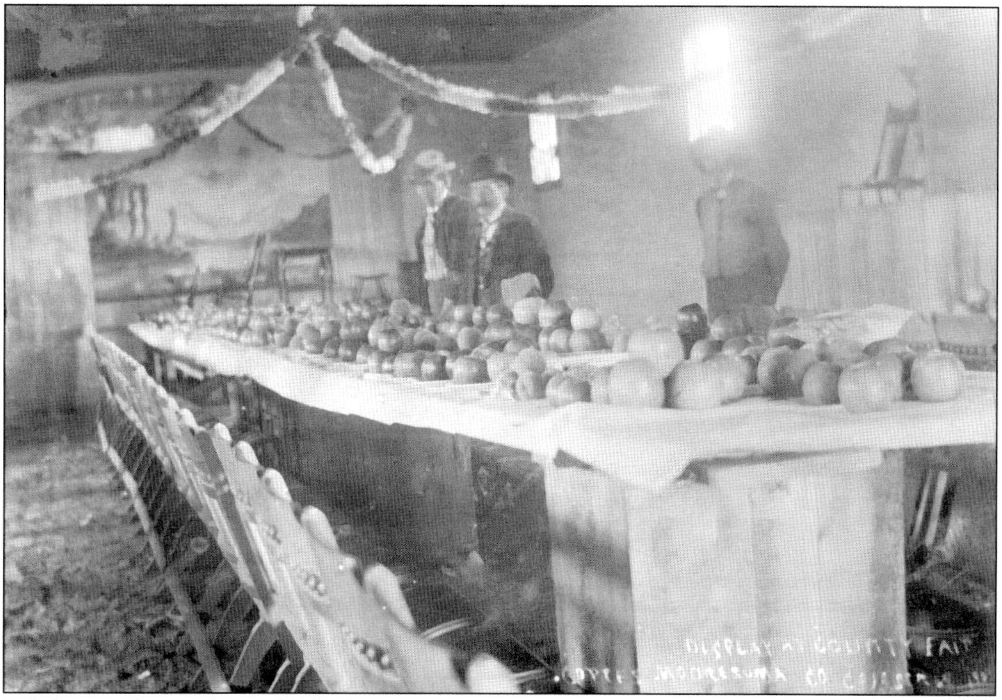

Exhibits at the newly established Montezuma County Fair included tables full of canned and fresh produce, dairy and bakery plates, needlework, and garden bouquets that were set up for judging in Woodmen Hall. Produce from Montezuma County in the first half of the 20th century was taken to various world fairs and often won numerous "best of" prizes. (Courtesy of Cortez Public Library.)

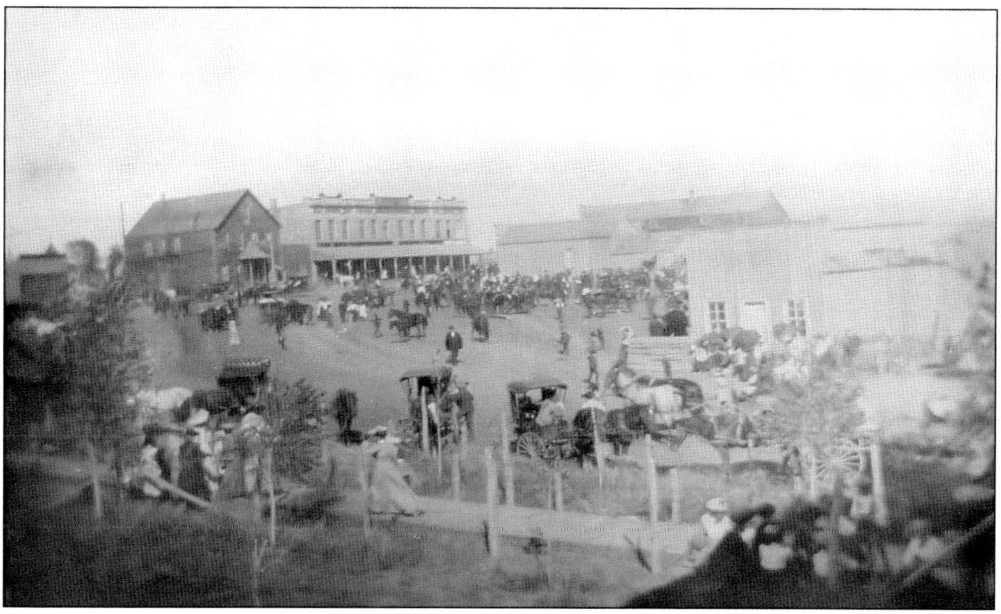

This bird's-eye view of people gathering for one of the first Montezuma County Fairs was taken from the top floor of Woodmen Hall. Outdoors activities were held at the fairgrounds on the west end of town where the school baseball field is now. (Courtesy of First National Bank of Cortez.)

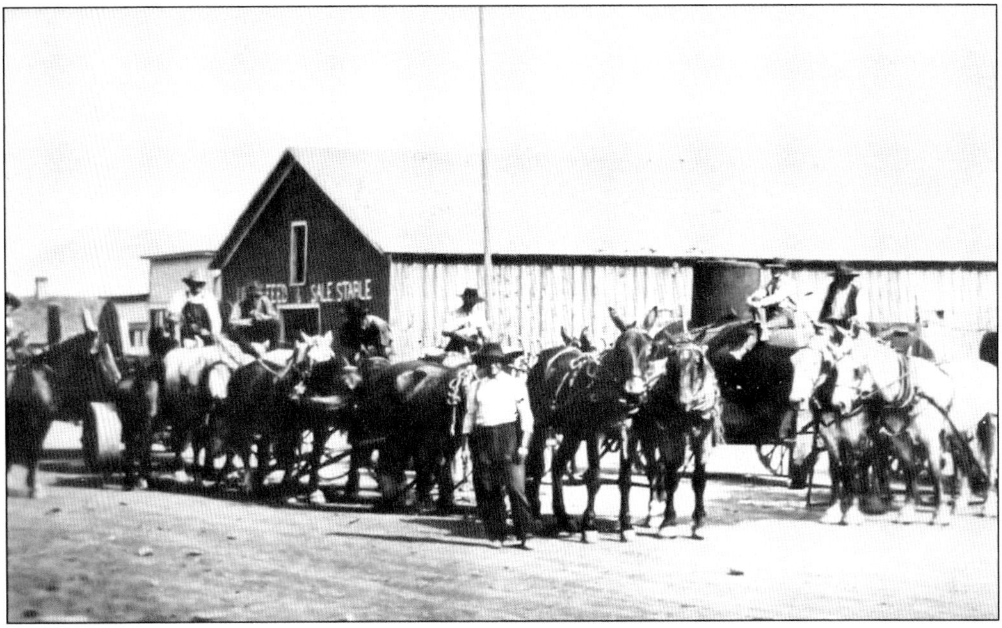

Men, mule and horse teams, and heavy equipment stand in front of Hi McEwen's Livery at the southeast corner of Main and Market Streets in this turn-of-the-century photograph. At this time, businesses constructed rough board sidewalks mounted on two-by-fours on dirt streets. The McEwen brothers were known for horse trading and racing and also were reported as having lost a Dolores River ranch in a poker game. (Courtesy of Duane Neal and First National Bank of Cortez.)

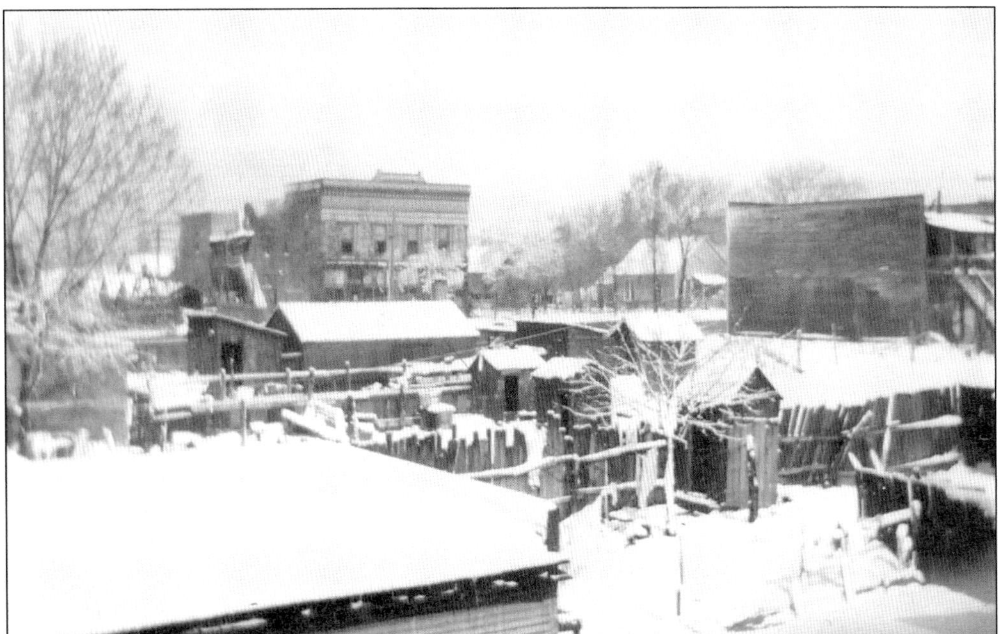

Edward R. Lamb and his wife endured three separate fires at their mercantile and millinery businesses. The cast-iron front of the last building, constructed in 1908, came from a St. Louis, Missouri, foundry. The E.R. Lamb Building at 25 North Market Street currently houses the Cortez Cultural Center. (Courtesy of Larry Hauser.)

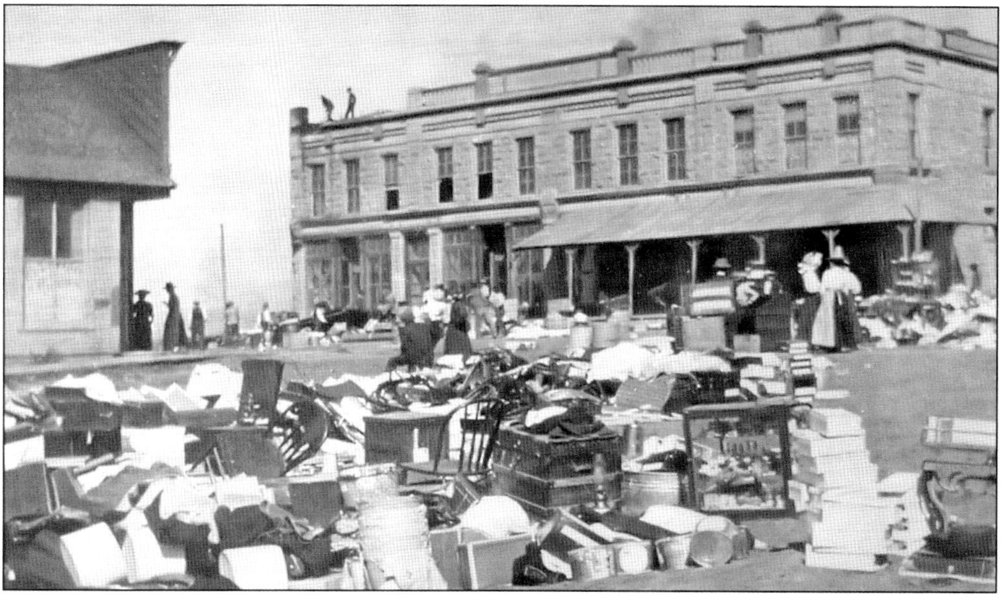

Smoke rises from the remains of the popular Clifton Hotel on West Main Street. Notice that portions of the wooden balustrade atop the neighboring Stone Block were removed. Opened in 1893 by Mr. and Mrs. Johnny O. Brown from North Carolina, the hotel escaped a large downtown fire in 1898 but burned to the ground in September 1908, along with several buildings to the west. Telephone lines were soon established between Cortez and Dolores to aid in requesting emergency assistance. (Courtesy of Herma Watson and First National Bank of Cortez.)

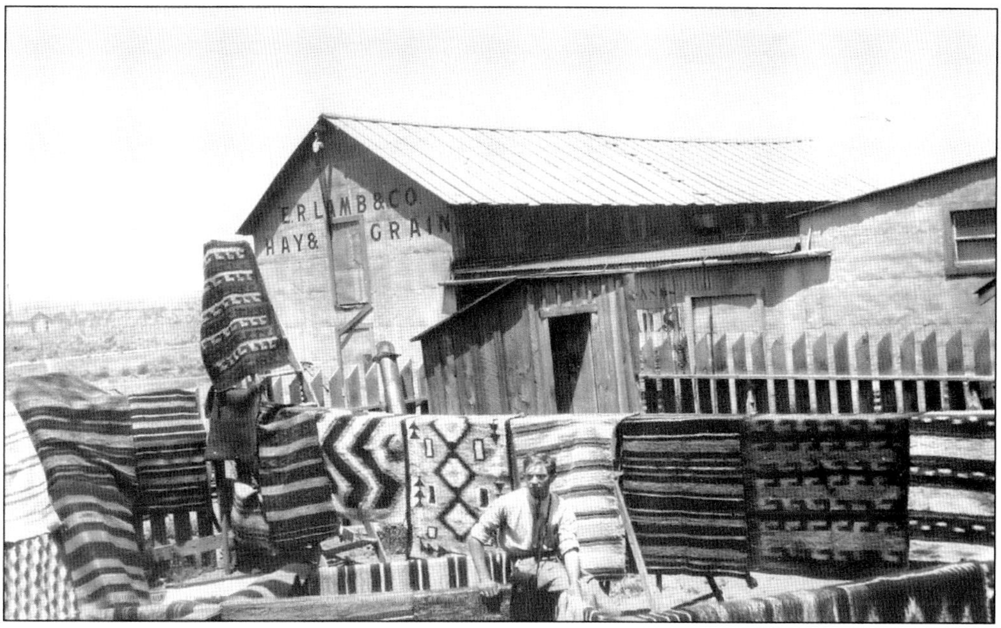

Navajo rugs drape fences behind the Stone Block and near the E.R. Lamb warehouse in the fall of 1908. Gladys Hart said her father, Herm Guillet, soaked Navajo rugs with water and laid them on the roof of the Stone Block to prevent the spread of the Clifton Hotel fire. The Guillet brothers, Herm and Pete, were partners in a trading post in Utah, flour mills in Cortez and Mancos, and a mercantile in Cortez. (Courtesy of A.L. Guillet family and First National Bank of Cortez.)

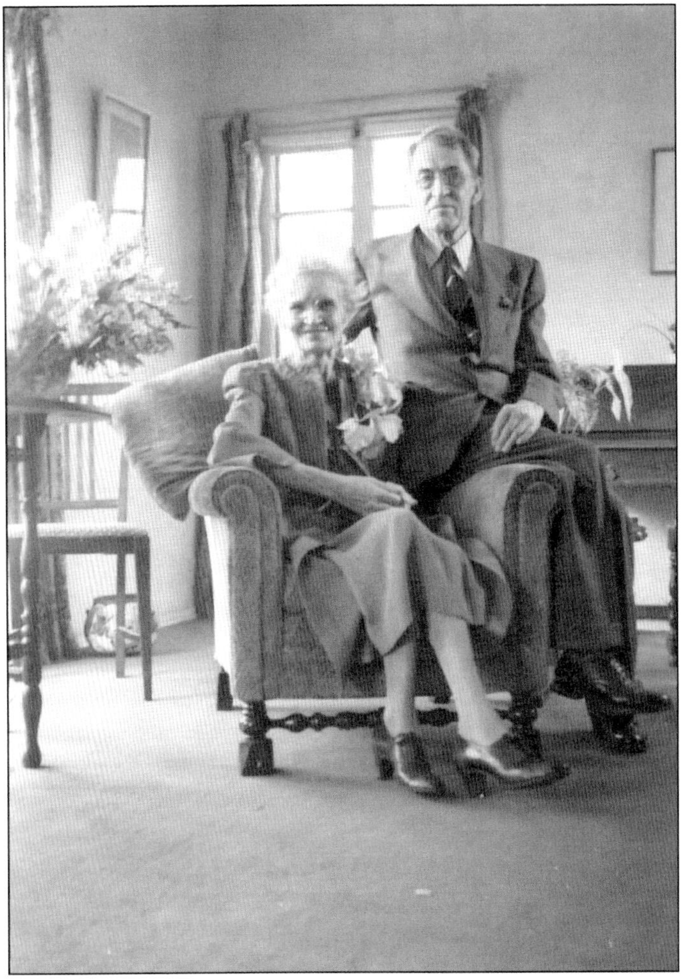

P.T. "Pete" and Margaret Guillet pose for their 50th wedding anniversary in 1942. The Guillet brothers came to Cortez from Missouri, but also lived in Brazil and California. Peter said he was not quite 10 when Lincoln was assassinated, and the family watched the funeral procession in New York City on their way to South America. Pete served as mayor and as a member of the school board, the Masonic lodge, and the First Methodist Church in Cortez. Margaret (née Morgan) from Iowa, taught at Blue Door School for a time. (Courtesy of Herma Jean Watson.)

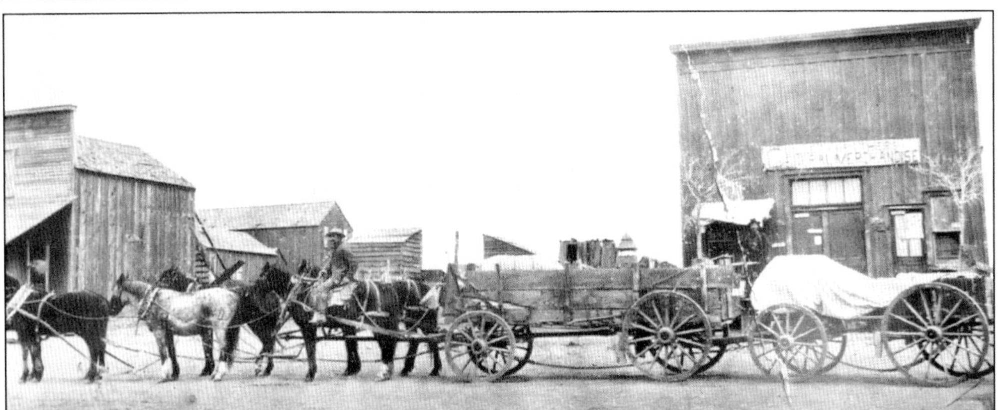

Sterl Thomas's tandem wagon readies a load of freight from Guillet Brothers General Merchandise in Cortez to the Guillet's trading post at Riverview (now Aneth), Utah. Lee Kelly was the freighter, with the teams broken to the jerkline. The trip usually took six weeks in good weather. Today's travel time would take a little more than an hour. (Courtesy of Duane Neal and First National Bank of Cortez.)

Johnny O. Brown, owner and manager of the Brown Palace Hotel, sits in a lawn chair with a hat in his lap. He and his wife built the Brown Palace Hotel after the Clifton Hotel burned. Brown had owned the Clifton, but it was managed by C.L. Plethebridge. (Courtesy of Cortez Public Library.)

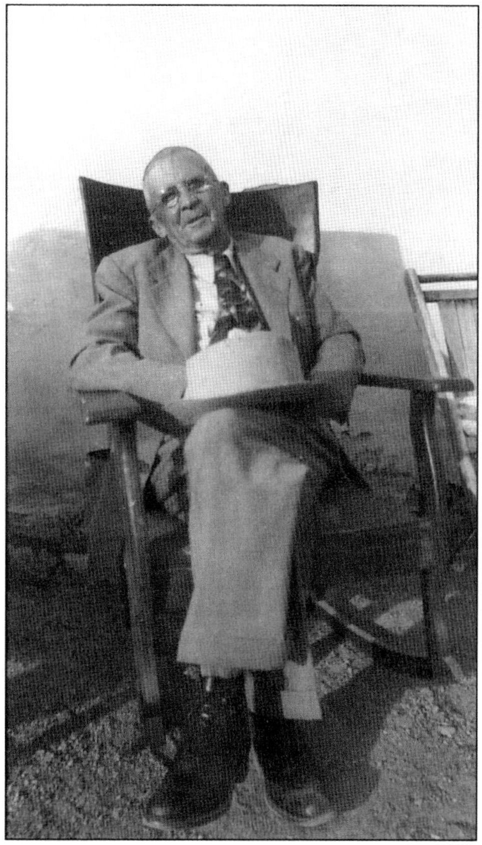

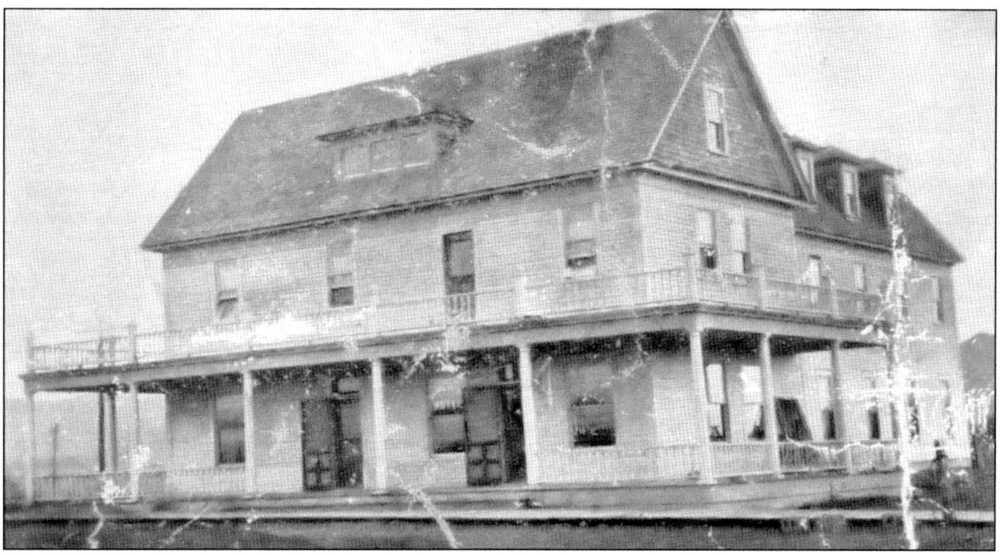

In 1909, the three-story, 40-room Brown Palace Hotel set the border for the east end of town at the corner of Main and South Washington Streets. It gracefully offered tourists and businessmen a wide veranda on three sides. In later years, its name changed to Hotel Cortez and the wooden facade was covered with stucco. The hotel was a landmark and a community gathering spot until it was demolished in 1986. (Courtesy of Hurschel Coppinger and First National Bank of Cortez.)

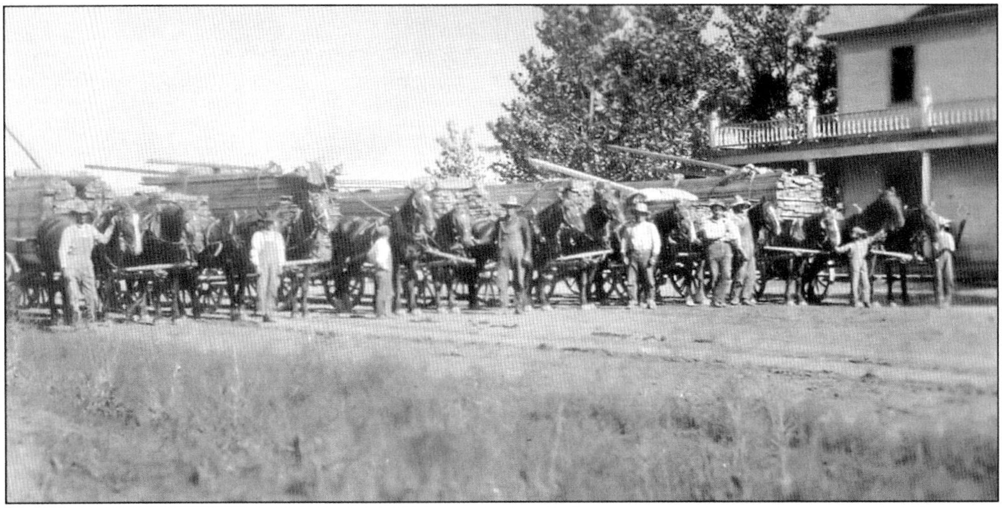

Seven wagonloads of lumber arrive in Cortez to supply a building boom in the early 1920s. They straddle Main Street in front of the Brown Palace Hotel. Just down the street at the corner of Main and Beech Streets, Dungan Gibson managed Gibson Lumber, formerly Mead-Hengstler Lumber Company, which operated two sawmills. Plentiful timber in the La Plata Mountains supported many sawmills. (Courtesy of Herma Watson and First National Bank of Cortez.)

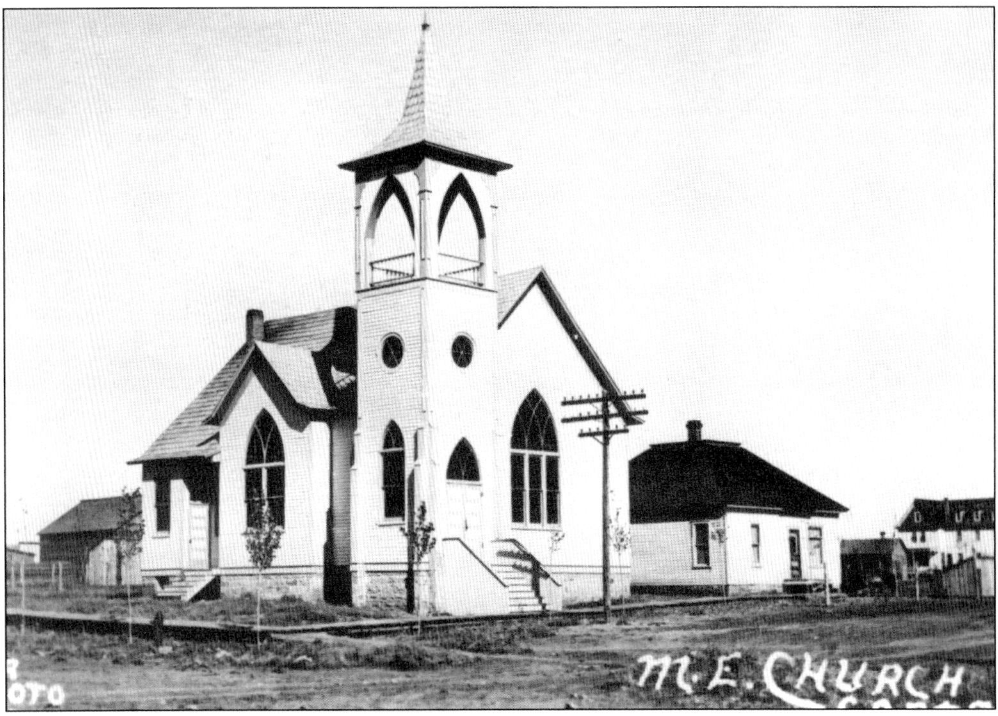

Grandma Bozman, president of the Ladies Aid Society, laid the cornerstone for the Cortez Methodist Church in November 1908. Built at the corner of South Beech and First Streets in the next two years, the first services were held in 1910. Membership was about 50. The parsonage was added soon after to the east, facing First Street. The Brown Palace Hotel can be seen to the far right. (Courtesy of Lucy Hadley.)

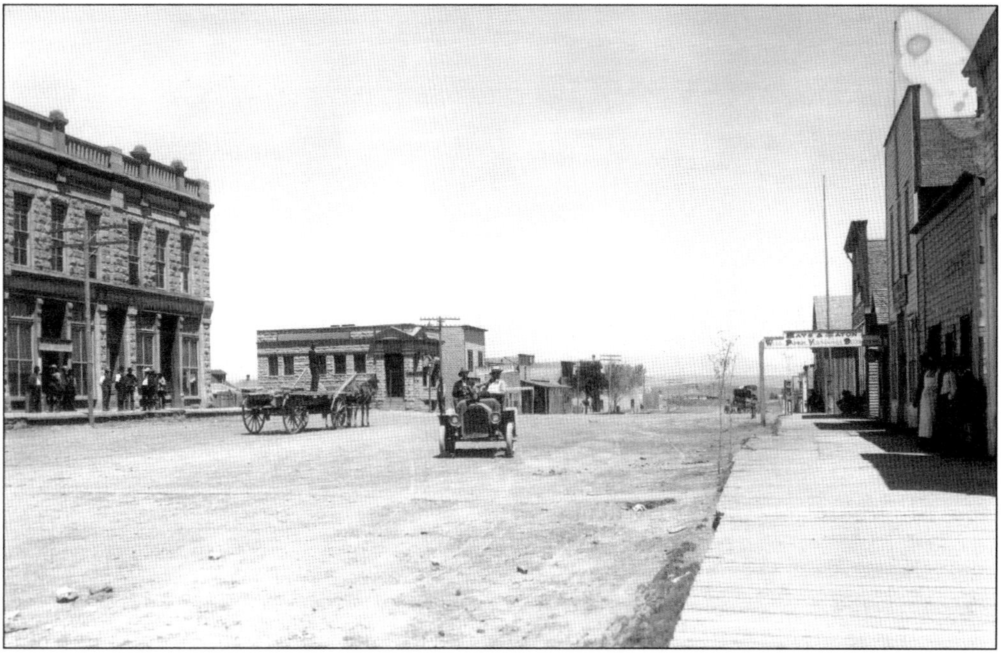

Looking east on Main Street from approximately the southeast corner of Main and Chestnut Streets, this photograph, taken between 1887 and 1910, shows early boardwalks, few trees, the original Montezuma Valley Bank building, the Stone Block, a horse-drawn wagon, and a lone automobile. (Courtesy of History Colorado, George Beam Collection, Scan No. 20004411.)

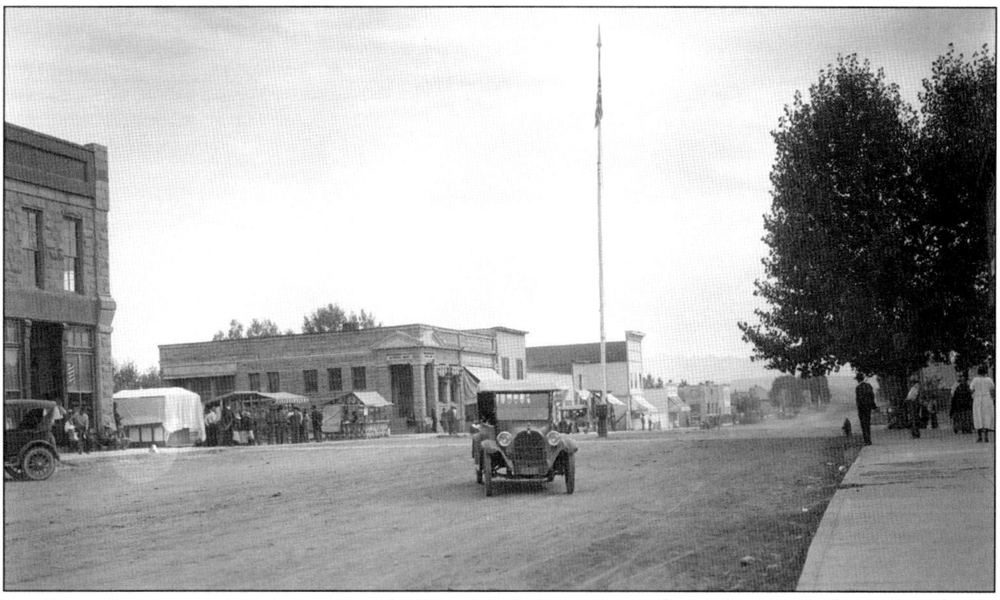

In a later photograph, taken between 1910 and 1920 from about the same spot as the image above, there are more and fairly large trees, a fire hydrant, concrete sidewalks, the flagpole at Market and Main Streets, taller buildings on Main Street, an addition to the Montezuma Valley Bank, no wooden balustrade atop the Stone Block, more automobiles, and a street fair. In 1909, Cortez installed a water system with fire hydrants to ensure good fire protection. (Courtesy of History Colorado, Denver & Rio Grande Collection, Scan No. 20005325.)

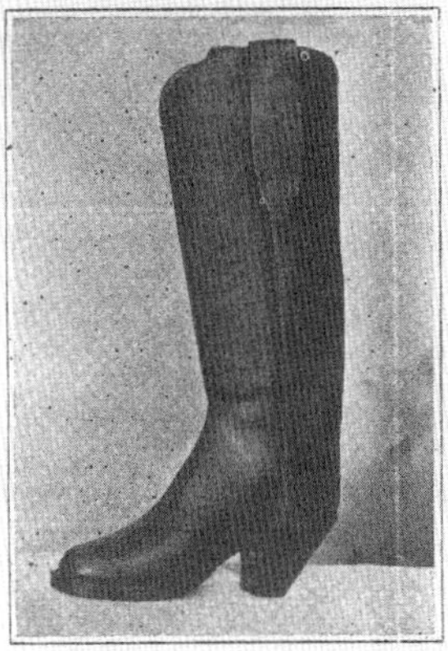

L. G. GRASSE

MANUFACTURER OF AND DEALER IN

FINE HAND-MADE BOOTS

FINE COWBOY BOOTS A SPECIALTY

P. O. BOX 2

CORTEZ, COLORADO

French Calf or Kip, pegged, $18.00
French Calf or Kip, sewed, $20.00

Ladies' and Men's Boots of any kind and style and of any kind of leather, made to order and satisfaction guaranteed.

Size Usually Worn ....

Ball of Foot ....

Instep ....

Around Heel to Instep ....

Calf of Leg ....
(Over Pants or as tight as you want them.)

Small Ankle ....

Toe .... Heel ....
(State kind of toe and heel wanted.)

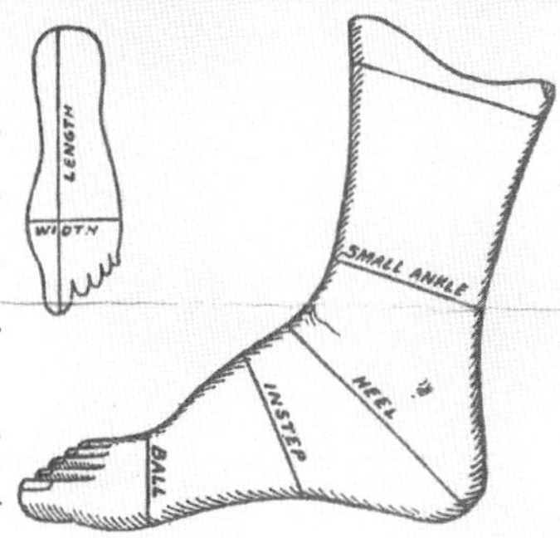

Name .... City of ....

County of .... State of ....

ALL BOOTS POSTPAID WHEN CASH IN FULL ACCOMPANIES ORDER. Be sure to write your name, county, state, postoffice and description of boots you want VERY PLAINLY.

All Orders Filled To Any Part Of The United States, Canada Or Cuba.

Be careful of snide shoemakers who claim they make a cowboy boot. We are the original and only makers of cowboy boots, and guarantee satisfaction.

All new customers are required to pay in advance at least one-fourth the price of the goods ordered. In case you pay but a part of the price in advance you must pay the postage on the goods and return charges on money.

We make all kinds of Boots, but we do not warrant any term of service for alligator or tan leather boots. French Calf and Kip are the most serviceable leathers and we warrant the same.

Directions for measuring: In ordering Boots, I can guarantee a perfect fit if the following directions are attended to. Place the foot on other side of this sheet and mark all around it, holding the pencil straight up. This will be the exact length and spread of the foot, as shown in the small cut. Then measure with a tape line: Ball, Instep, Heel, and the height of boot as shown in larger cut. When you want any particular style, state plainly what you want.

If you follow instructions for measuring as given above, and you favor me with your order, I will guarantee you a pair of boots, stylish and comfortable in fact a PERFECT FIT; however, should it happen that the boots you order and receive from me, do not fit satisfactorily, return same, advising plainly where the trouble lies, whether too large or too small, and I will immediately make another pair in place of the ones returned, THAT WILL FIT.

All C. O. D. Orders must be accompanied by one-fourth of price.

Leo Grasse used this handbill to advertise his boot, saddle, and harness business. (Courtesy of Paul Crawford.)

Leopold and Augusta Grasse, both of German heritage, moved to Cortez in 1909 from Paonia, Colorado, where they had owned a bicycle shop. (Courtesy of Paul Crawford.)

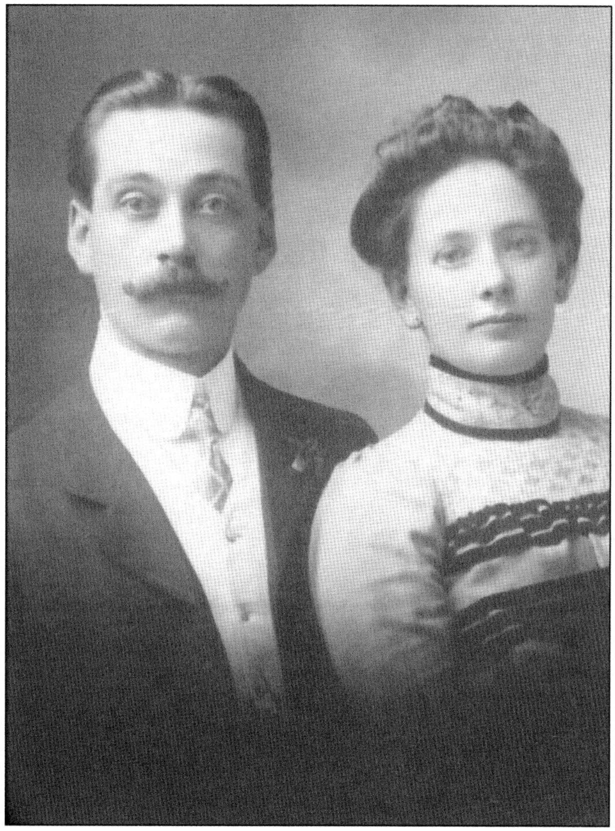

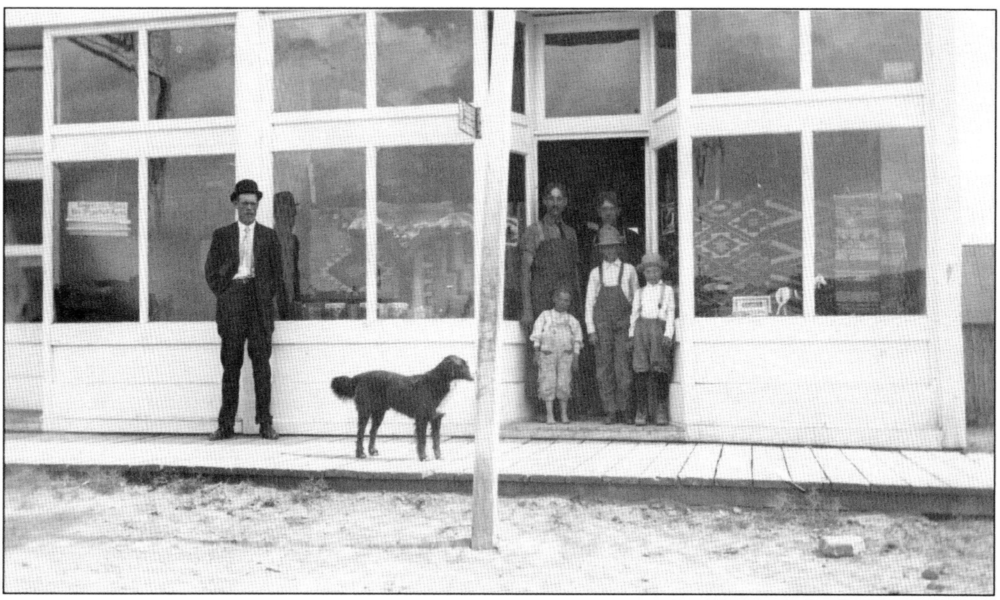

Leopold Grasse stands in the doorway of his boot and harness shop on East Main Street. Grasse had inherited some money from his grandfather. He briefly considered starting a liquor store in Lake City. The local temperance society physically ejected them from that town, so they opened this business in Cortez. (Courtesy of Paul Crawford.)

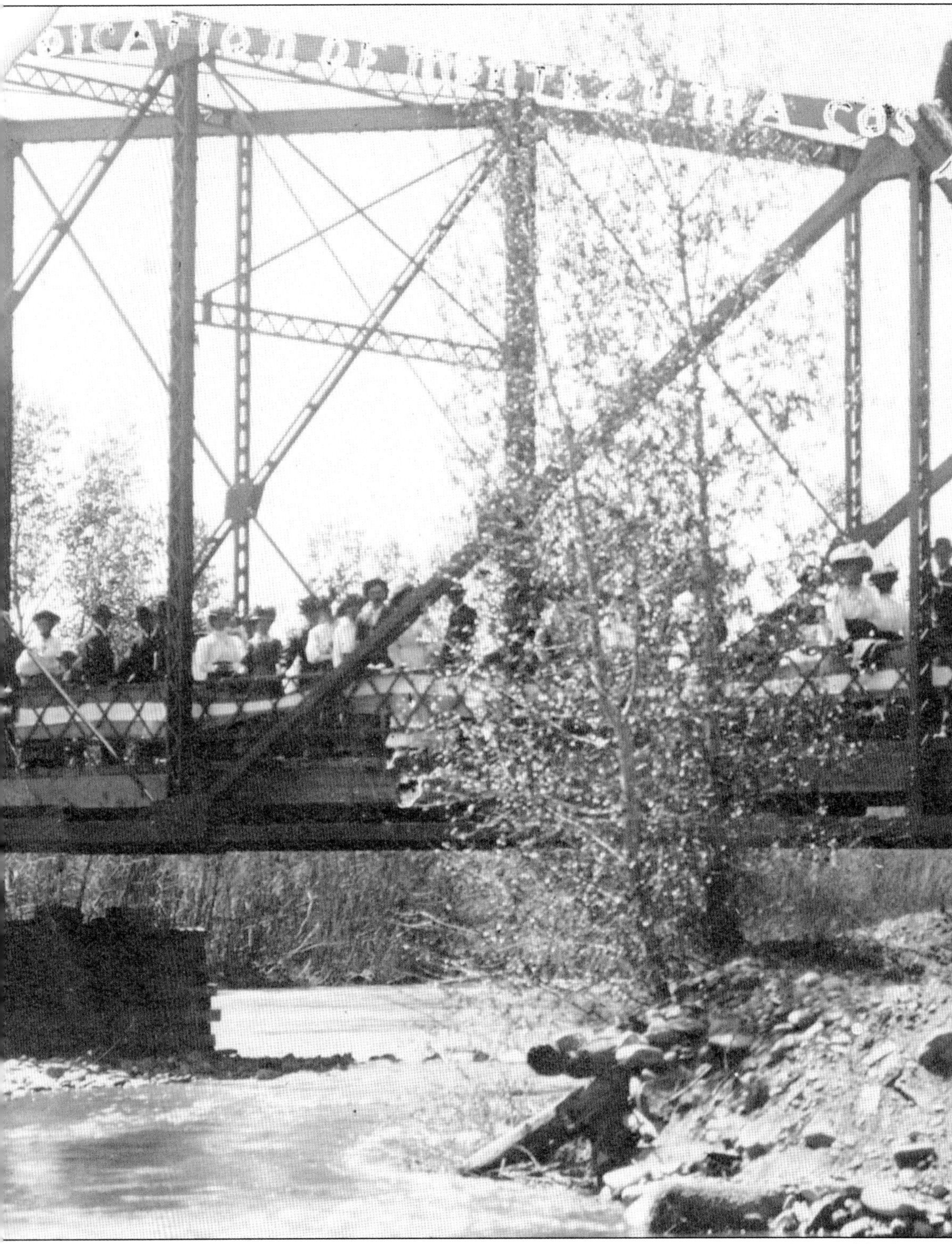

Folks from all around gathered to celebrate the dedication of Montezuma County's first steel bridge over the Dolores River on June 8, 1910. This particular image was made into a postcard, a typical

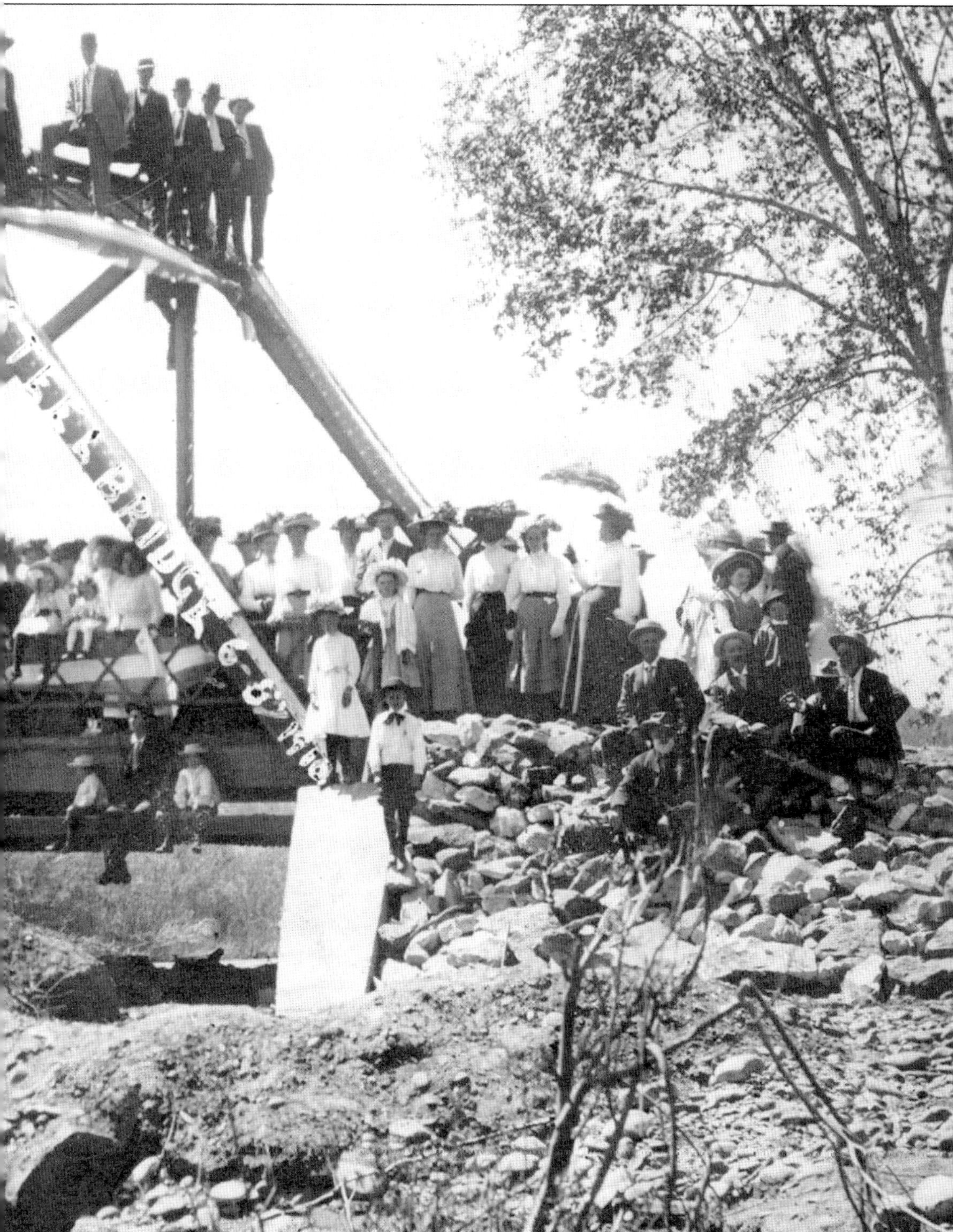

way to promote the newly developing West. (Courtesy of Anasazi Heritage Center.)

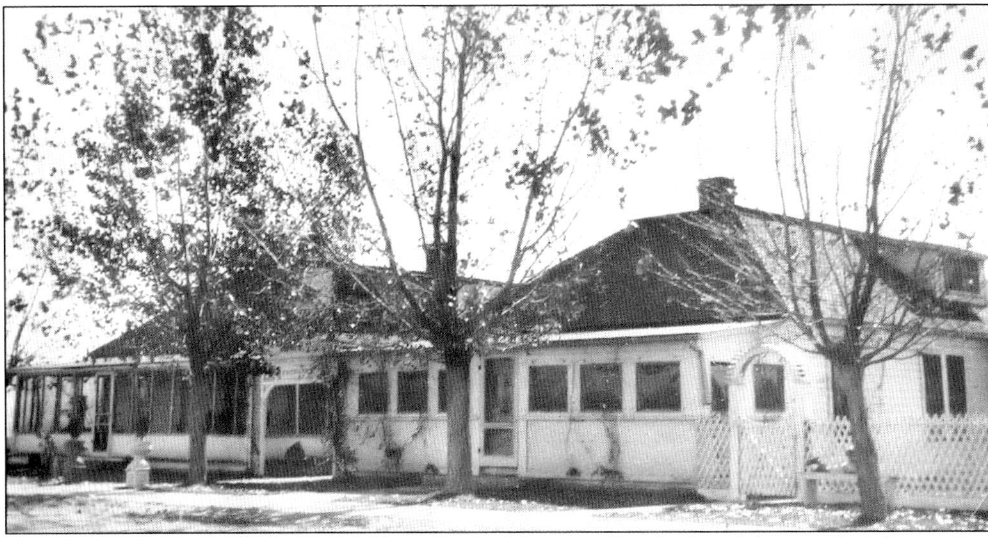

In 1917, Dr. Emil E. Johnson purchased these two cottages to serve as Cortez's first hospital. A Swedish immigrant, Johnson graduated from the Chicago College of Medicine and Surgery and purchased a Cortez medical practice in 1912. He reared his family, served on community boards and commissions, and aided in the establishment of electric power in Montezuma Valley, along with practicing medicine and taking patients into his living quarters when hospital beds were full. (Courtesy of Ingrid Hartley and Eugene Johnson, and First National Bank of Cortez.)

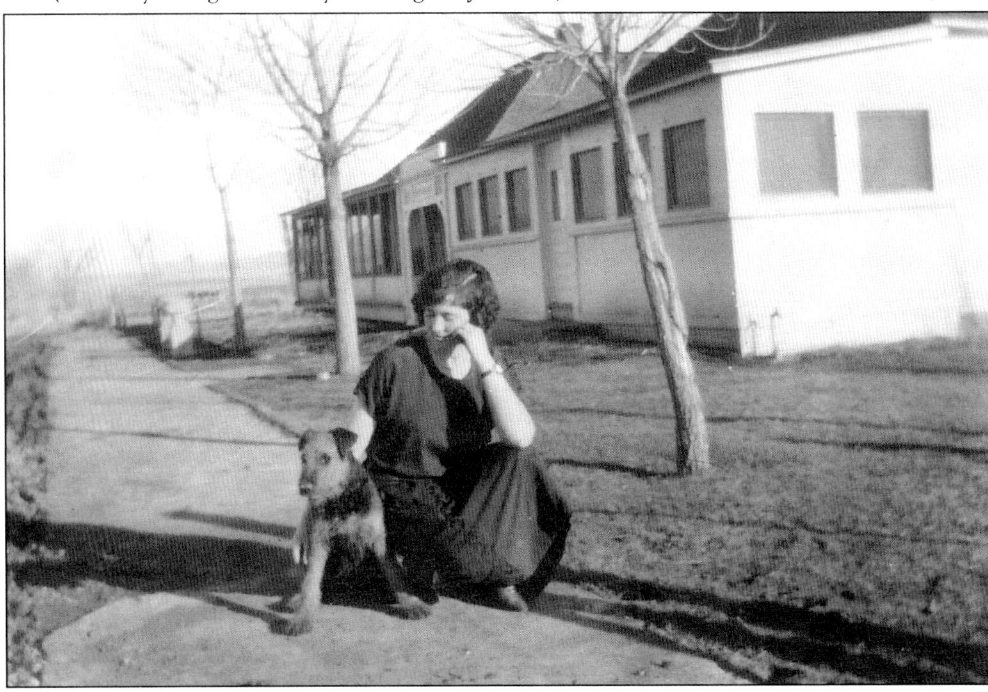

Virginia Norman Johnson, wife of Doctor Johnson, poses in front of the hospital on East Main Street. Virginia worked as a nurse in the doctor's practice and hosted the Crown Prince of Sweden when he visited Mesa Verde. In 1915, Doctor Johnson left his Cortez practice for 26 days to attend to two injured members of a Ute-chasing posse in Bluff City, Utah. Collecting on his bill of $502 for fees, board and room, and livery for his team proved difficult. (Courtesy of Larry Hauser.)

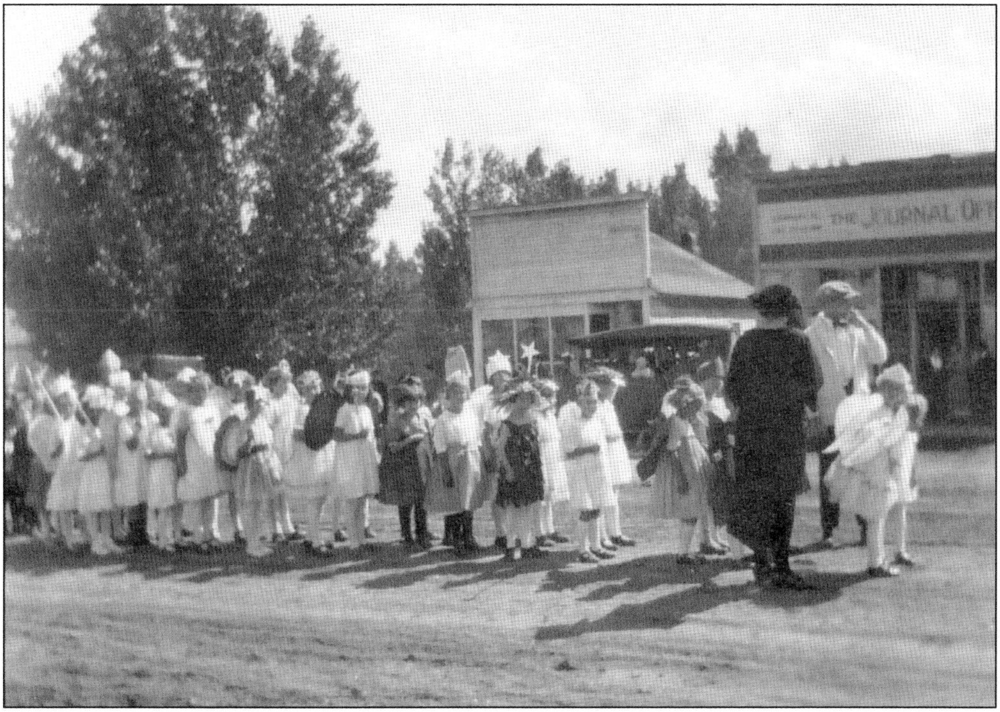

Teachers ready their schoolchildren for an old-fashioned parade down East Main Street, probably around the mid-1910s. The Journal Office on the south side of Main Street between Beech and Market Streets stands behind them. (Courtesy of Larry Hauser.)

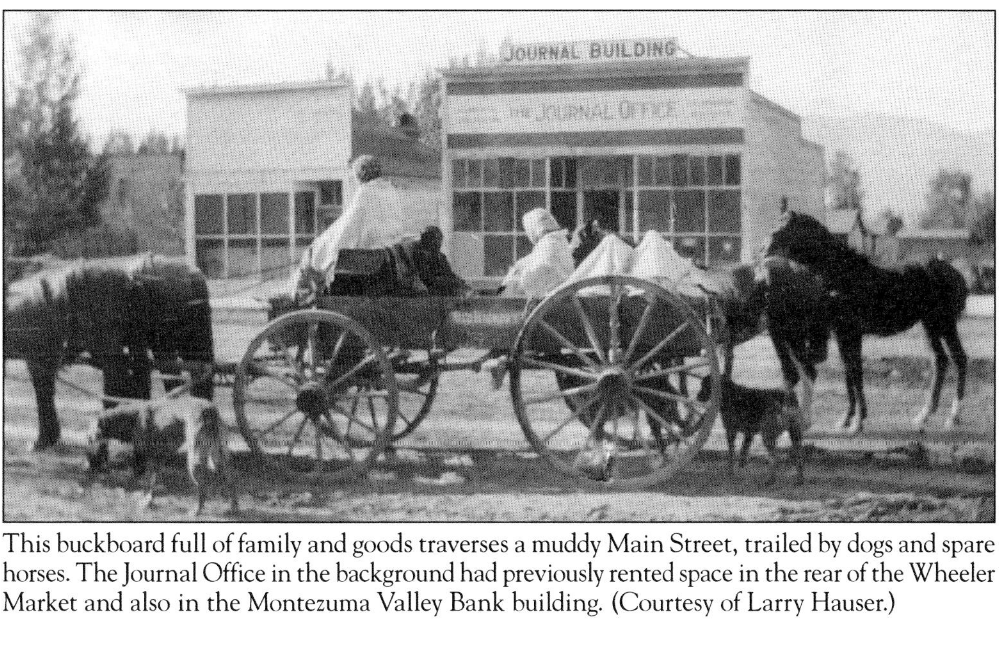

This buckboard full of family and goods traverses a muddy Main Street, trailed by dogs and spare horses. The Journal Office in the background had previously rented space in the rear of the Wheeler Market and also in the Montezuma Valley Bank building. (Courtesy of Larry Hauser.)

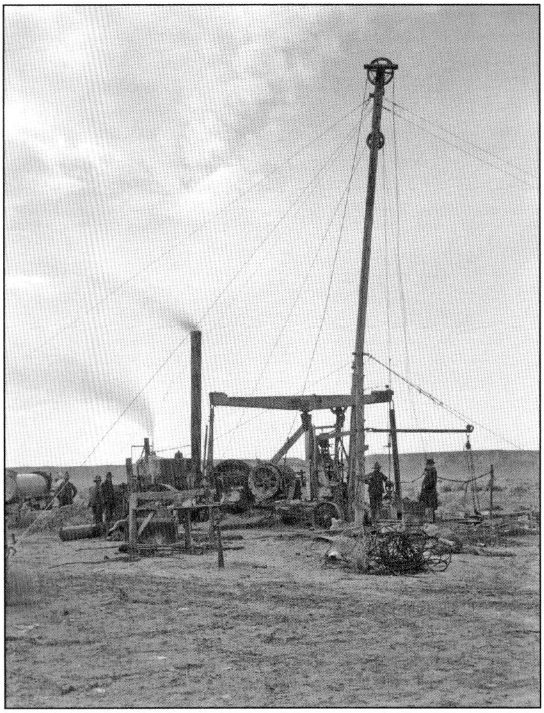

George Lytle Beam photographed this steam-powered drilling rig on the Colorado-Utah border between 1922 and 1935. Finding oil was a dream for many entrepreneurs as soon as its potential for energy use was deemed commercially viable in the mid-1800s. In 1908, oil was found near the Colorado-Utah border, both northwest and southwest of Cortez. (Courtesy of Denver Public Library, Western History Collection, GB-7119.)

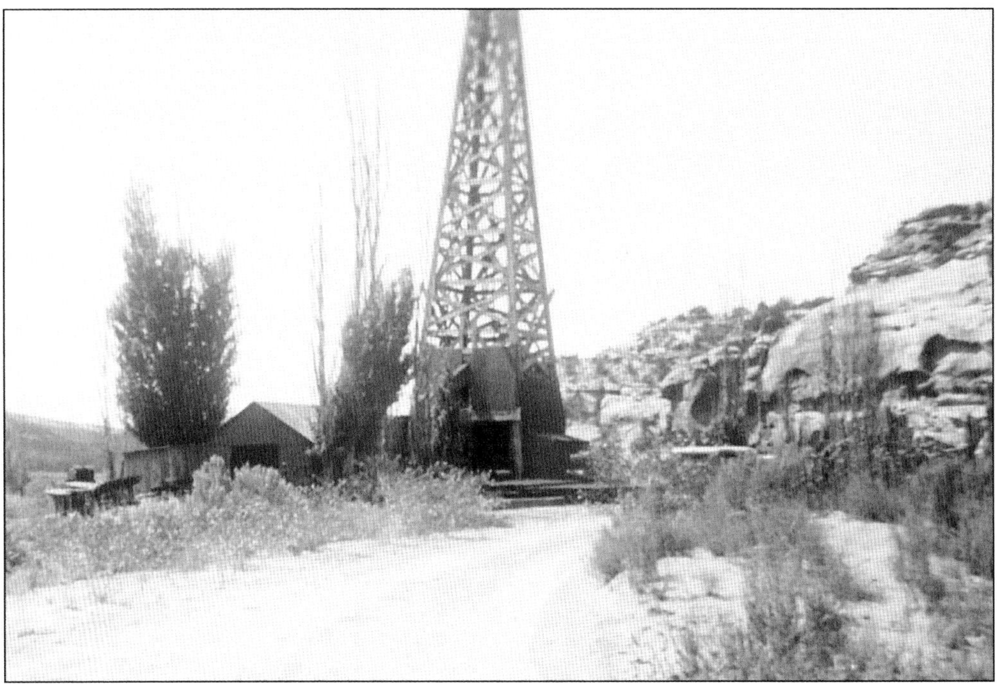

This photograph of a drilling rig appears to be in McElmo Canyon. In the summer of 1911, Mesa Verde Oil and Gas Company drilled a test well four miles south of Cortez. Also in 1911, Big Four-San Juan Oil and Development Company drilled a well at Battle Rock that came in at 150 feet. The flow was light but the oil was good. Another Big Four drill struck water at 500 feet, which hampered efforts to retrieve the oil. (Courtesy of Cortez Area Chamber of Commerce.)

In 1911, civic leaders and farmers recruited agriculturist, writer, and former politician William B. Ebbert to manage and stabilize the Montezuma Valley Irrigation District, a position he held until 1920. In 1889, prior to moving to Cortez, Ebbert was elected to the state legislature, representing Pueblo and Otero Counties. He later represented Montezuma and Dolores Counties. (Courtesy of Brian Ebbert.)

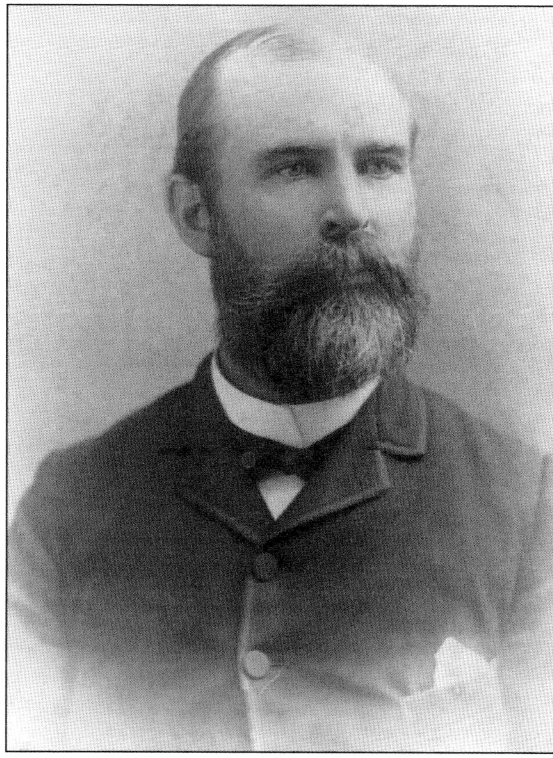

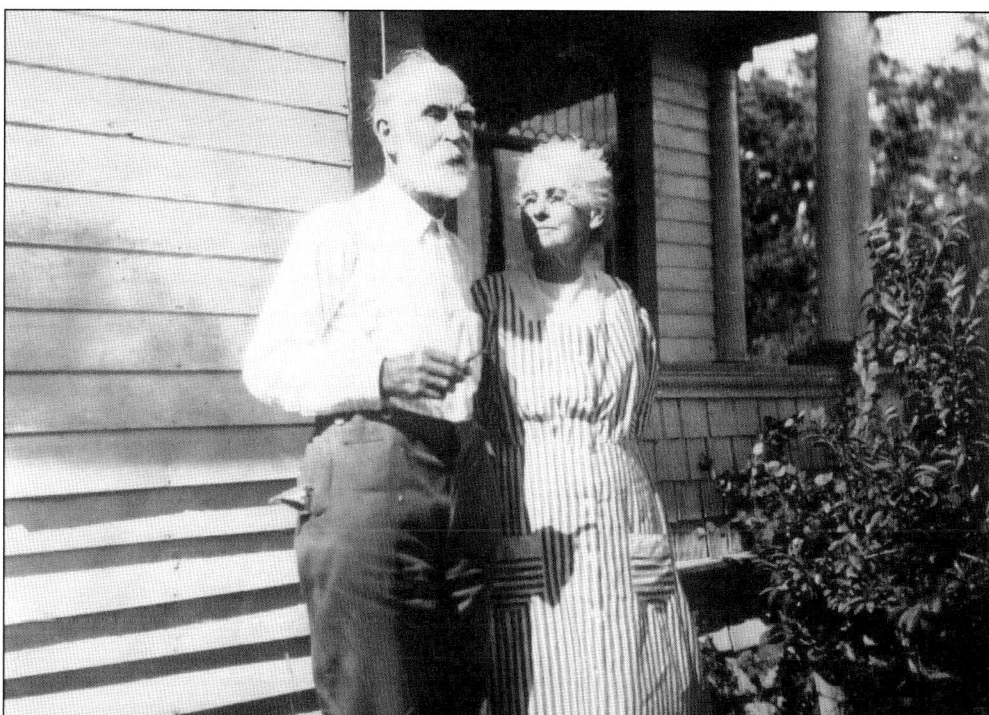

Post-retirement, William Ebbert and his second wife, Catherine, stand in front of their Arriola ranch house in this 1924 photograph. (Courtesy of Brian Ebbert.)

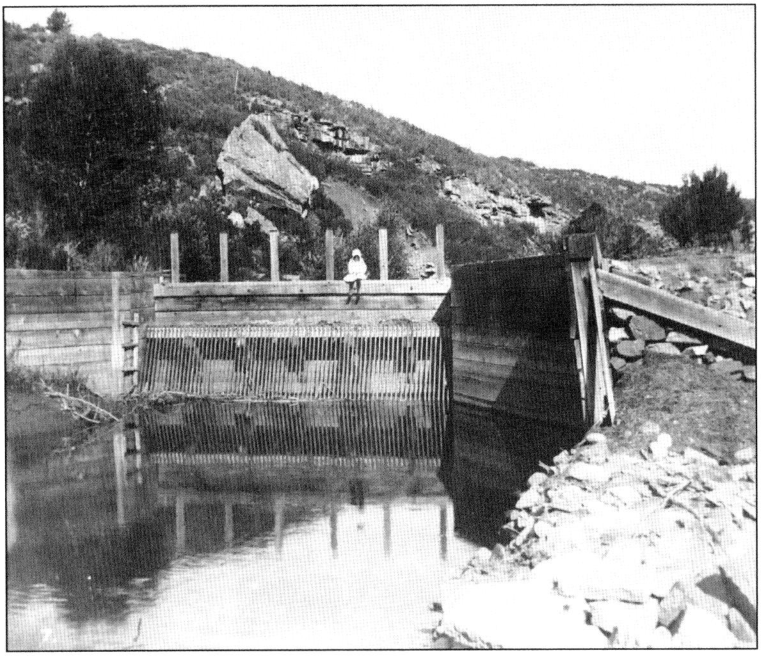

A little girl sits on one of the wooden headgates in the system. The initial cost of the Great Cut and Morton flume was about $700,000. The flume was 5,850 feet long by 18 feet wide by seven feet deep and ran between McPhee and Highway 145. These two parts of the canal were very expensive to maintain. (Courtesy of Anasazi Heritage Center.)

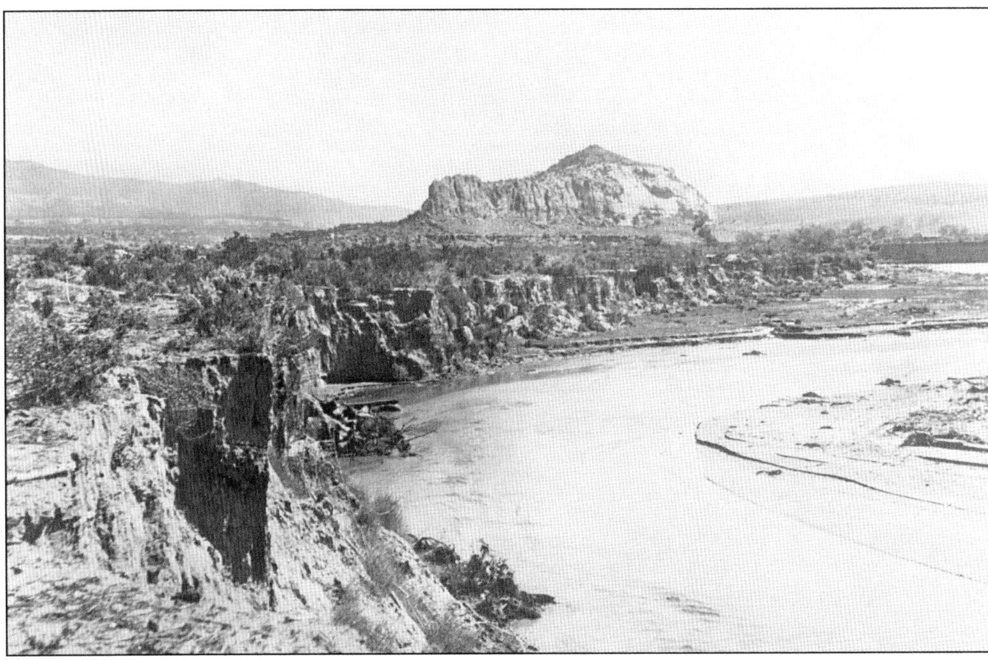

On July 10, 1911, floods cut a canyon within a canyon in McElmo. A ranch residence, parts of several orchards, 40 acres of wheat, and the big wooden bridge were washed away. Flumes washed out, and large laterals broke in a dozen or more places. Again, on October 5, a steady downpour covered most of the San Juan basin, where the San Miguel, Dolores, Mancos, La Plata, Animas, Pine, Piedra, San Juan, Navajo, and Chama Rivers all flooded, cut new channels, took bridges, and washed out highways and railroads. One of these storms washed out Groundhog Reservoir, which was completed in 1910 but was not rebuilt for 20 more years. (Courtesy of Denver Public Library, Western History Collection, P-1071.)

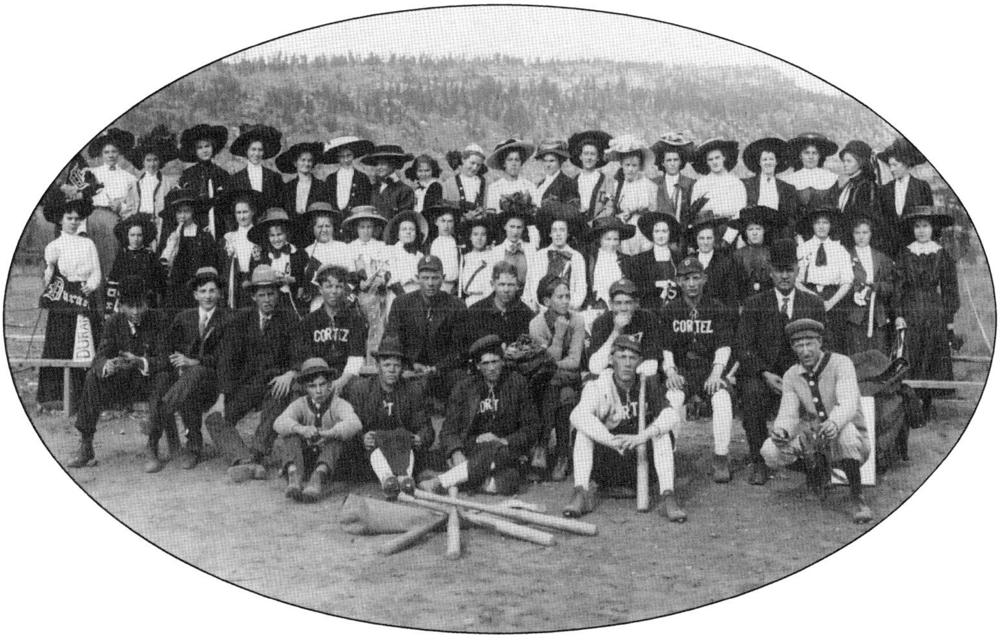

The boys from Cortez High School and their fans gathered for this photograph after soundly trouncing Durango's baseball team against hometown odds in the spring of 1910. Cortez and Durango have always been rivals, from Montezuma County's secession to vying for the relocation of Fort Lewis College. (Courtesy of Richard Lindsay.)

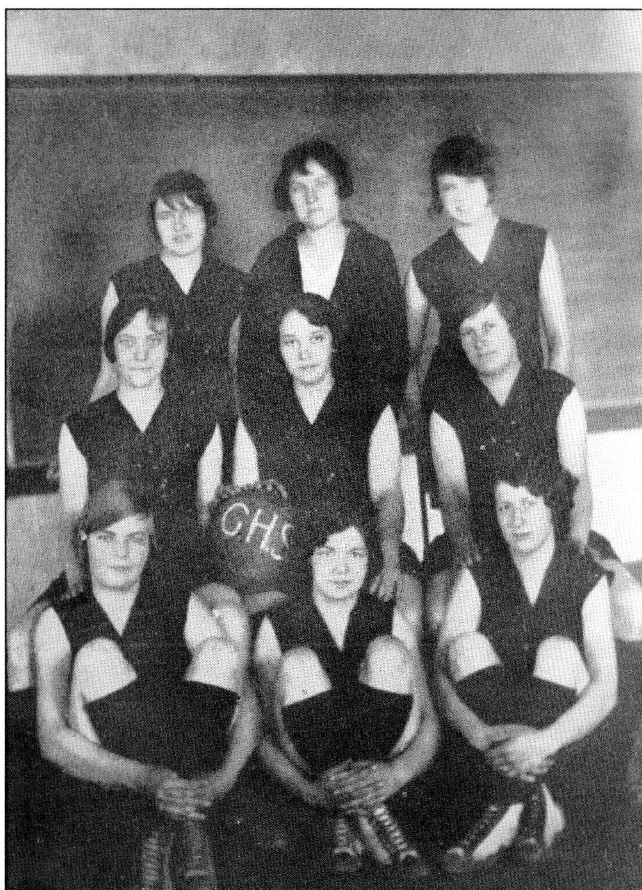

The 1926 Cortez High School annual listed the girls' basketball team by the players' last names, all of which were prominent families in the 1950s and 1960s. Included in the photograph are, from left to right, (first row) Larimore, Bowen, and Kirk; (second row) Major, Longenbaugh, and Veach; (third row) Honaker, Nelson (coach), and Hickman. (Courtesy of Larry Hauser.)

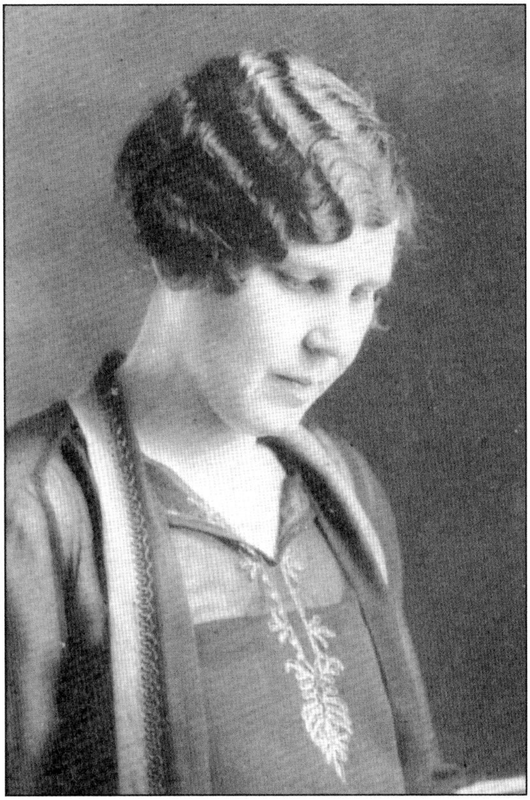

Anna Downing Henry was considered a dear friend and teacher to many, both in and out of school. The 1926 edition of the *Sleeping Ute,* the Cortez High School annual, was dedicated to her. She served as teacher, Ute Mountain Study Club officer, and community leader up until her death in the 1960s. (Courtesy of Larry Hauser.)

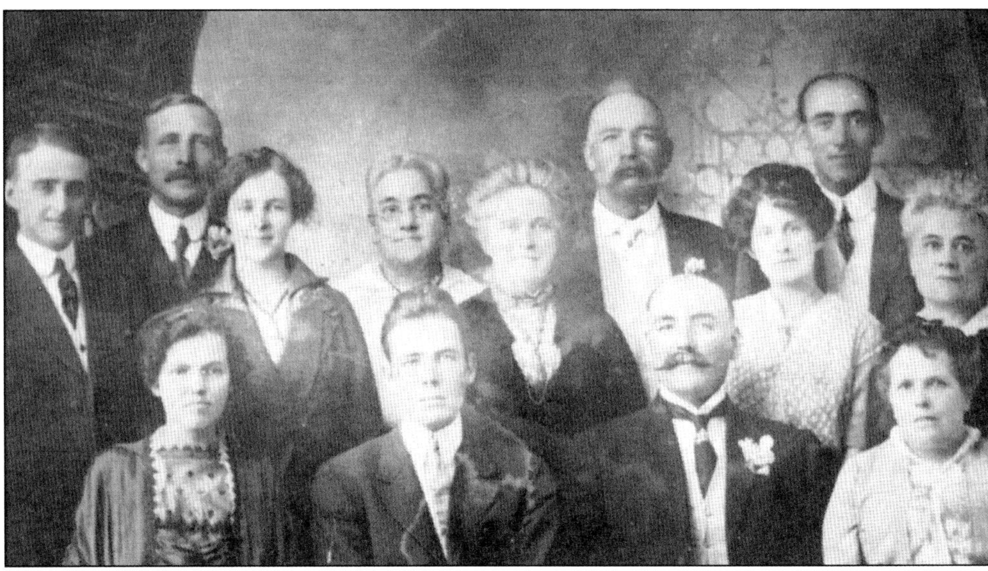

The Kermode family posed for this c. 1913 photograph. R.C. "Dick" Kermode owned a livery and stage line and guided trips into Mesa Verde. He was later joined by Alph Kermode in a farming enterprise, and Allen Kermode, who owned a bakery. R.C. was elected sheriff in 1907. They and their descendants owned a garage, dairy, bakery, and bookstore, fought in World War I, went into banking, and ranched, along with generally contributing to the welfare of the community. (Courtesy of Cortez Newspapers.)

Three

Automobiles Drive New Business

Growth began to strain Cortez's infrastructure. New telephone and electric services and automobiles began to change people's expectations of how business should be done. Fires and floods continued to periodically deplete resources. Residents wanted reliable water, better forms of communication, and improved roads.

The town built a new reservoir on three to five acres near the corner of Market Street and Montezuma Avenue. In 1916, the Cortez Board of Trustees passed a water ordinance. Work continued to expand and stabilize reservoirs in the high country and the valley. By 1937, Cortez had two water systems to provide more water taps.

In September 1920, the defaults of the water company and landowners caused the district board to work on a plan to put the indebtedness on an individual liability basis. When put to a vote, the new plan passed with 209 for and 20 against. Preparations were made to liquidate the irrigation district and form a new mutual ditch company under the name Montezuma Valley Irrigation Company (MVIC), incorporated under the laws of Colorado. Former state representative William Ebbert facilitated the district through this transition into MVIC. Economic development was renewed.

In 1910, the Mancos to Cortez highway was designated US Highway 160. In 1920, the federal government spent $20,000, the state added $10,000, and the county provided $10,000 to straighten bends and prepare the Cortez to Dolores road for gravel. The Cortez to Dove Creek road received $30,000 for improvements.

In 1913, automobile owners met with county commissioners to propose improving roads. The county began to grade county roads as they dried in the spring and after heavy rains. Main Street was graveled in 1922. The county purchased a crawler tractor to work on the Cortez to Dolores road. The county contributed $13,500 and the state $6,500 for road maintenance.

In 1914, the Cortez to Gallup highway received an appropriation of $15,000, quickly followed by another $15,000. In 1921, existing roads from Gallup to Moab formed a highway that generally followed the Old Spanish Trail. In 1932, Gov. William "Billy" H. Adams signed a budget including $60,000 for construction on Highway 160 between Mancos and Cortez.

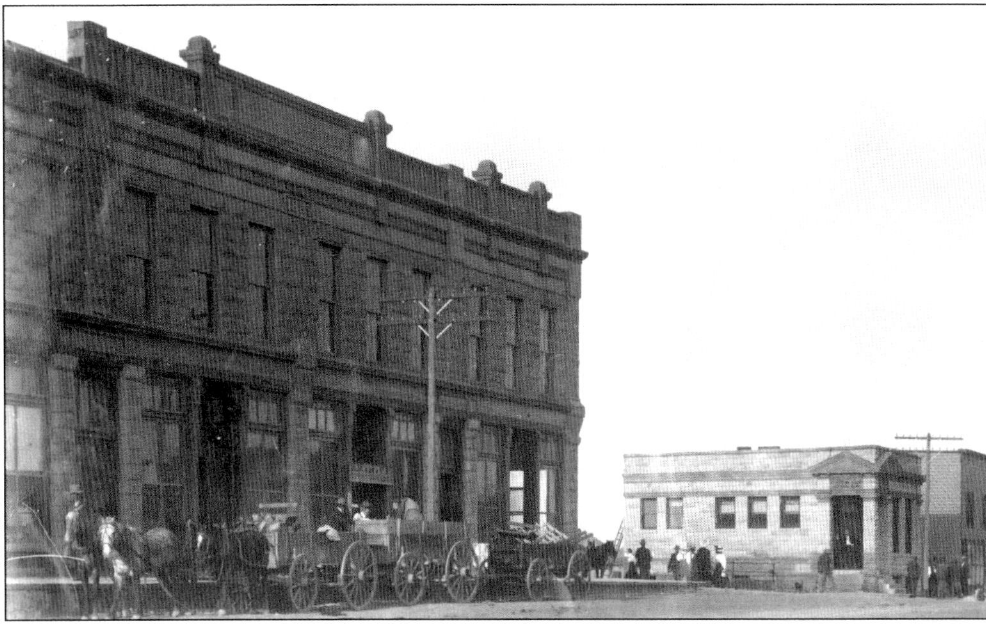

The Stone Block and Montezuma Valley Bank building stand as cornerstones for Cortez's city center. Poles for electricity or telephones are new additions, since the Montezuma Telephone Company, a local cooperative, completed the line from Mancos to Cortez in August 1905. As more businesses requested electricity, Cortez's first power plant was built in 1909. (Courtesy of Cortez Area Chamber of Commerce.)

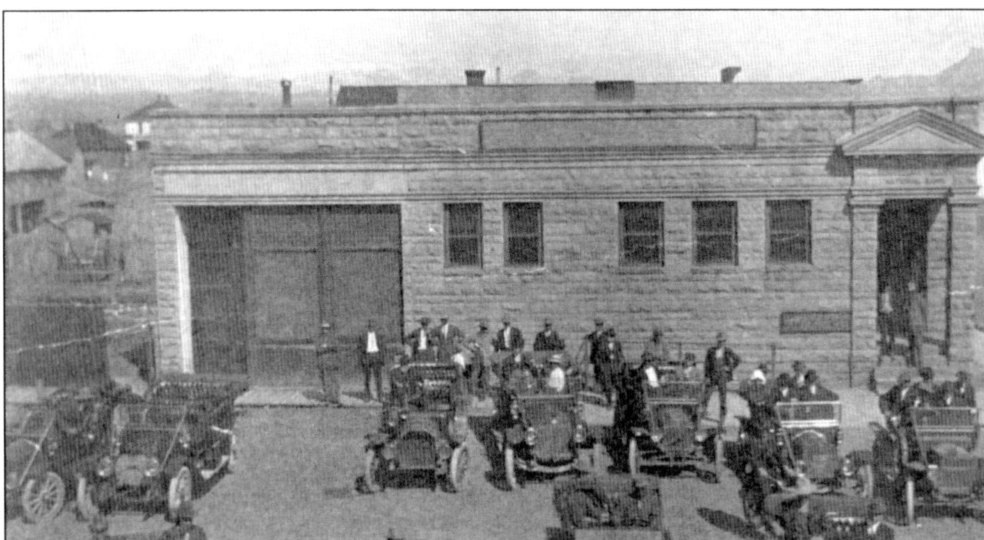

The Montezuma Valley Bank and its 1910 addition stand behind a group of cars touring through Montezuma County. In March 1908, realtors Blatchford and Bozman and livery owner Hi McEwen bought the first automobiles. McEwen subsequently sold the livery in June, but retained the stage and mail route. In 1916, Dick Kermode purchased the first motor truck in the county to haul freight. The number of cars and trucks nearly doubled in the next year, from 130 to 256 automobile registrations in Montezuma County. (Courtesy of First National Bank of Cortez.)

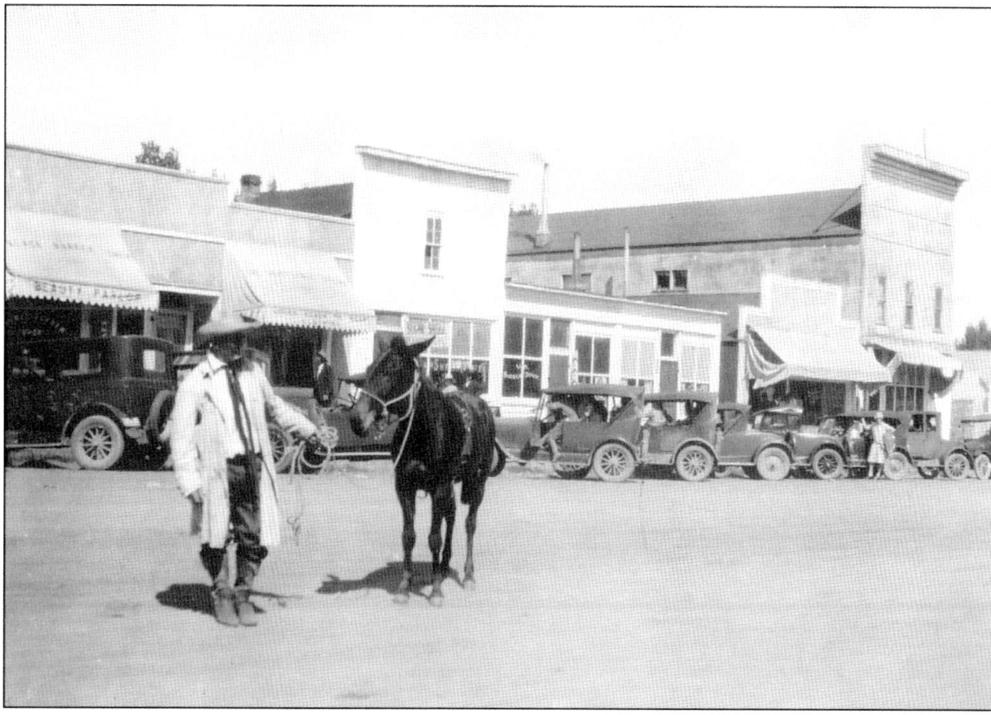

Main Street in Cortez has always had a mix of transportation types. Sometimes the beast carries the man. (Courtesy of Larry Hauser.)

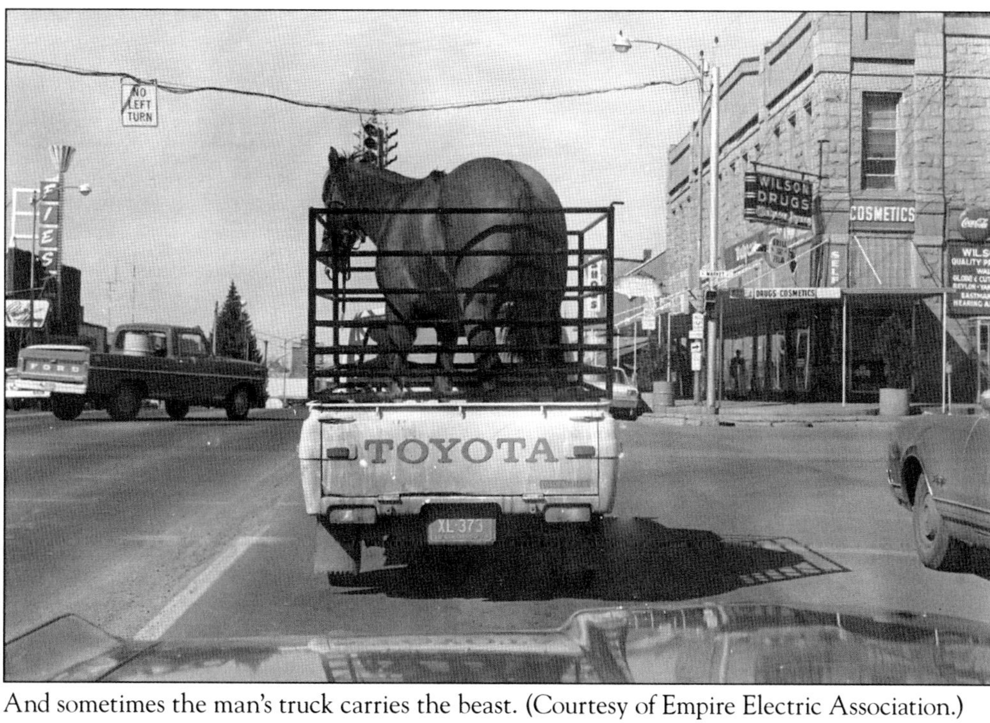

And sometimes the man's truck carries the beast. (Courtesy of Empire Electric Association.)

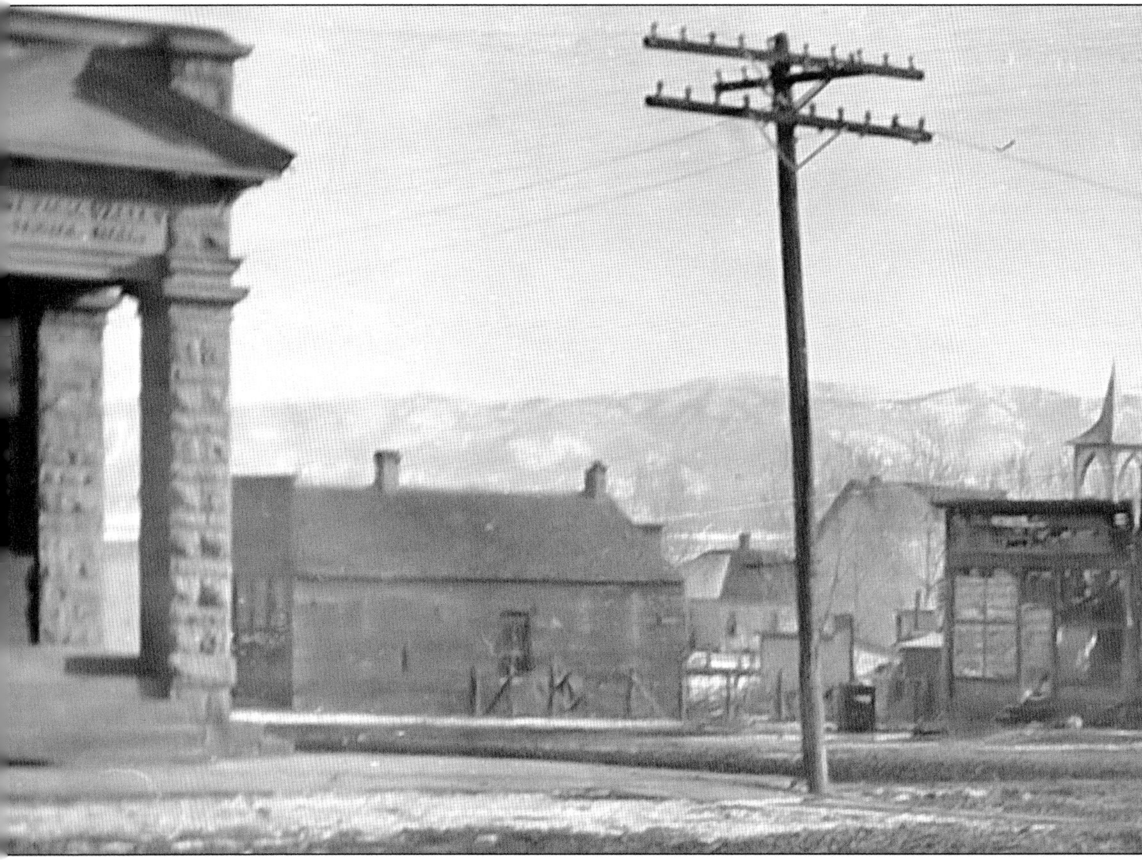

Kermode's Garage burned on December 26, 1918. A week later, an arson fire destroyed the Bozman Garage and the neighboring Carlile building. The still smoking ruins are pictured here. A total of 32 cars were lost; all but four were insured. R.C. Kermode lost all his cars and the Kissell truck. The Lipscomb brothers lost their delivery truck and Dodge cars. Bozman lost six cars. The Smith

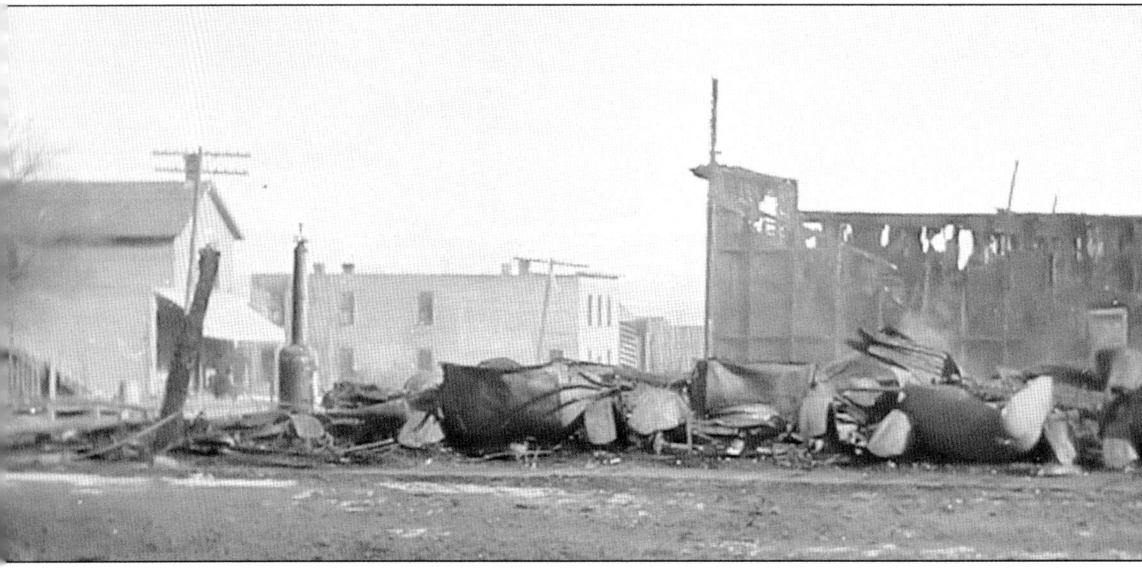

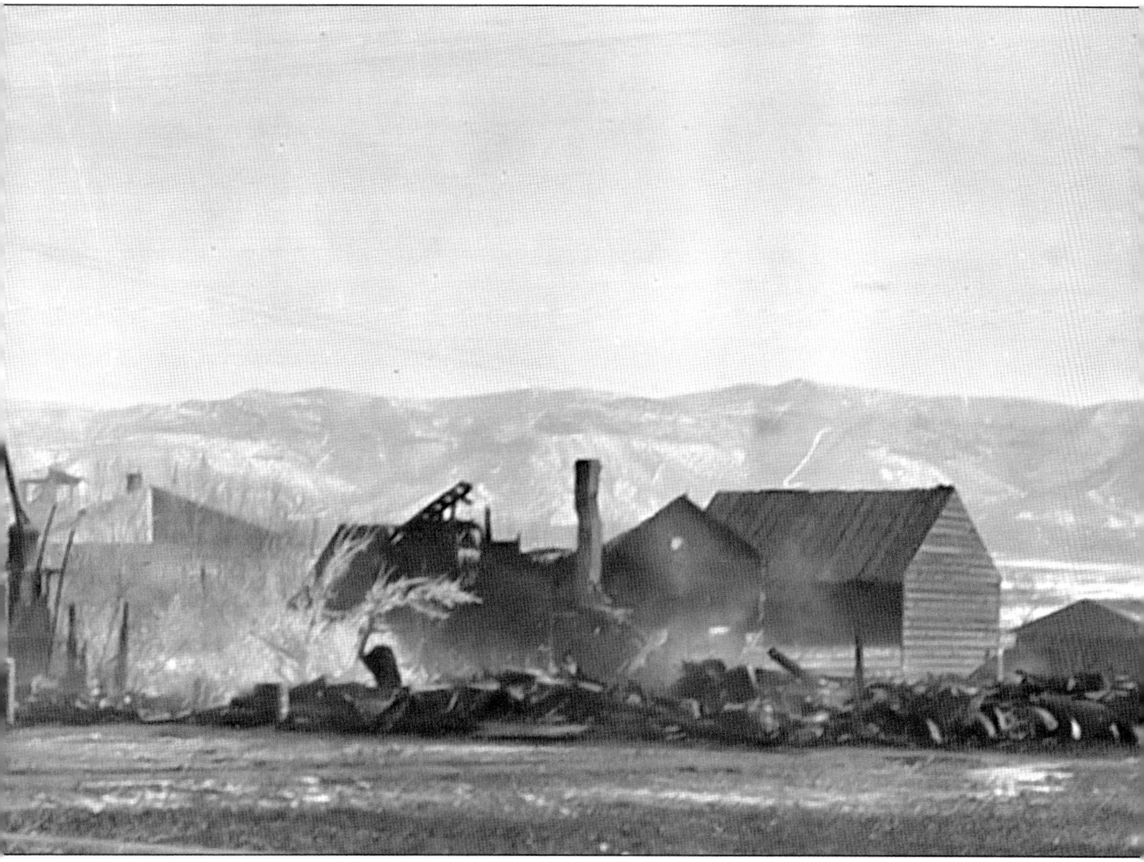

brothers lost two cars, and others lost one each. Bozman was partially insured with $2,500. Carlile had $800 insurance on the barbershop. The building, owned by Hattie McEwen's heirs, was insured for $2,500. Hi McEwen, the estate administrator, bought the lot and replaced the building with a fireproof structure. (Courtesy of First National Bank of Cortez and A.L. Guillet family.)

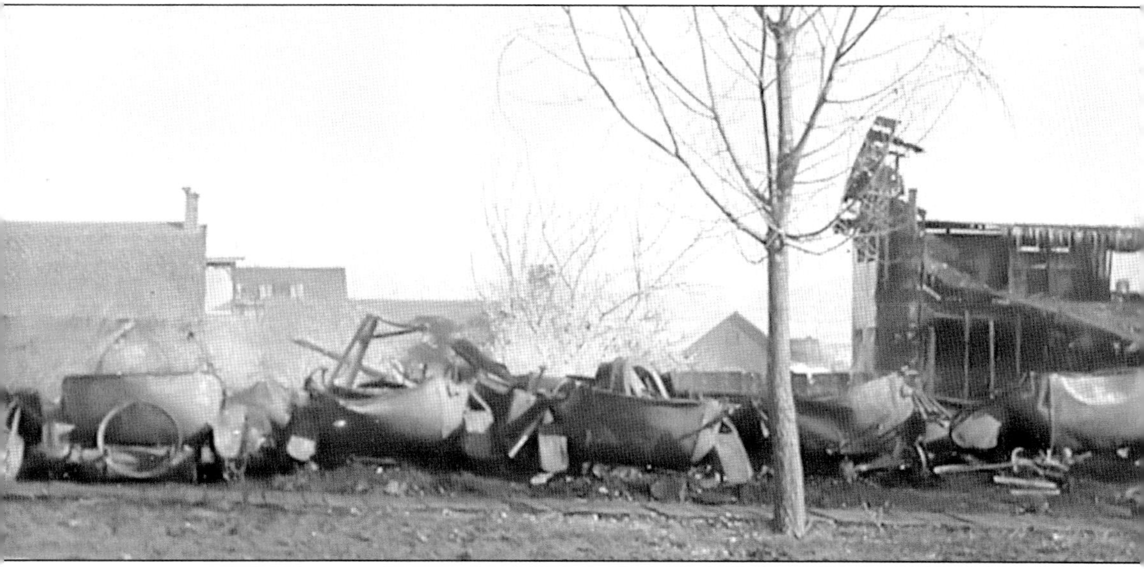

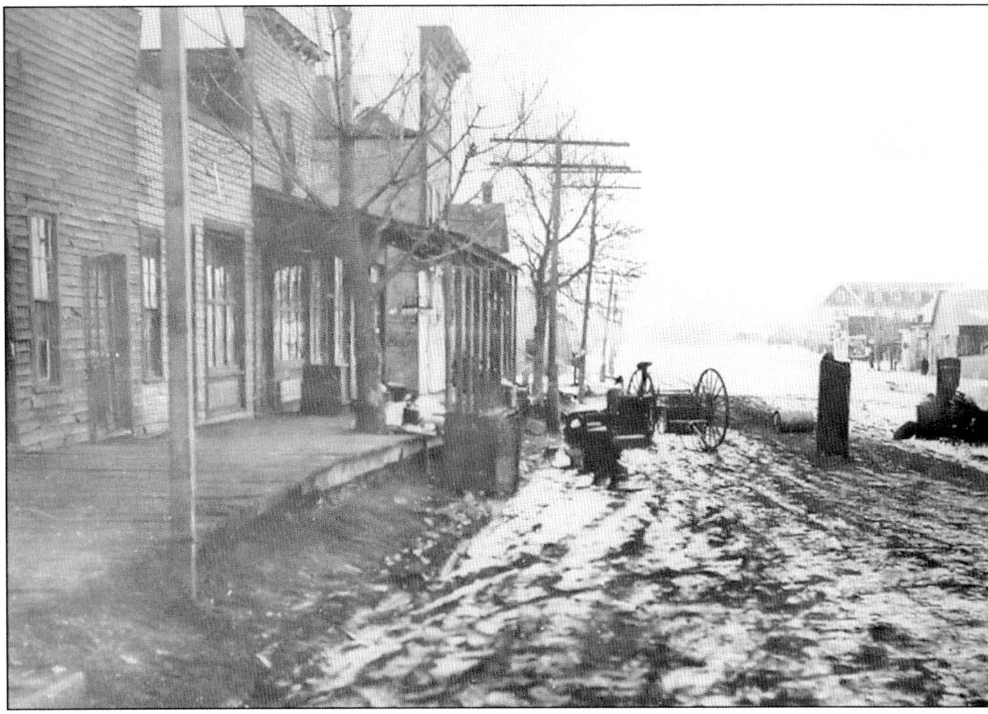

In 1911, the Cortez Volunteer Fire Department was organized. Cortez purchased fire equipment. This wintertime photograph could be of the aftermath of the Bozman Garage fire. The two-wheeled cart, ladder, and rolled hose were pulled by human, horse, or automobile and were stored behind the Stone Block. A siren was installed behind Montezuma Valley Bank. Sheriff Jim Gawith was elected fire chief and Tom Omo secretary. Guy Harrison and city councillors assisted Omo with the department's financial records. Other volunteers included George Rowe, Bill Belcher, Elmer Belcher, Jake Duckshir, Bill Maelis, Joe Stavely, Virgil Armstrong, Walter Hayes, George Eaton, and George McEwen. (Courtesy of First National Bank of Cortez.)

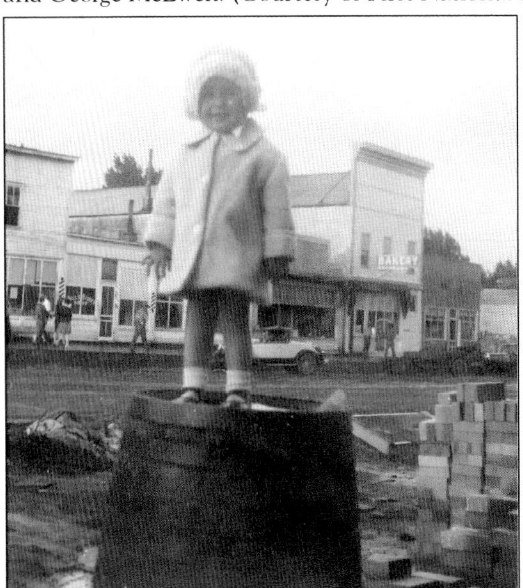

This little girl was put on top of a barrel, apparently to keep her safe. Bricks were used to replace the burned Bozman Garage to prevent future fires. This photograph was taken in front of the ruins, facing northeast, during construction of the building that replaced the garage. (Courtesy of Larry Hauser.)

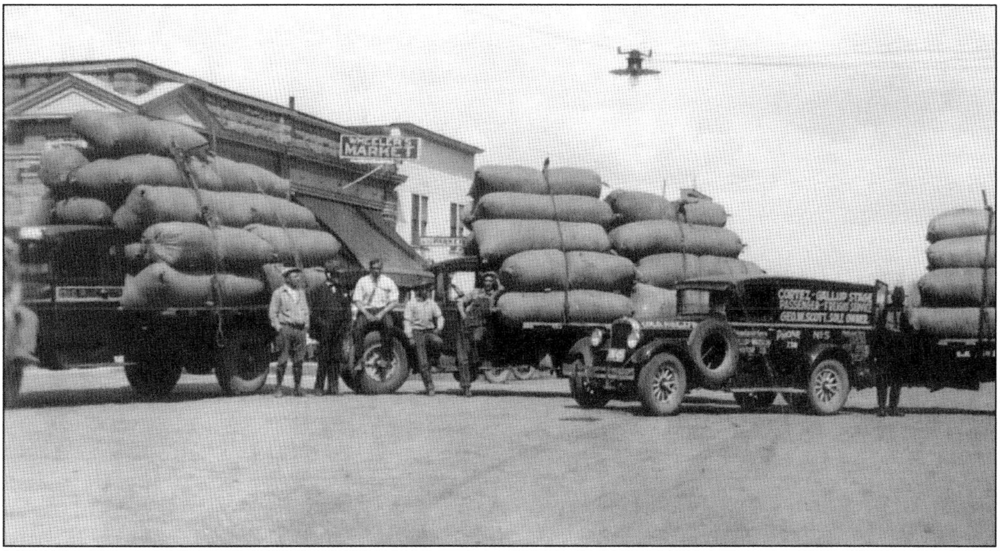

Main and Market Streets were aptly named. Two of the Hinton brothers' trucks are loaded sky high and are ready to roll from the primary business intersection. George W. Scott hauls a trailer behind his motor coach. The Gallup rail station shipped carloads of wool from the Navajo reservation and from sheep ranchers in all four states to fabric mills. (Courtesy of Duane Neal, Larry Hauser, and First National Bank of Cortez.)

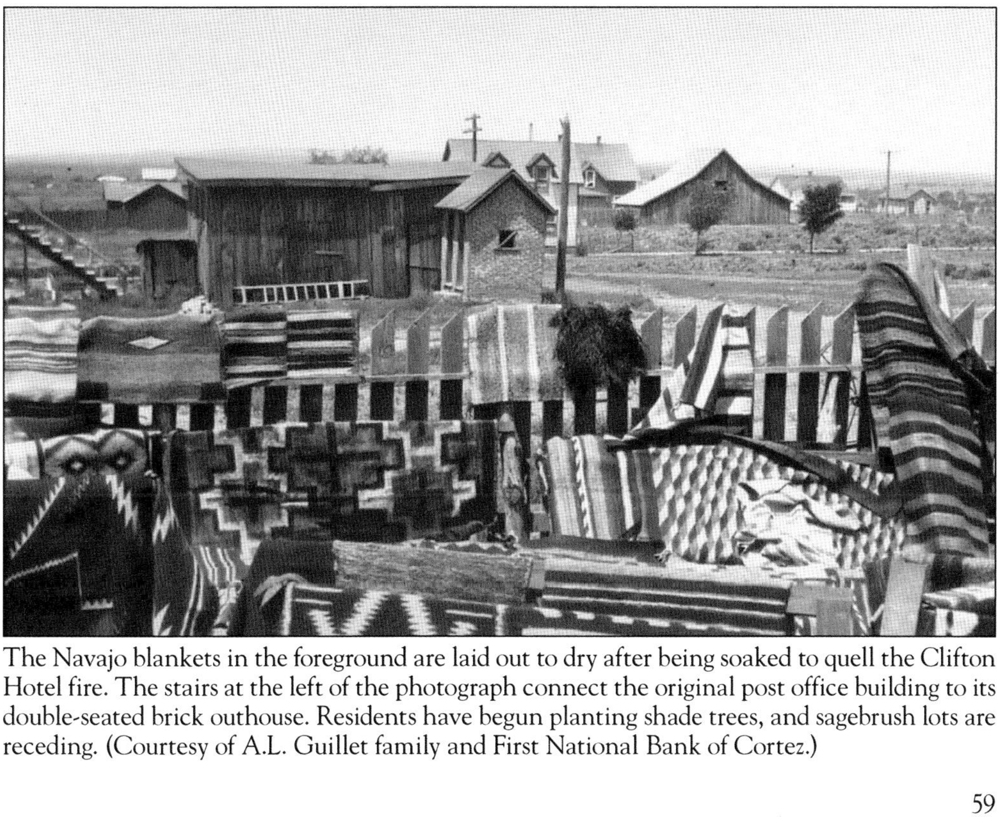

The Navajo blankets in the foreground are laid out to dry after being soaked to quell the Clifton Hotel fire. The stairs at the left of the photograph connect the original post office building to its double-seated brick outhouse. Residents have begun planting shade trees, and sagebrush lots are receding. (Courtesy of A.L. Guillet family and First National Bank of Cortez.)

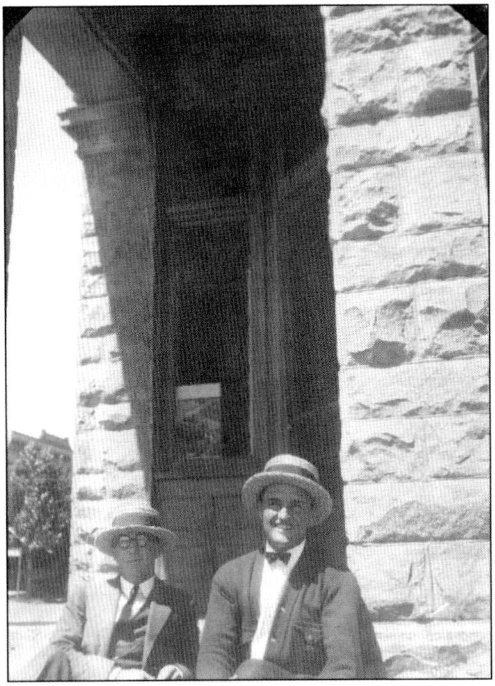

Brothers Bill (left) and Arnold Kermode (right), young lions in the banking industry, sit on the steps of Montezuma Valley Bank in 1924. Emery S. Turner and partners opened Cortez's first bank in 1887 in this stone building constructed by Peter Baxstrom. Baxstrom built the courthouse (1886–1888), the post office on Main Street (1887), the Stone Block (1888–1890), the schoolhouse on Montezuma (1890), the first third of Union School (1909), Battle Rock Schoolhouse (1915), and other local stone structures. (Courtesy of Barbara Breternitz.)

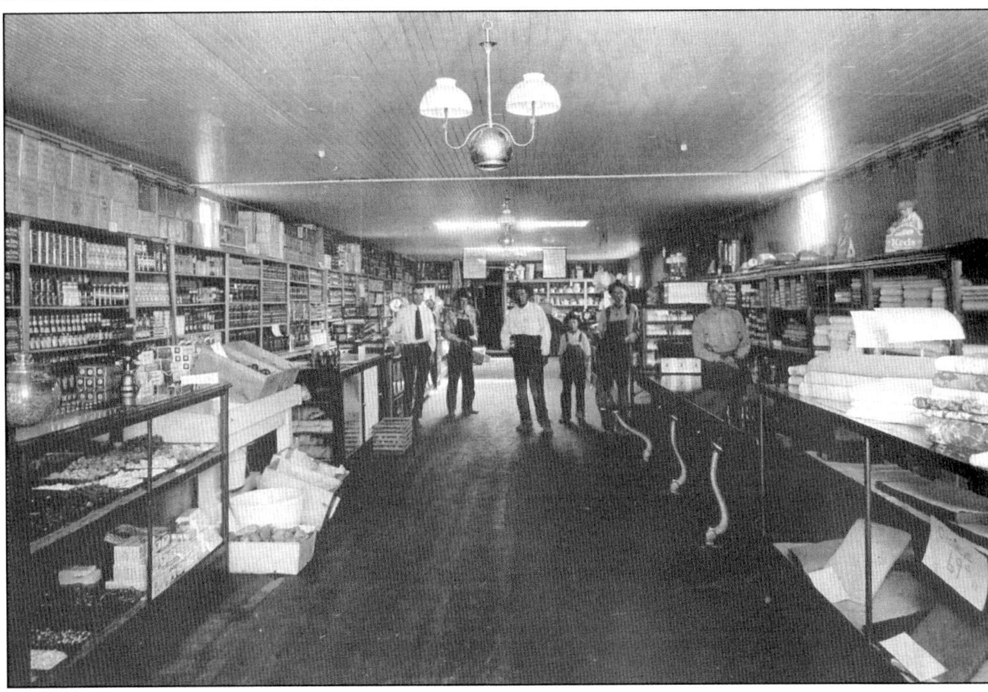

Cortez Mercantile was located on the southwest corner of Main and Market Streets. Groceries were offered on the left, dry goods on the right, and hardware at the back. Included in this photograph are, from left to right, Steven Girard, owner Sam Walker, John Hinton, two unidentified customers, and Regie Kermode. Note the overhead electric light styled like a gas lamp. In 1909, Cortez businessmen built a power plant that used flour mill engines on South Market Street. By 1923, Cortez Light and Power provided electricity citywide. (Courtesy of the Optical Shoppe.)

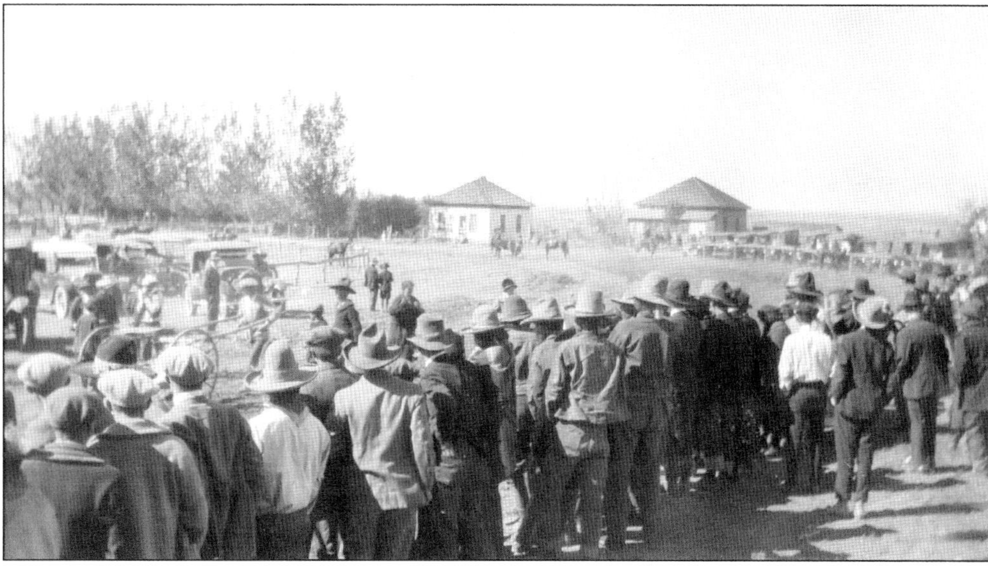

People worked hard and played hard. Inner and outer side rails for the racetrack protected spectators from flying hooves and racehorses from errant vehicles. Horseracing was popular, in spite of its seedy side. Butch Cassidy reportedly raced his fine horses throughout western Colorado—a slightly more respectable activity than robbing banks and yet another way to make "easy" money. (Courtesy of Barbara Breternitz.)

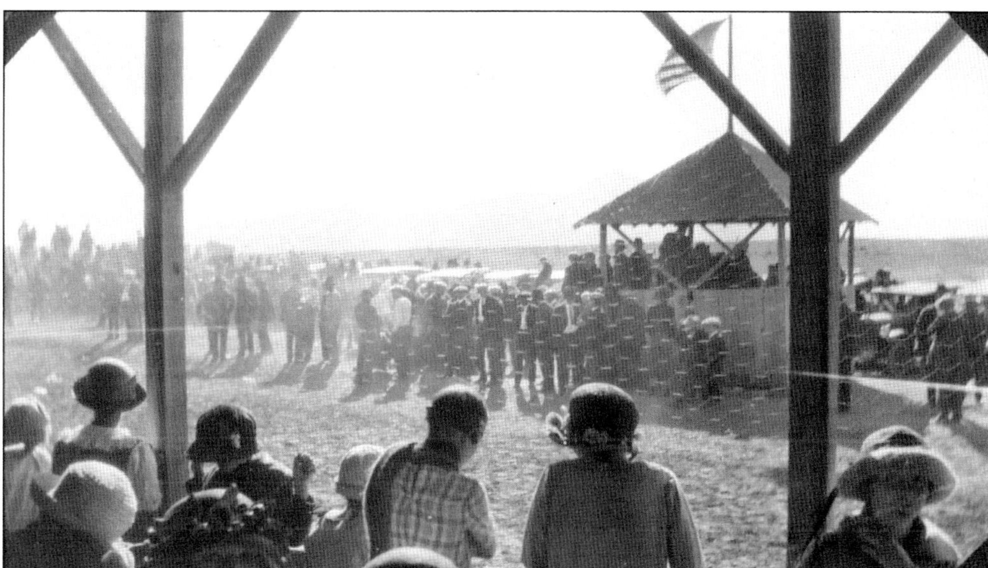

Sleeping Ute Mountain lies behind the grandstand and announcer's podium at what was probably the county fairground on the west end of town. Young and old, American Indian, white, and Hispanic congregate to watch horses and people challenge each other in fun sports. (Courtesy of Barbara Breternitz.)

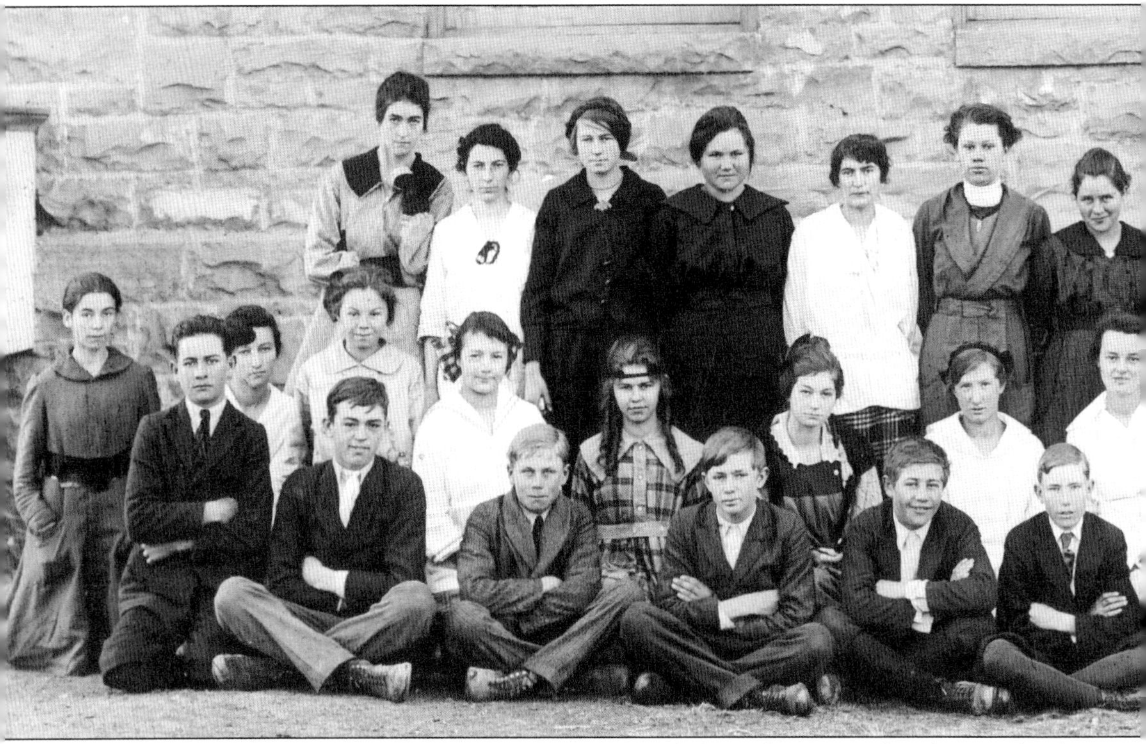

Cortez High School students (grade levels listed) pose with their educators in this photograph taken on a warm January 1918 day. Pictured from left to right are, (first row) Ray Gingles, 8th; Emery Wilson, 8th; Louis Demore, 9th; ? Hindmarsh, 9th; Jay Pim, 8th; Walton Knight, 8th; Dewey Smith, 8th; Elmer West, 8th; Frank Coppinger, 8th; Jimmy Wark, 8th; Frank Todd, 8th; James Clark, 10th; and Rex Talcott; 10th; (second row) Marjory Lewey, 8th; Beth Wark, 8th; June Frederick, 8th; Alice Demby, 9th; Mildred Wade, 9th; Olive Wilson, 9th; Alma Beaber, 9th; Hazel Leavette, 12th; Verna Pim, 11th; Edith Towser, 10th; Helen Smith, 11th; Alta McEwen, 11th; Clair Winship 11th; Mary

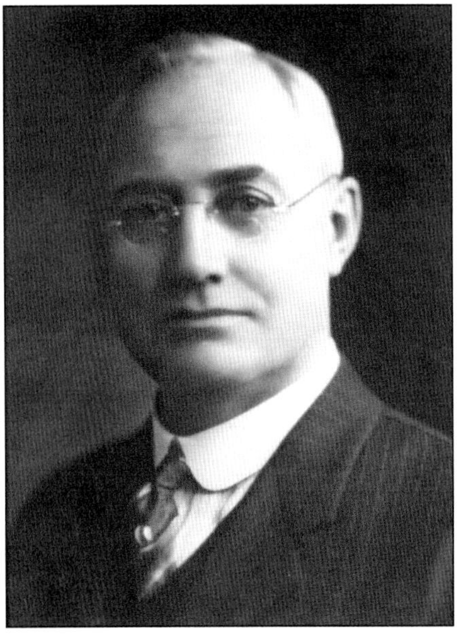

Dr. Royal William Calkins was the physician for the Ute Indian agency. Serving the entire county through the 1918 influenza epidemic, he lost only six patients out of 468. From 1926 to 1932, Calkins served in the state house of representatives and was unanimously elected Speaker of the House in 1929. A reelection brochure stated that Calkins helped pass highway and cooperative marketing legislation, introduced and helped pass the Colorado River Compact Bill, supported the auditing of educational institutions, and fought graft through his work on the House Appropriations Committee. When a new high school was built in 1946, the stone school became Calkins Junior High. (Courtesy of Montezuma-Cortez School District Re-1.)

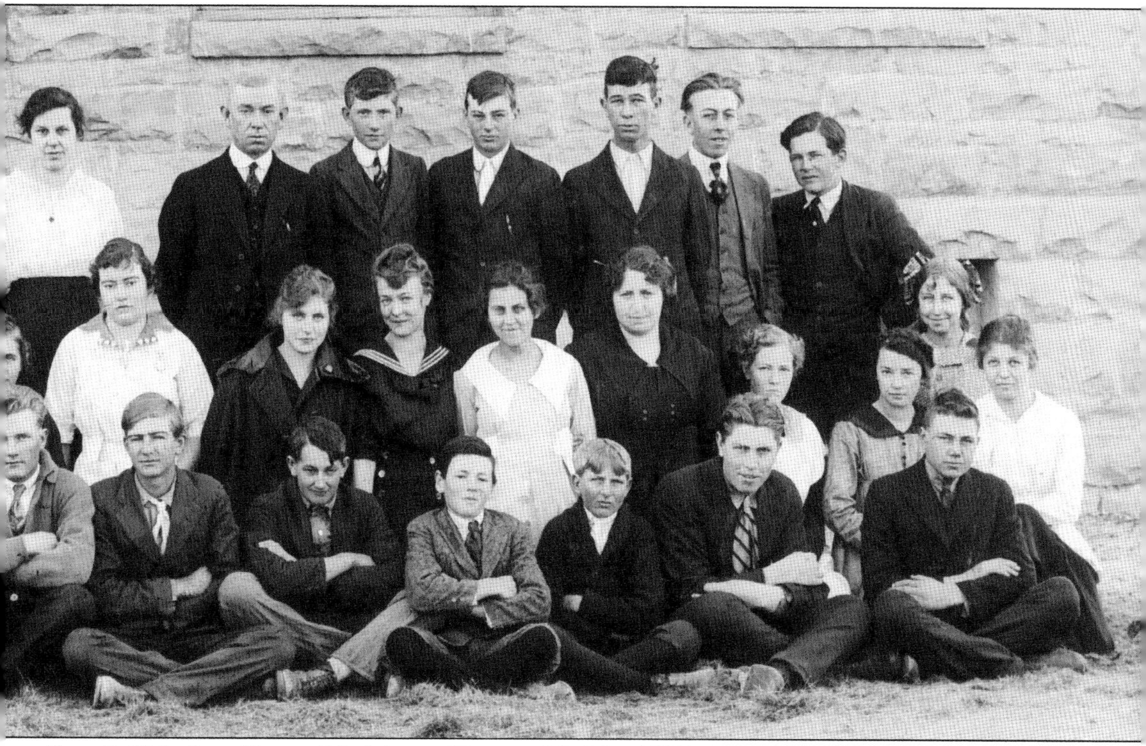

Purcell, 10th; Lucy Eaton, 8th; Marian Hopper, 8th; Hazel Wilson, 10th; and Ernestine Thomas, 8th; (third row) Marcella Lewey, 10th; Manty Eims, 8th; Ester Peterson, 9th; Alice Pig, 9th; Berdy Dennison, 8th; Muriel Davis, 12th; Dorthy Patterson, 8th; Emma Brinker, 8th; Anna Downing, teacher; Elza Needham, professor; Garner Beaber, 11th; Edwin Wilson, 11th; Henry Wilson, 12th; Charles Stabler, 11th; and Karl Wesh, 11th. Students listed as absent on the back of the photograph include: Mary Townsend, 12th; Ralph Hickey, 11th; Katherine Willis, 9th; Velva Hall, 10th; and Arlie Coppinger (no grade listed). (Courtesy of Cortez Public Library.)

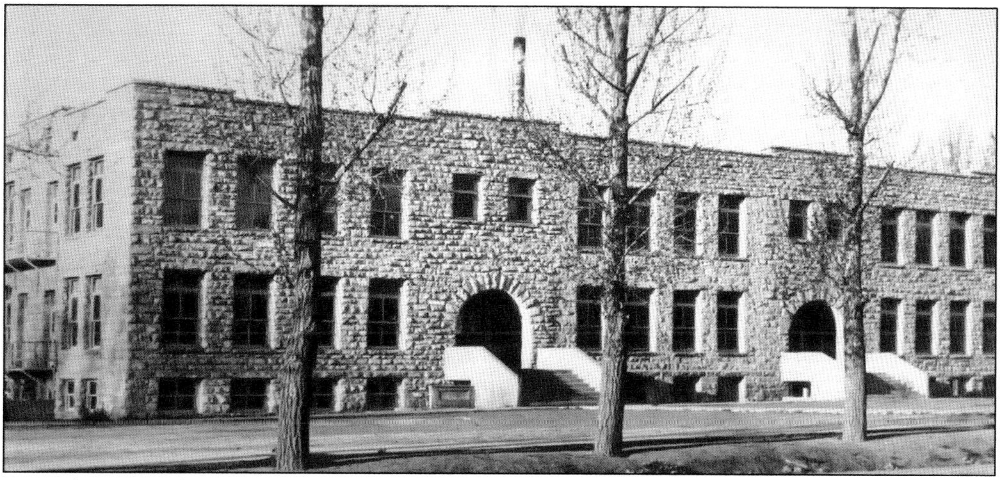

Over the years, the school received complementary additions for the growing population. This photograph was taken in the mid-1940s. That decade's graduation classes proudly and actively support the area's history. Currently, the building awaits additional renovation funding, and until recently it housed the district's administration. (Courtesy of First National Bank of Cortez.)

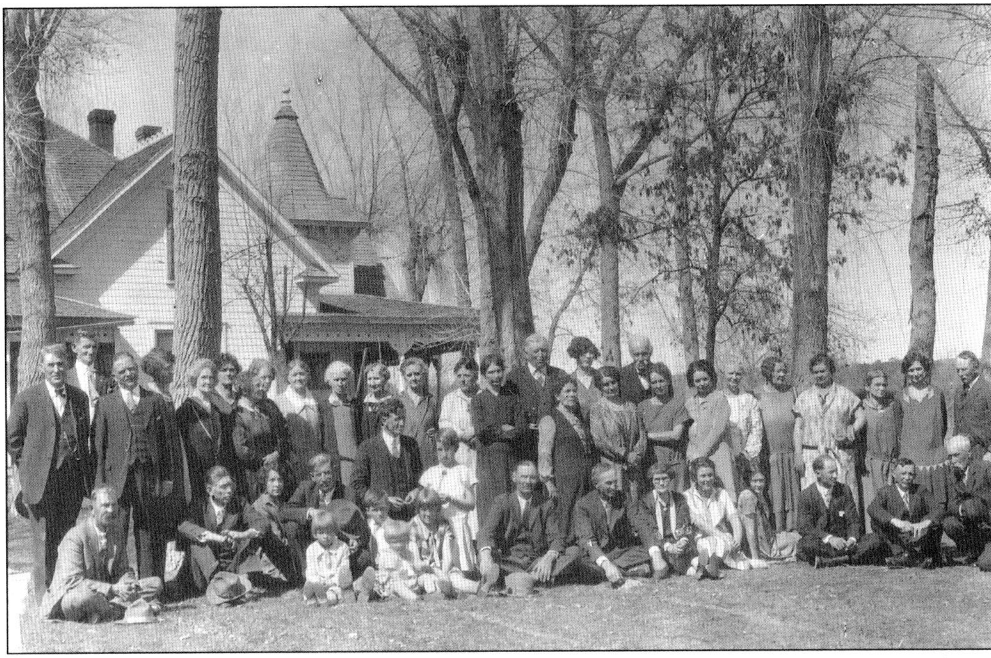

Family and friends of the Mylers gather on a warm spring day in 1927. Their farm was located near what is now the intersection of State Highway 145 and County Road P. Myler and other rural residents were and continue to be successful farmers, merchants, and community activists. Myler's Corner has been a landmark for locals for more than a century. (Courtesy of Cortez Public Library.)

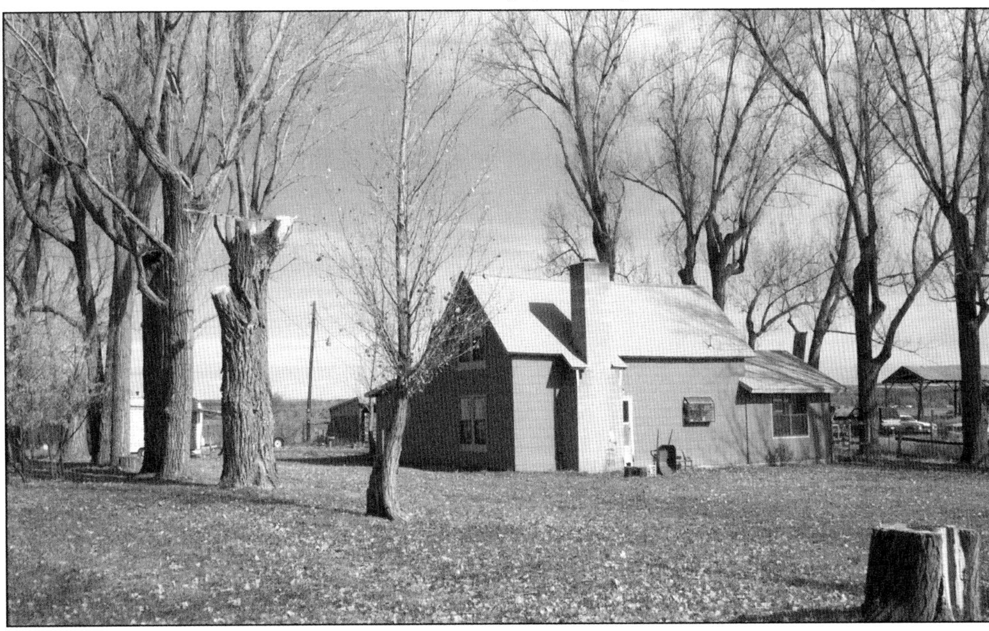

The Walter Longenbaugh family, unrelated to Dave M. Longenbaugh, lived and farmed from this house on County Road L just north of Cortez. Walter recalled that as a lad he was asked to take eggs, flour, coffee, and supplies to a dugout near Cortez. Butch Cassidy, partner of Harry Longabaugh (the Sundance Kid), supposedly owned an undeveloped ranch north of town. The family always said the Sundance Kid was not related to them. (Photograph by Barbara Grist Photography.)

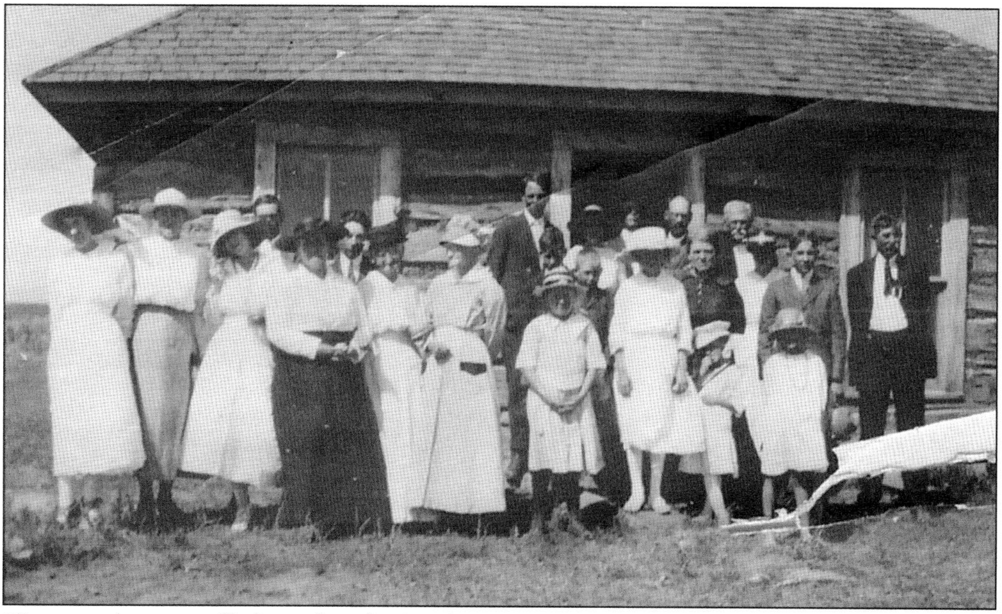

These residents are all cleaned up for Sunday meeting in 1918. This group poses in front of the sturdy Fairview log schoolhouse that was also used for church services. Fairview School was located northwest of Yellow Jacket. (Courtesy of Cortez Public Library.)

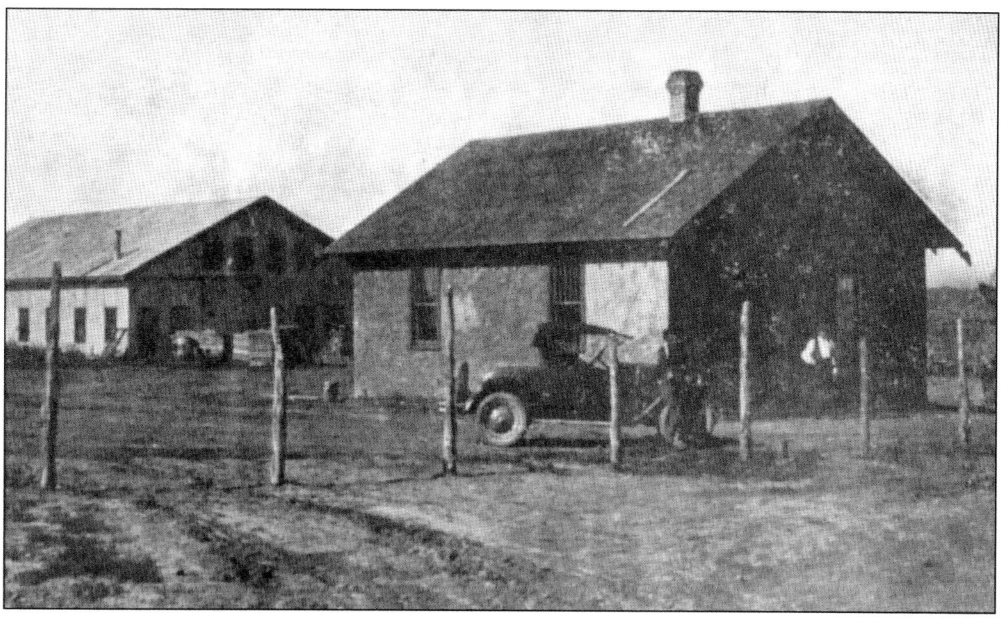

The Montezuma Valley Irrigation (MVI) office was a humble building on East Main Street in Cortez until the district expanded enough to need more land for equipment and office space. MVI first moved downtown in 1980 to share space with the Dolores Water Conservancy District. In 1986, MVI moved to its new headquarters three miles north of Cortez on US Highway 491. (Courtesy of Cortez Newspapers.)

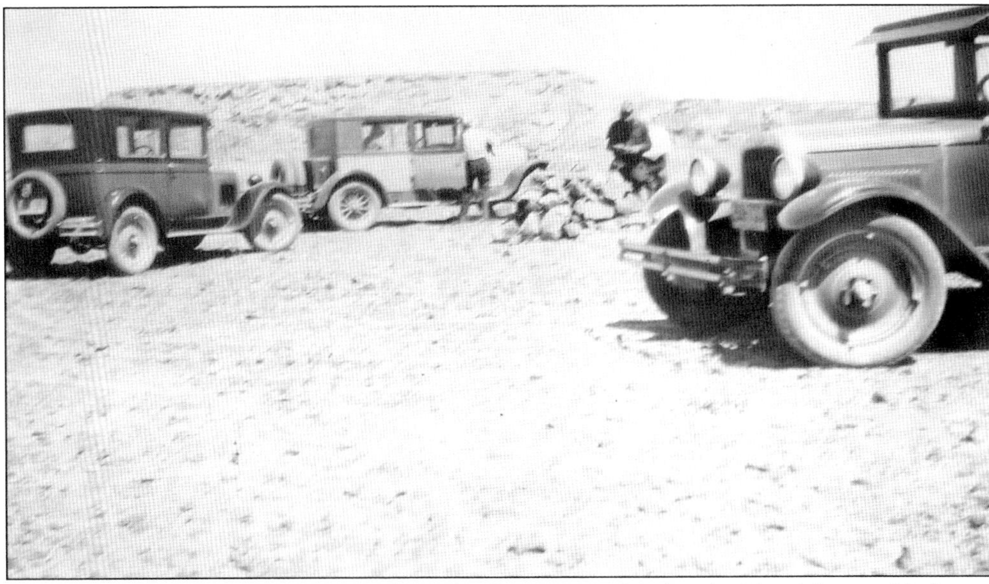

In 1928, a marker was constructed where the four states of Colorado, New Mexico, Utah, and Arizona join at a single point, the only place in the United States where this happens. (Courtesy of Carl and Guyrene Skoog and First National Bank of Cortez.)

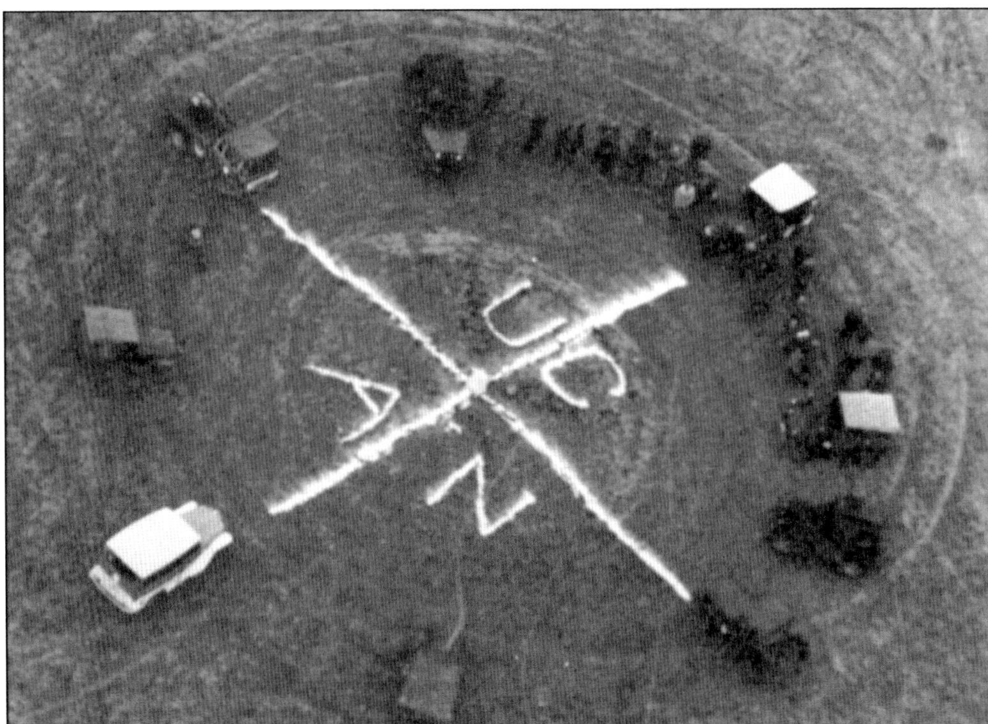

An aerial photograph in July 1949 captures the full impact of the monument, with white chalk marking the four state lines for the dedication ceremony. All four governors attended: W. Lee Knous of Colorado, Thomas J. Mabry of New Mexico, Dan E. Garvey of Arizona, and J. Bracken Lee of Utah. Judge James M. Noland spoke. (Courtesy of Larry Hauser.)

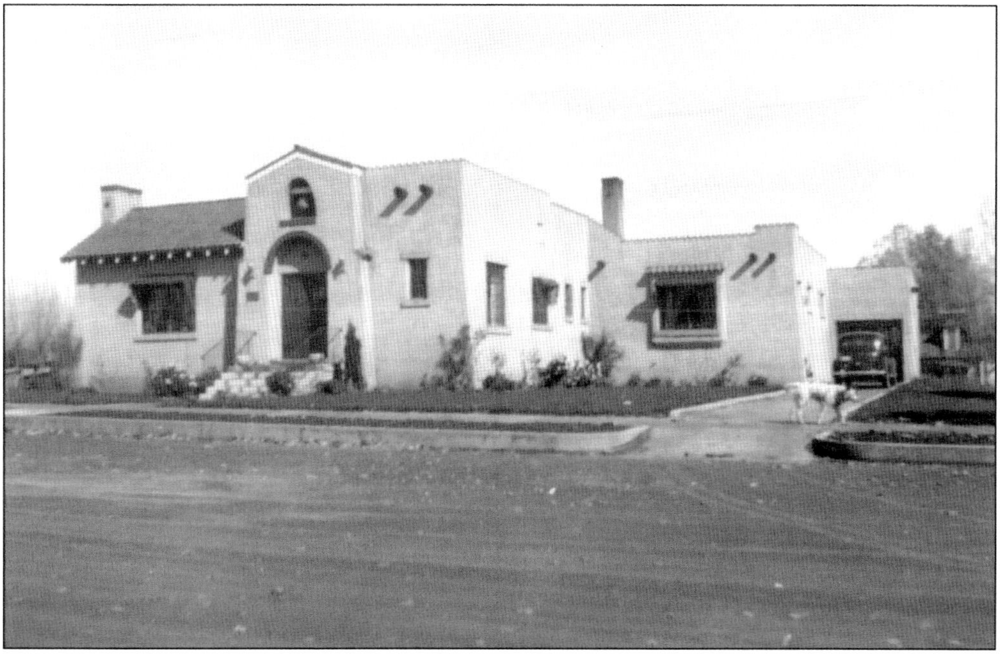

In 1921, J. Walter Ertel purchased three Ames and Omo Funeral Homes in the area. In 1933, he consolidated them into one and started planning to build a new facility in Cortez. In 1936, the Southwestern-style stucco building was complete. In 1995, the building was added to the National and Colorado Registers of Historic Places. (Courtesy of Ertel Funeral Home.)

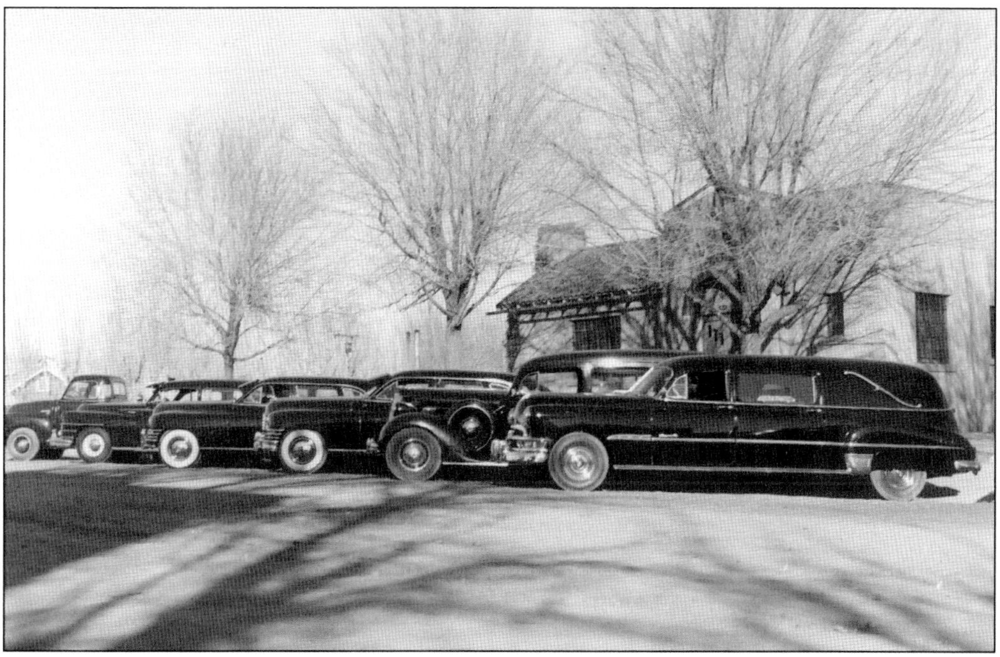

A couple of decades rolled by, and the funeral home was able to serve the community in fine style with two elegant hearses and three limousines for families of the deceased. (Courtesy of Ertel Funeral Home.)

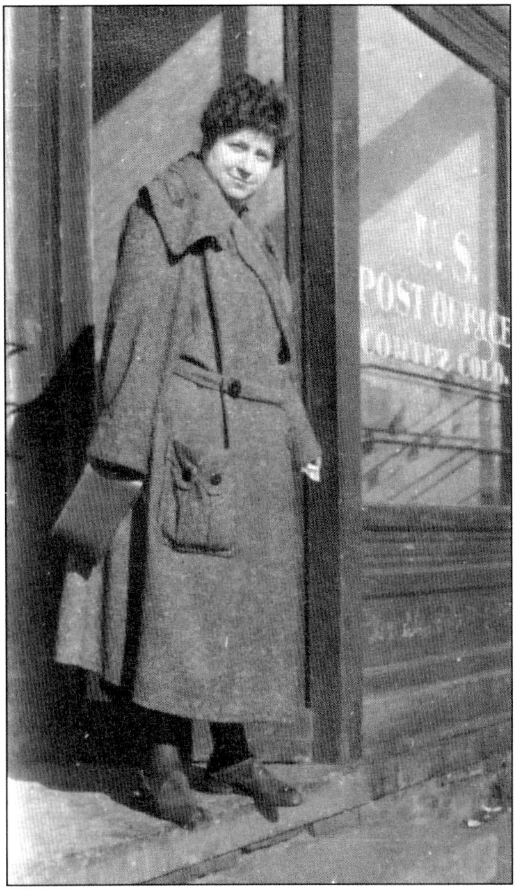

Mary Purcell steps out of the Cortez Post Office at 34 West Main Street in this 1924 photograph. The post office was first established on June 21, 1887, in Dr. Bernard J. Byrnes's drugstore in the courthouse. Major E.H. Cooper was the first postmaster appointed by President Benjamin Harrison. The post office moved several times in the next decade because of postmaster changes. (Courtesy of Barbara Breternitz.)

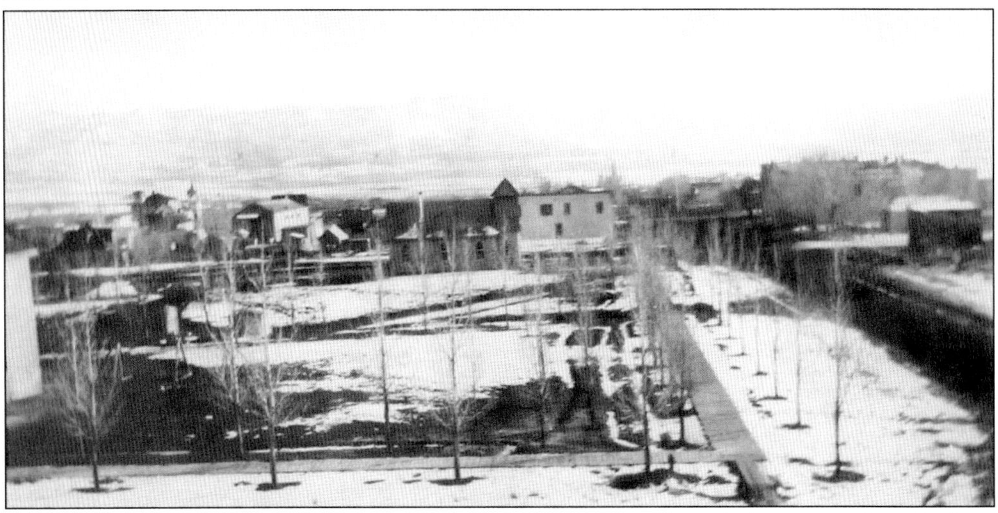

Trees were important to the townspeople. Rows of cottonwoods and elms were planted along roadways to provide shade. They also took the edge off the stark landscape of sage and open plains. Montezuma Avenue, pictured in the foreground, was conceived with a canal to carry water from the irrigation system to town. It also created a pleasant neighborhood for downtown's merchant class. (Courtesy of First National Bank of Cortez.)

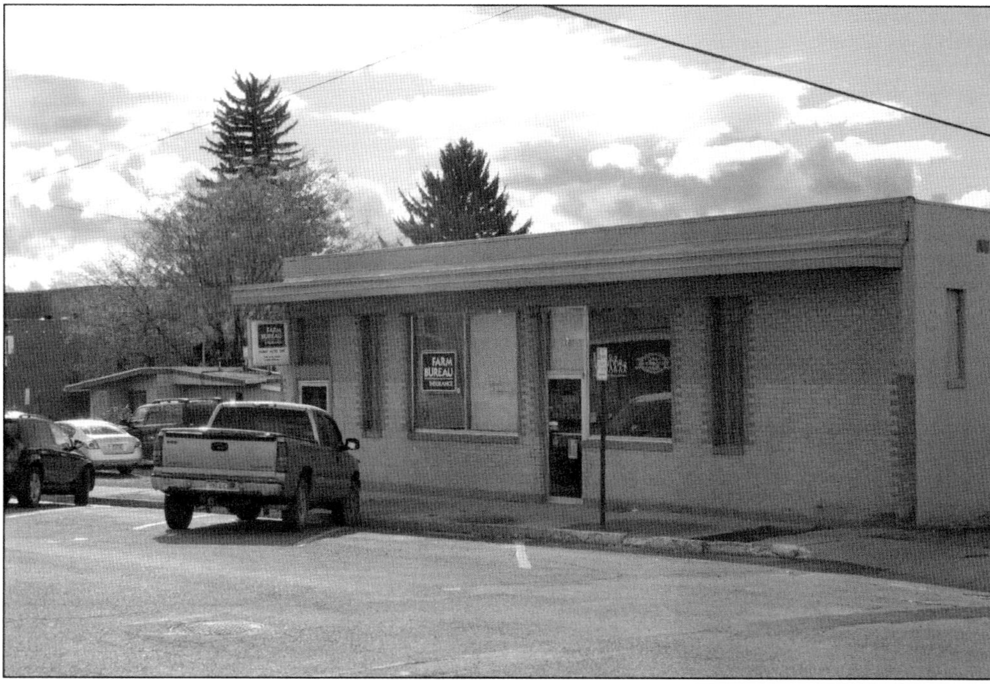

This building served as Cortez's post office through the 1950s. The building has also served as a bank and is currently home to Farm Bureau Insurance and a social service business. Behind it to the left are Pippo's Café and the 1937 courthouse on West Main Street. (Photograph by Barbara Grist Photography.)

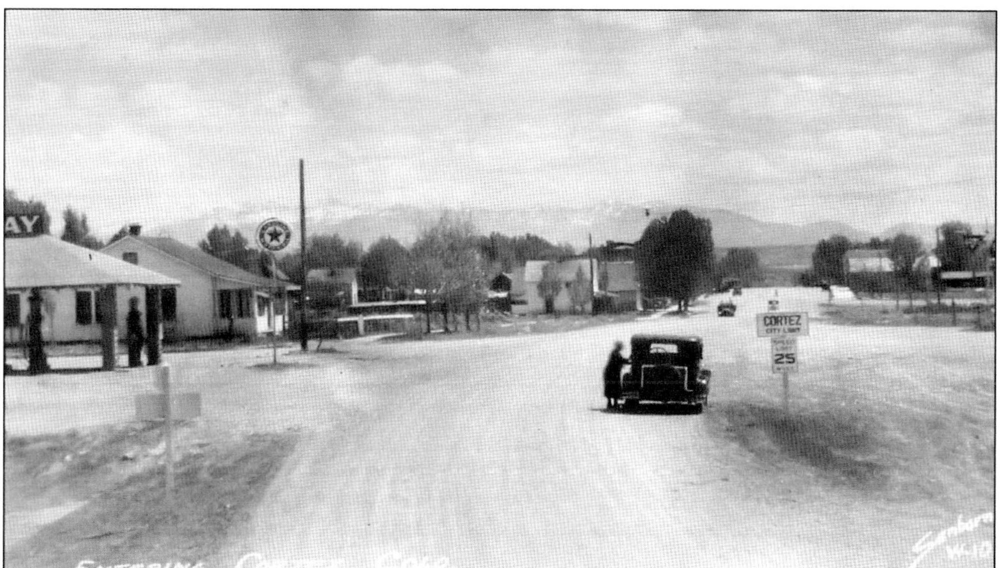

Visitors coming to Cortez from the west had this view of a comfortable town beneath the snowy rise of the La Plata Mountains. (Courtesy of Ross Durant and First National Bank of Cortez.)

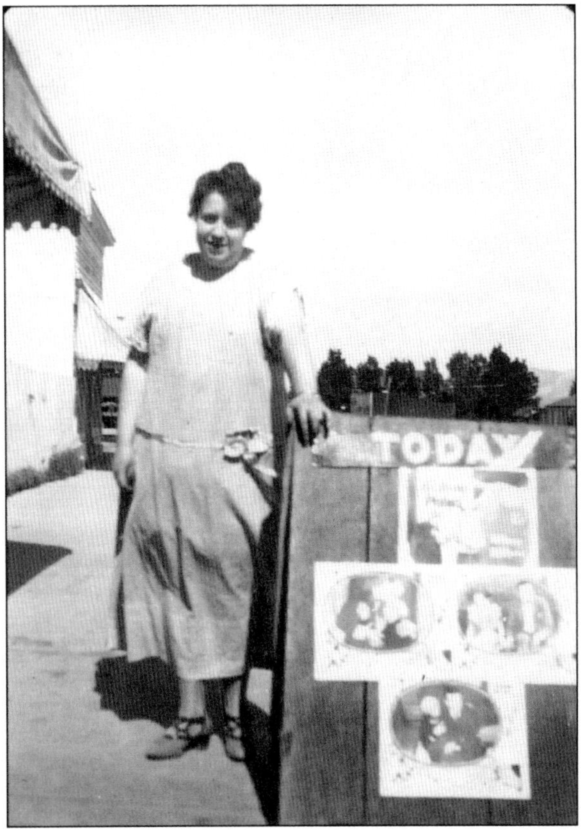

Mary Purcell poses in front of the Muse-U Theater with a signboard announcing the evening movies in 1924. Cortez's first movie theater was built by George McEwen in 1911, and Harry Freeman supplied the projector. (Courtesy of Barbara Breternitz.)

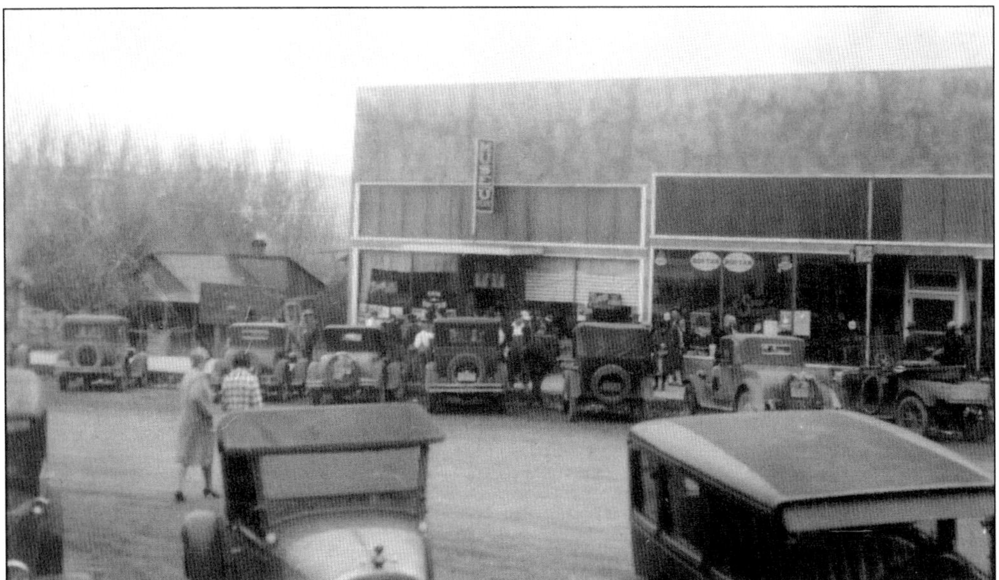

On a Saturday night, many in the county headed for the Muse-U Theater on East Main Street for a good time and a little relief from reality. It cost 10¢ to get into family night in the late 1920s and 1930s. Mom and Pop Purcell, Mary's parents, owned the theater and soda fountain. Everyone in town knew the Purcells. (Courtesy of Larry Hauser.)

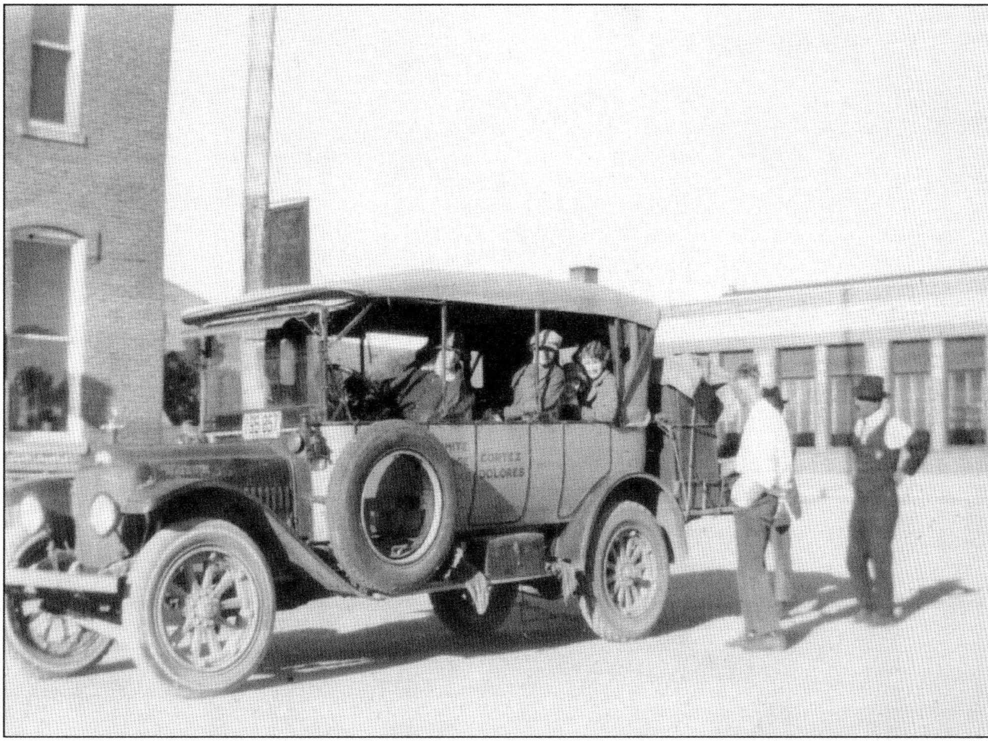

Motor coaches quickly replaced horse-drawn wagons to transport people to work, on shopping trips, and to visit people and other places. Judging from the buildings in the background, this photograph was taken in Durango. The side of the coach lists Cortez and Dolores as two of its destinations. (Courtesy of Barbara Breternitz.)

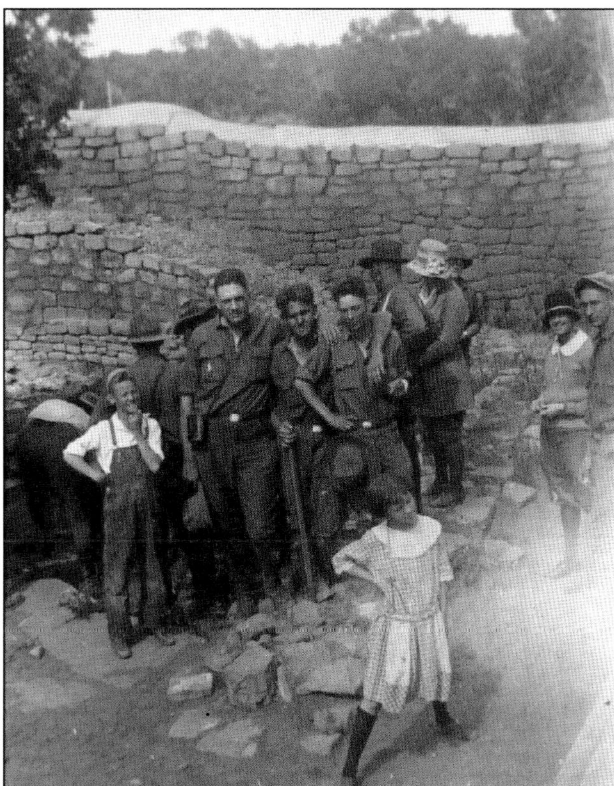

Barbara Moser and her friends and family visit Mesa Verde National Park in June 1924. The Mesa Verde ruins have been a destination for tourists from all over the world since their discovery by white settlers in the late 1800s. Cortez's *Montezuma Journal* wrote about Mesa Verde cliff ruins regularly from 1899 on to promote tourism and the establishment of a national park (accomplished in 1906). (Courtesy of Barbara Breternitz.)

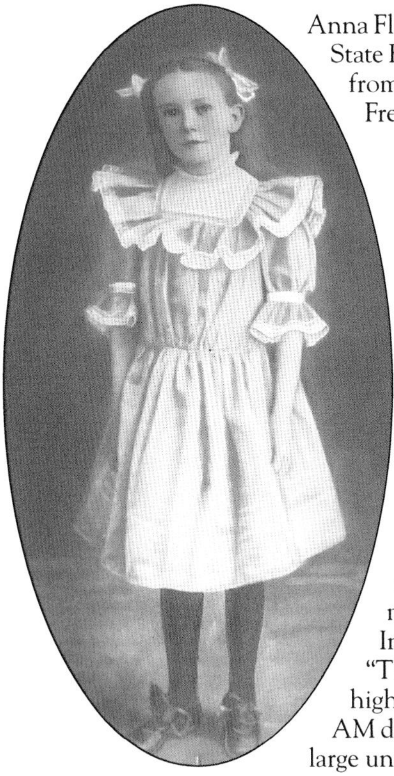

Anna Florence Robison, a Cortez resident, worked for the Colorado State Historical Society. In 1934, she began to collect oral histories from people who lived in Montezuma Valley. (Courtesy of Fred Blackburn.)

F. William Robison, wife Mary, and daughter Anna Florence moved to Colorado from Edmond, Oklahoma. The family moved to Tin Cup, Colorado, and then to Montezuma County. In an introduction to her oral histories, Anna Florence stated, "The writer of this note and a classmate graduated from the high school at Cortez in 1916, and later each obtained AB and AM degrees from standard colleges and did postgraduate work at large universities." (Both courtesy of Fred Blackburn.)

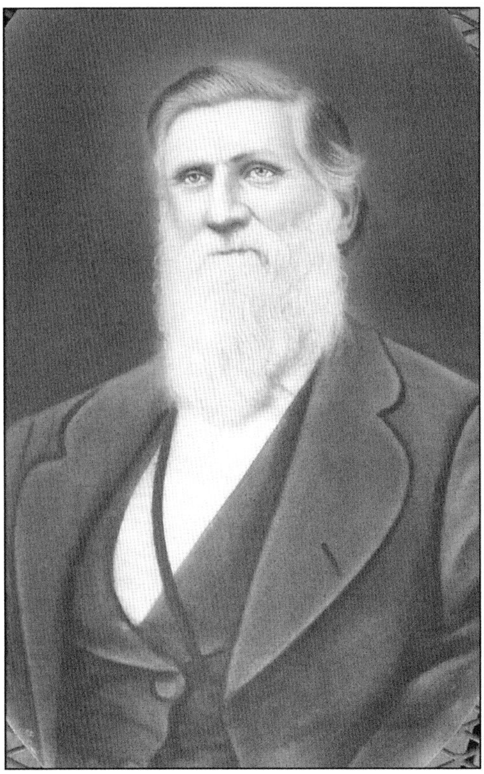

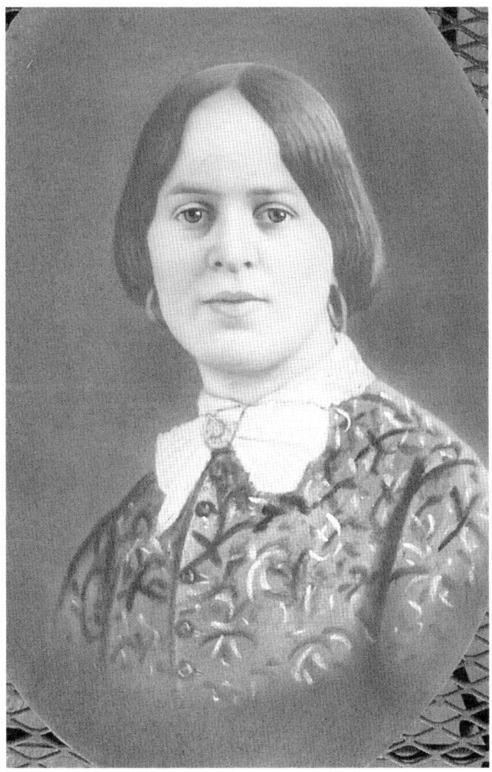

Four

Going Modern

The 1930s held promise but also dashed hopes because of the nationwide Depression. Businessmen needed foresight and perseverance to take advantage of government assistance and programs and changing technologies. Gasoline engines and airplanes changed how people and products were transported. Power and telephone lines changed how people connected for business and for fun.

For those who needed assistance, the government distributed flour and feed for stock. Women sewed bedding out of Red Cross–donated clothing. Churches set up soup kitchens.

The Roosevelt administration closed banks, including Montezuma Valley National Bank (perhaps unnecessarily) and Mancos Bank. Another bank, Citizens State Bank, opened with government-insured deposits.

Weather continued to send either too much water or too much drought. Water rights were a hot topic statewide. Montezuma Valley Irrigation Company received an 11,086-acre-feet appropriation of water in 1929. Montezuma County farmers decided to accept government money to rebuild Groundhog Reservoir, which was adjudicated for water storage. The town installed new eight-inch water lines. Cortez got its first official swimming pool.

Farm prices fell before and rose after 1935. Cattle were culled and shot or sold. Milk and egg money often did not fill the sugar jar. County extension agents came and went. In 1934, Colorado congressman Edward T. Taylor sponsored the Taylor Grazing Act, which helped with range depletion but also removed government land from homesteading.

New homes were built. Businesses and commercial buildings changed owners. The lumber mill in McPhee closed, reopened, and then closed completely. Highland Utilities consolidated area power plants under their management.

Anna Florence Robison collected oral histories for the state historical society. Murder and mayhem continued between law-keepers and law-breakers. The McDaniels brothers shot a sheriff and were brought to justice.

Highway construction and Works Progress Administration (WPA) projects hired able workers. A new school addition was built. A new courthouse was funded and built. The railroad discontinued passenger service. The Galloping Goose and motor coach businesses stepped into the void. Men purchased trucks and started freight companies.

The Congregational Church burned. St. Barnabas Episcopal Church held its first services. A public health service was established.

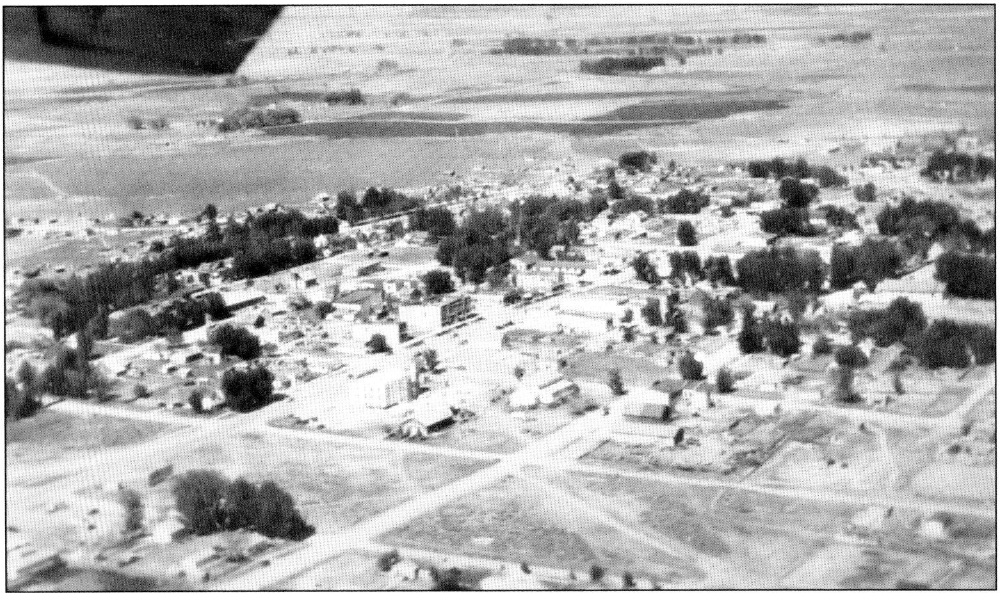

Airplanes finally let people see from a bird's point of view. Looking east over Cortez, one can see the new courthouse under construction in 1936, just to the left and down from the center. The large building to its right is Woodmen Hall. The Clifton Hotel lot, between the post office and the Stone Block, is still vacant. The canal and line of trees along Montezuma Avenue are evident at the far edge of town on the left side of the photograph. (Courtesy of First National Bank of Cortez.)

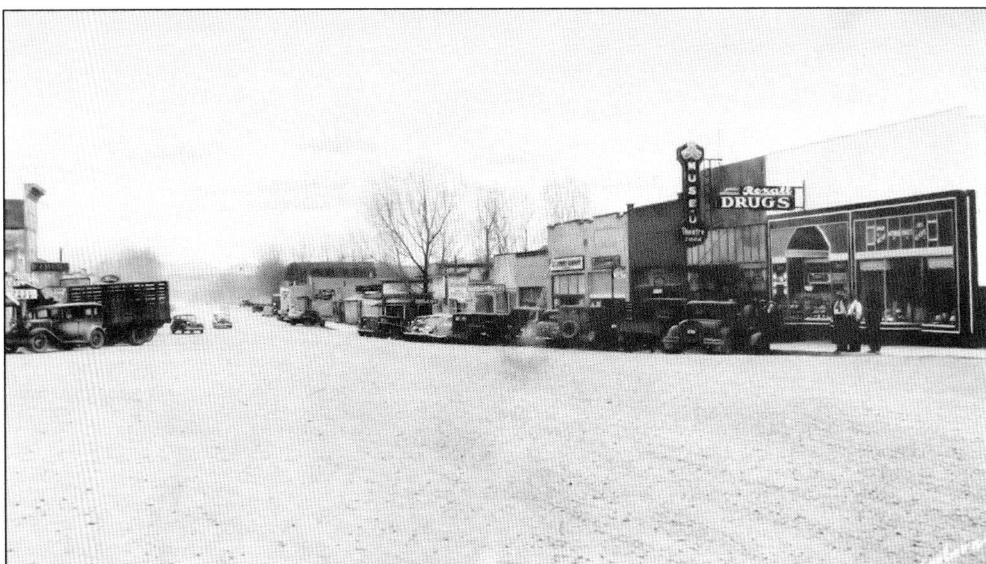

Downtown begins to look more civilized in spite of Main Street's lack of pavement. Glass, metal, and concrete are replacing wood. In 1930, the state removed all the poplar trees on Main Street to widen it after its designation as US Highway 160. (Courtesy of Ross Durant and First National Bank of Cortez.)

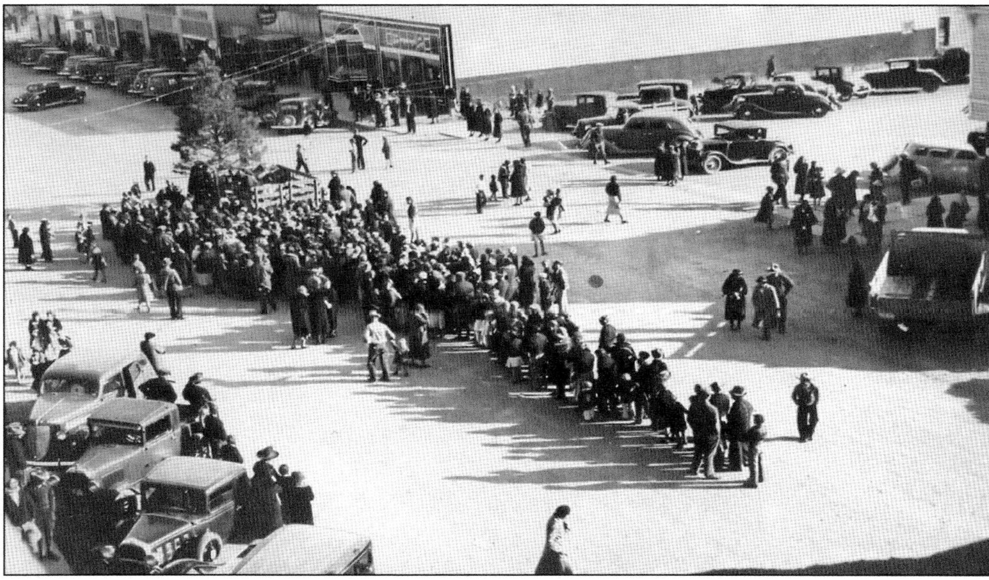

The center of Cortez at Market and Main Streets is hopping with Christmas shoppers. Kids are lined up to see all the doings that the American Legion provided along with the decorated tree. The plentitude of vehicles points toward the area's growing financial success and also the necessity of getting from farms to commercial centers. Pearl Kirk said this photograph was taken about 1937. (Courtesy of First National Bank of Cortez.)

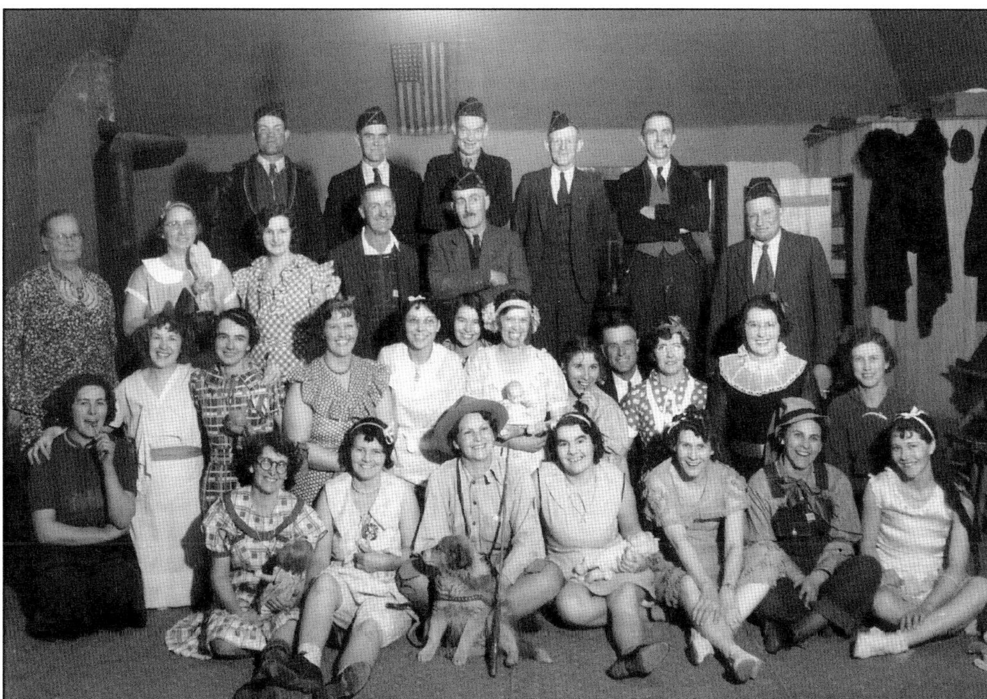

Members of the American Legion and Ladies Auxiliary got together for a "Tacky Party" at Woodmen Hall in 1932. The men were apparently less eager to be tacky and kept their dignity intact. (Courtesy of Cortez Public Library.)

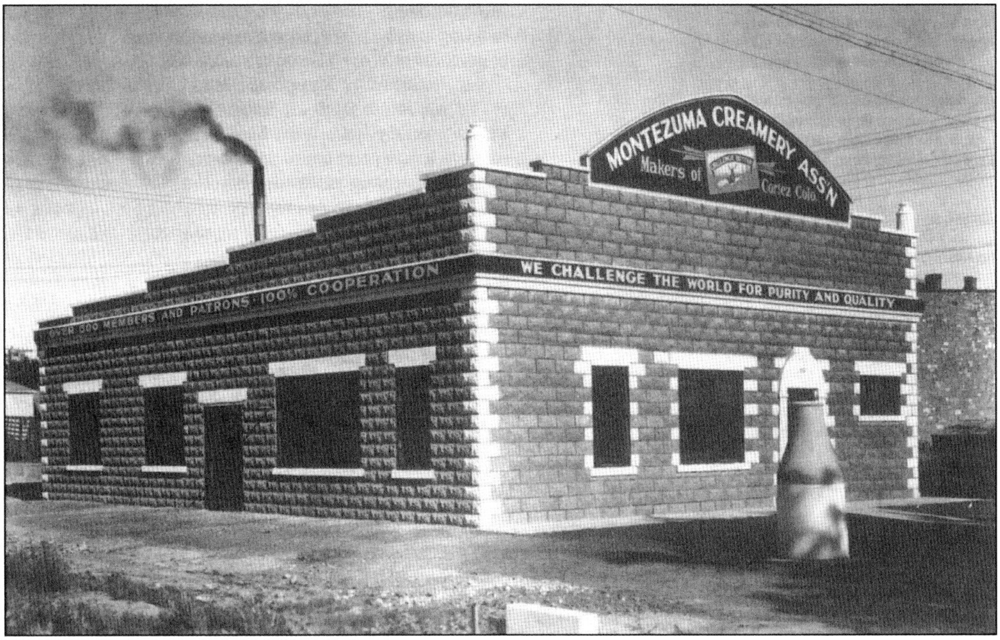

The Cortez Creamery, one of the country's earliest refrigerated creameries, was conceived as a cooperative and opened in 1931. The building was constructed and equipped with up-to-date equipment on North Chestnut Street. P.T. Kuhre was hired as manager, Walter Carpenter as operator, and Bill Runck as refrigeration mechanic. Within two months, it had shipped 5.5 tons of butter to Los Angeles. Area producers included Tom Cox, Tony Suckla, Gerald Neal, Earl Hart, John Carver, Francis McCabe, Jerry Prior, Pete Katzendorn, and Gordon Maness. (Courtesy of Cortez Area Chamber of Commerce.)

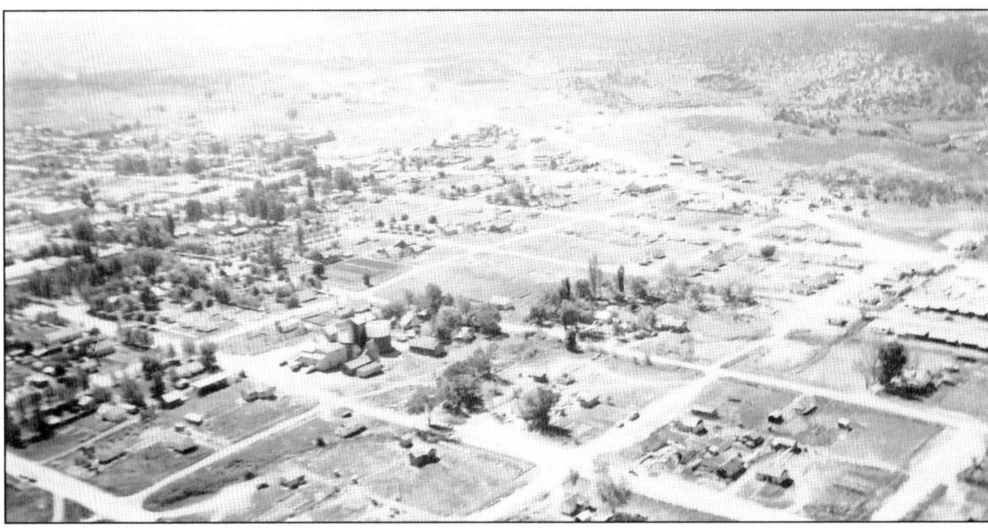

Much of Cortez continues to be rural, with farmsteads scattered throughout the city, as seen in this aerial photograph looking southwest. Members of the dairy association outnumbered that of the cattlemen. Broadway/US Highway 666, now 491, marks the west side of town. The flour mill on Market Street is clearly recognizable in the front, just left of the center. The Civilian Conservation Corps (CCC) camp sat just outside the photograph's right edge. (Courtesy of Montezuma County Historical Society.)

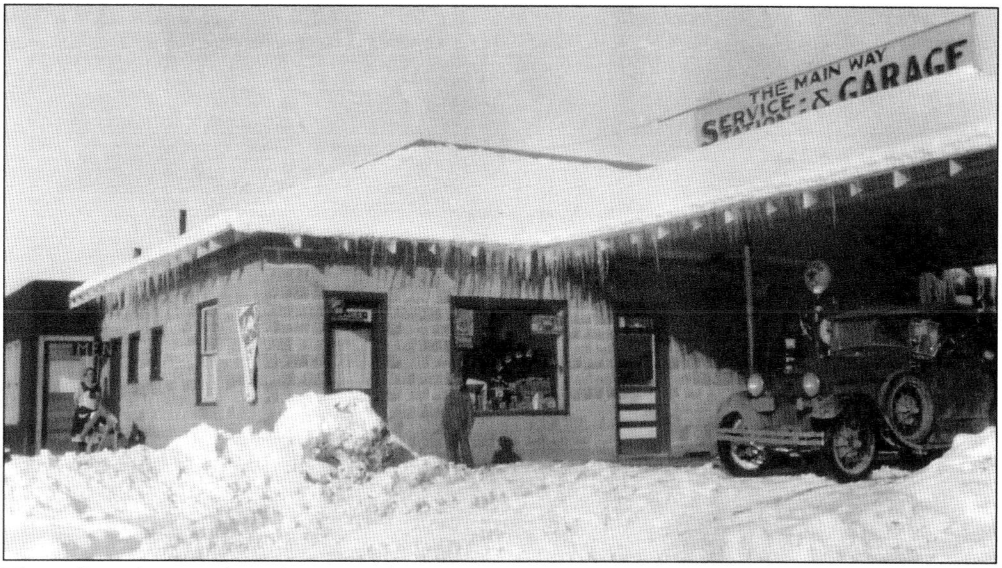

The influx of cars and trucks meant that livery businesses were being replaced by service stations and garages. The Bill Kuenzler family owned the Main Way Garage at Maple and Main Streets on the west end of town. Bill immigrated to the United States from Switzerland in 1903 and ended up in Cortez in 1930. Labor for the garage was provided by people who were in debt to Bill from a business he had owned before. Young John Kuenzler stands in front. (Courtesy of City of Cortez and Montezuma County Historical Society.)

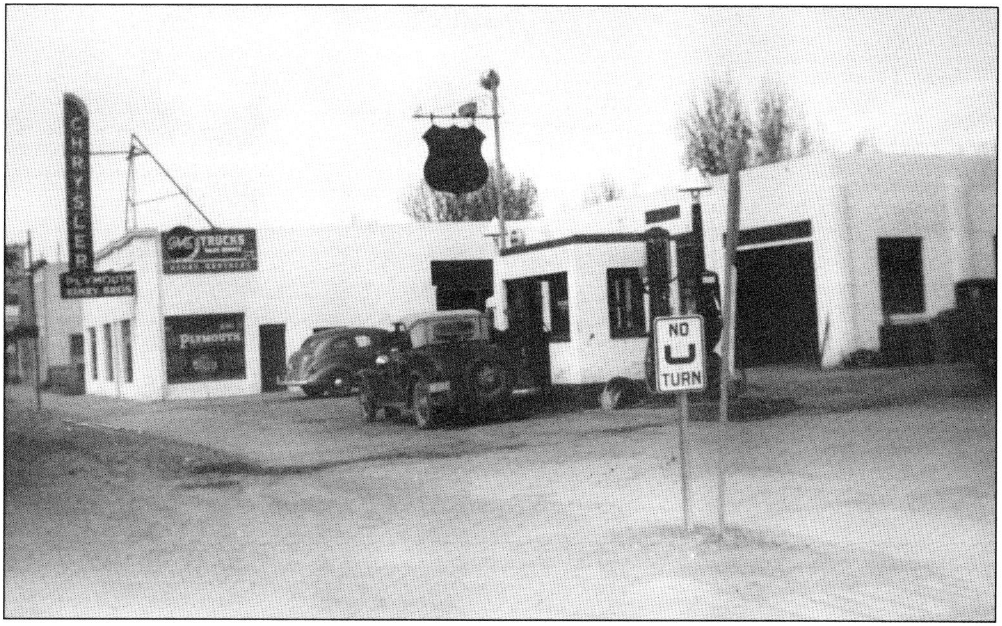

Ted and Jim Henry started the Henry Brothers Garage, located on the northwest corner of Ash and Main Streets, in the 1920s. In the late 1930s, Hunter Motor Company bought the business and expanded to sell Chrysler, Plymouth, GMC Trucks, and John Deere. The name changed in 1946 to reflect new owners' names. Car sales continue to be big business in Cortez, and the larger lots have moved from the center to the periphery of town. (Courtesy of City of Cortez and Montezuma County Historical Society.)

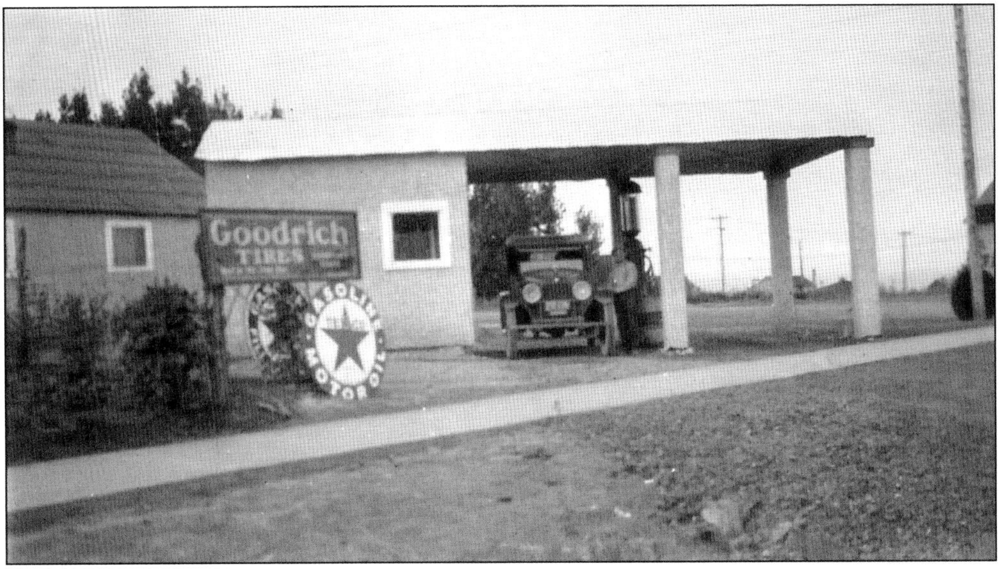

Automobiles allowed the citizenry to more easily explore the rapidly developing nation. Service stations sprang up to replace livery stables. Garages that sold tires, gasoline, and motor oil replaced wheelwrights, harness makers, and hay and oats merchants. This Texaco station stood at the west end of town. (Courtesy of Larry Hauser.)

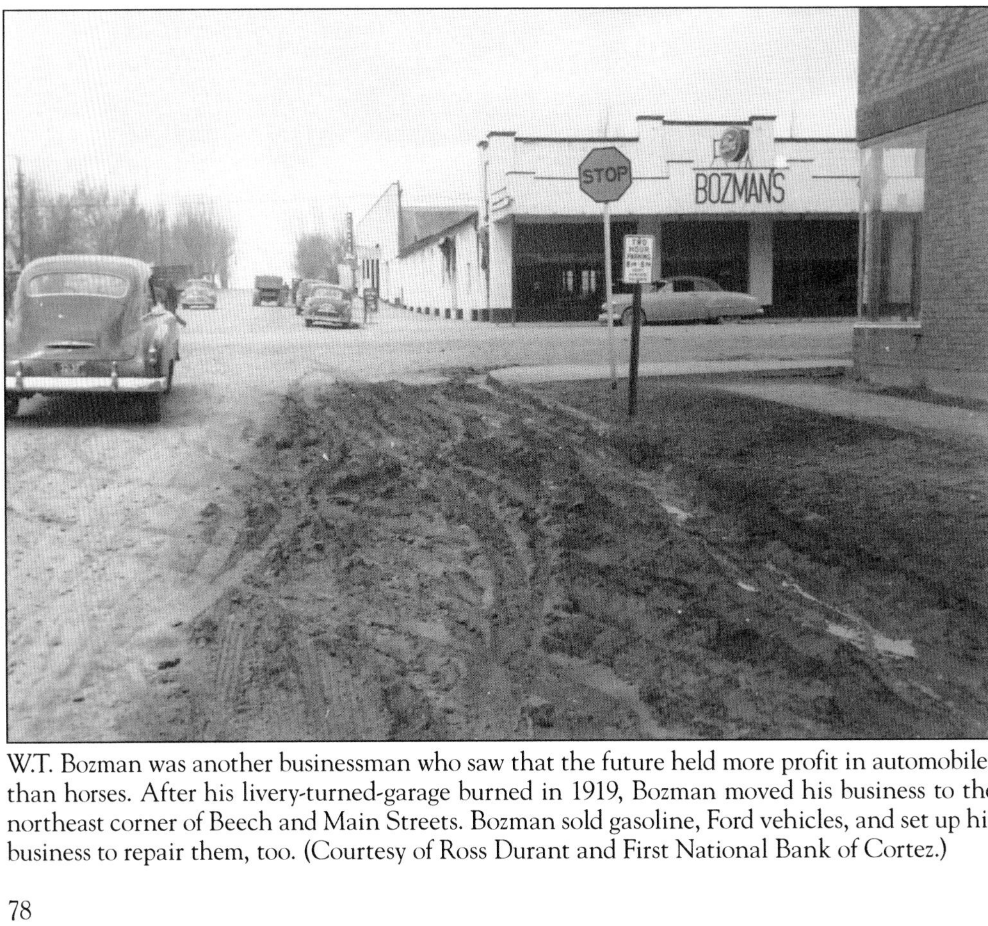

W.T. Bozman was another businessman who saw that the future held more profit in automobiles than horses. After his livery-turned-garage burned in 1919, Bozman moved his business to the northeast corner of Beech and Main Streets. Bozman sold gasoline, Ford vehicles, and set up his business to repair them, too. (Courtesy of Ross Durant and First National Bank of Cortez.)

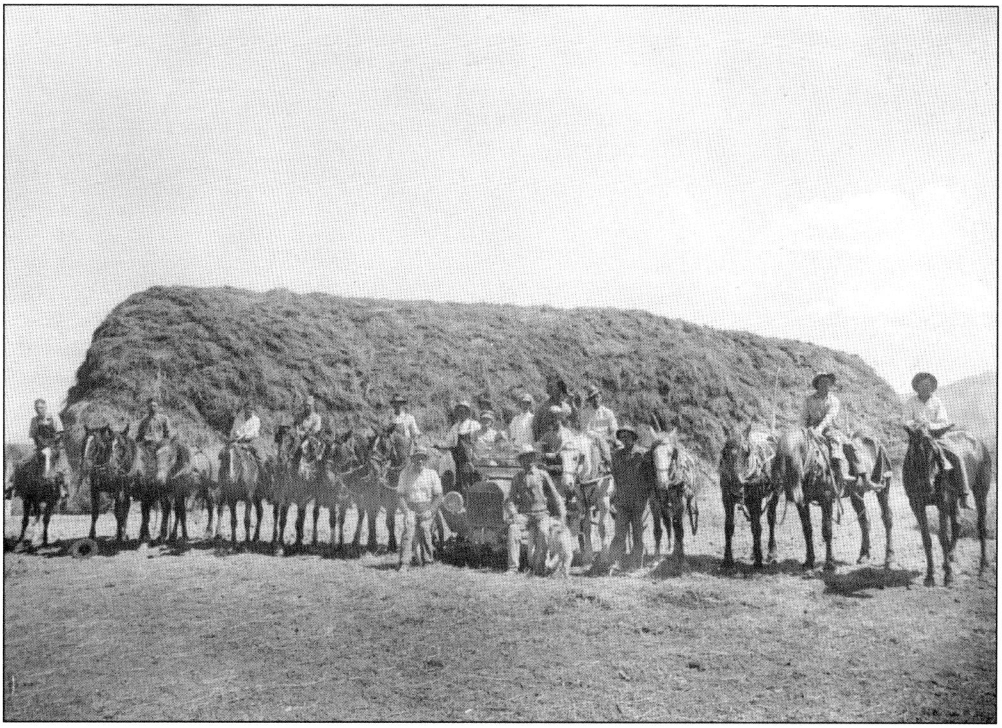

Tourists and merchants were not the only people taking advantage of gasoline engines. This crew put up a passel of hay with the hard work of men and horses. The one vehicle shown portends a new way of working that would involve a lot less sweat. (Courtesy of Cortez Public Library.)

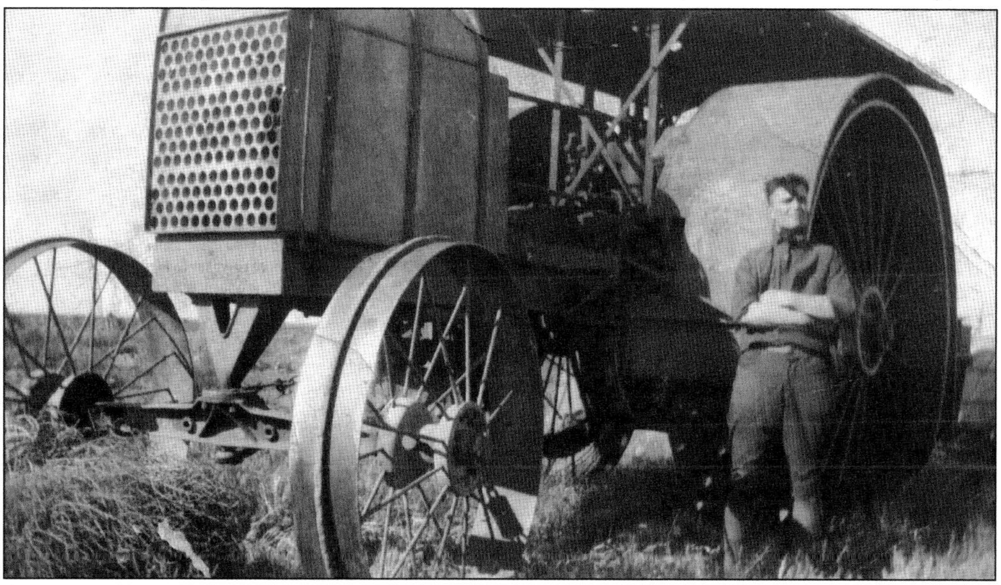

A steam tractor such as this was used alone or to power a baler or threshing machine using its PTO (power take-off, which allows power to be "taken off" the engine of one machine and used in another). In 1922, at Ackman (later Pleasant View), a Mr. James and C.B. Haney experimented and successfully grew pinto beans. The agricultural conservation program initiated by the Roosevelt administration in 1937 helped improve soil and slow erosion. (Courtesy of Cortez Newspapers.)

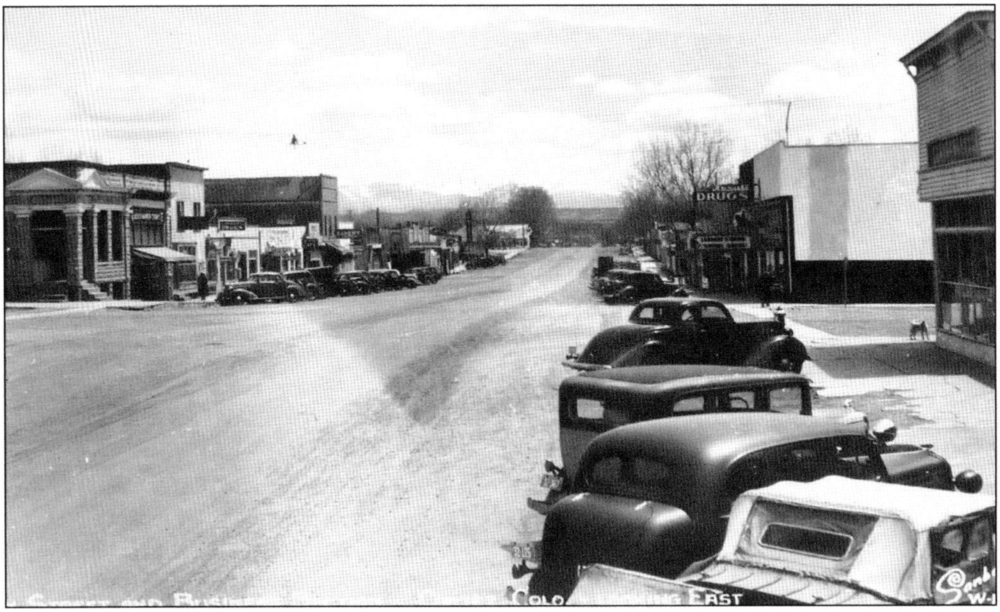

At Market and Main Streets, the electric light over the intersection shows the city's progress in providing utilities. The building at far right is Sam Walker's Cortez Mercantile. The convertible, canvas-topped car must have been a status symbol for someone. Across Market Street is the fireproof replacement to Bozman's Garage. Across Main Street are the bank, Farmer's Drugs, the café that still operates today as El Grande, and Kermode Bakery. (Courtesy of Pauline Sleeper and Denise Carver, and First National Bank of Cortez.)

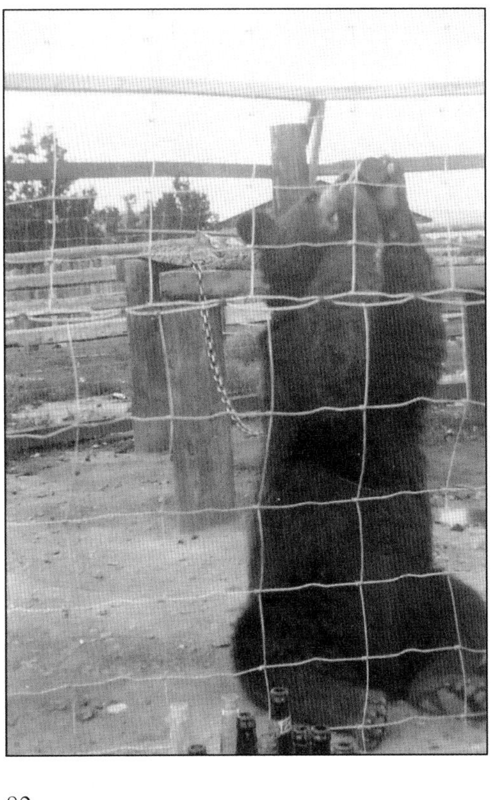

Early local attractions were not always sophisticated. The wayside station at Hallarville, 10 miles east of Cortez, sold soda pop and sundries. Many older locals remember giving Fred Hallar's pet black bear a bottle of orange soda pop. The bear was called Nehi, after the brand-name carbonated drinks. (Courtesy of Jack Winbourn.)

Five

Rural Cooperatives Build Energy Connection

Electricity changed how rural folks worked and played. In the 1930s, only residents of urban areas had access to central-station electric power. The Rural Electric Cooperative was an idea launched into reality through Pres. Franklin D. Roosevelt's New Deal.

Up to the 1930s, rural Americans did not have electricity as their urban neighbors did. Power companies viewed rural areas as too costly to serve due to the difficulty and expense of installing and maintaining lines. Sparsely populated farming communities also returned fewer profits.

In Montezuma County, a woman named Lulu Fitzgerald wrote a letter to President Roosevelt and asked how a Rural Electric Cooperative could be started. She received a response and presented the documents to the county. Planning board members set up community meetings to share information and gather support. Leaders in the community solicited charter members and secured the rights-of-way from landowners.

Empire Electric Association was incorporated in November 1939. Then, 18 months later, the initial line construction was completed and the switch turned on at 5:25 p.m., providing power to about 50 members of the cooperative.

Empire's first power source was a large diesel power generator near the small town of Lewis. It was noisy to some and sweet music to others, who were now able to light their homes at night without worrying about fires and soot from kerosene lamps.

Betty Porter from McElmo Canyon said the first thing her family purchased was a record player so they could play music and dance. For many to receive power, mules and horses had to drag poles and heavy electric lines up steep hillsides and across creeks. It was an effort that got the whole community excited.

Empire Electric Association has had its ups, including joining Local Union 698 of the International Brotherhood of Electrical Workers and closing the switch on the Dove Creek substation and a 44,000-volt transmission line. It also had its downs, including warehouse fires in 1948 and 1957 and severe snowstorm damage to much of the system in 1965. Throughout its 70-plus years, Empire Electric Association expanded its core lines and now serves parts of five large rural counties.

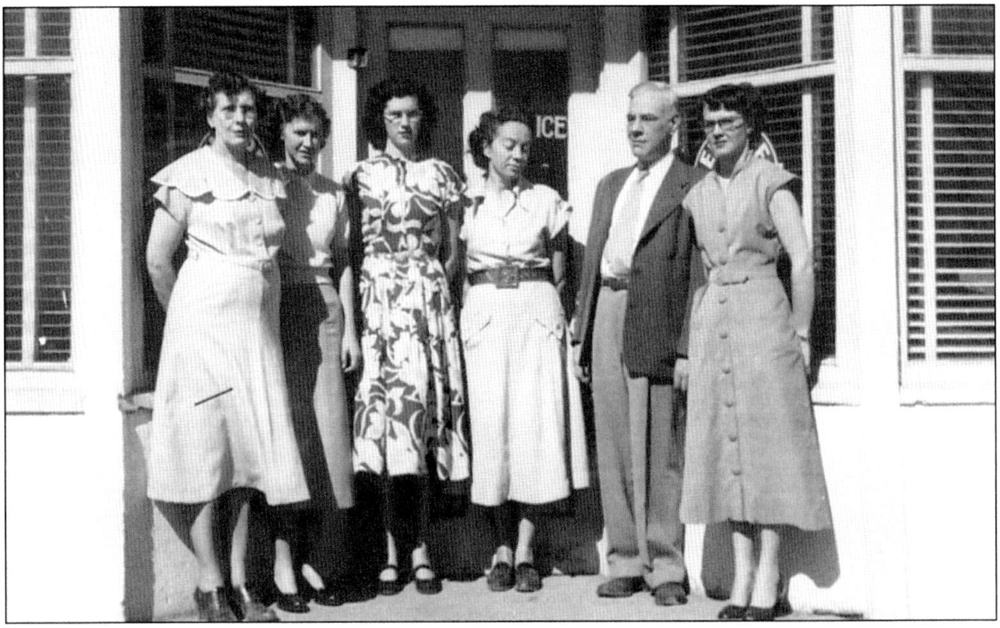

In 1955, Empire Electric Association offices were on North Market Street next to Montezuma Park. Standing in the doorway are, from left to right, Lula Todd Grasse, Bonnie Carter Rust, Mary Ellen Wilson McComb, June Cowan, office manager Robert C. Merkel, and Shirley Kirk Hanson. (Courtesy of Empire Electric Association.)

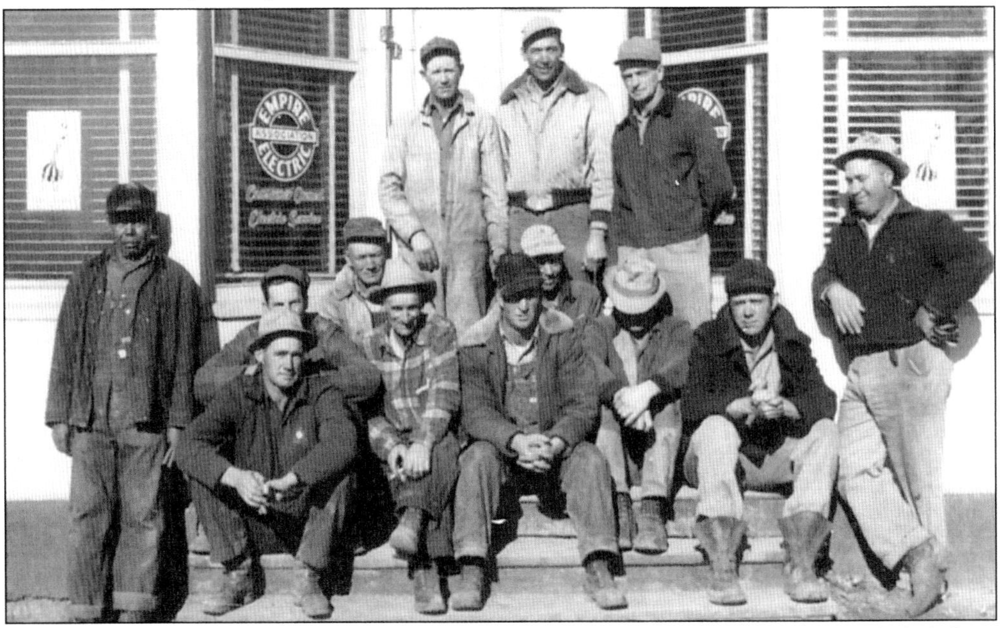

The men who managed the field work for the new Empire Electric Association included, from left to right, (first row, seated) Ray Patten; (second row) John Hayes (standing to left of Patten), Lovell Shepherd (behind Patten), Floyd Cox, Archie Jarrett, Bob Baer (hat brim hiding face) Frank Olson, and Bob Frasier (standing at right); (third row) Harley Graves and Howard Baxstrom (partially hidden); (fourth row, all standing) Claude Barker, Alex Archibeque, and Clarence Higman. (Courtesy of Empire Electric Association.)

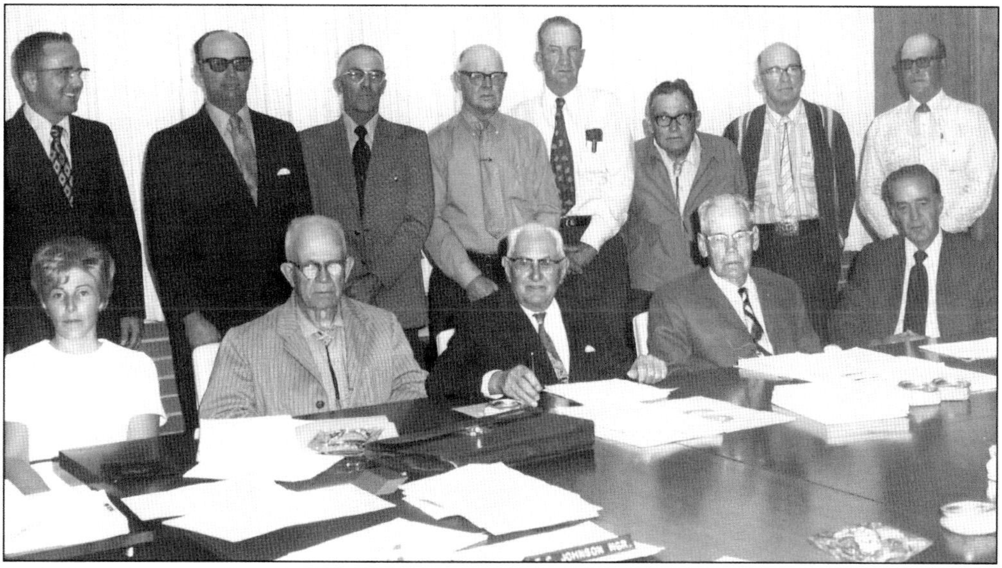

Both Dan Hunter and J.C. (Calvin) Denton pushed hard to establish Empire Electric Association. November 15, 1939, turned the tide in Montezuma and Dolores Counties with the formal incorporation of the Empire Electric Association. Board members of a later year include, from left to right, (first row) executive secretary Gloria Heald, J.C. Denton, Creighton Rauh, Hugh Rauscher, and attorney George Dilts; (second row) manager Everett Johnson, Wilson Brumley, Raymond Doyel, Ernest Watson, Wayne Rogers, Thomas Brennan, Charles McAfee, and Clarence Everett. (Courtesy of Empire Electric Association.)

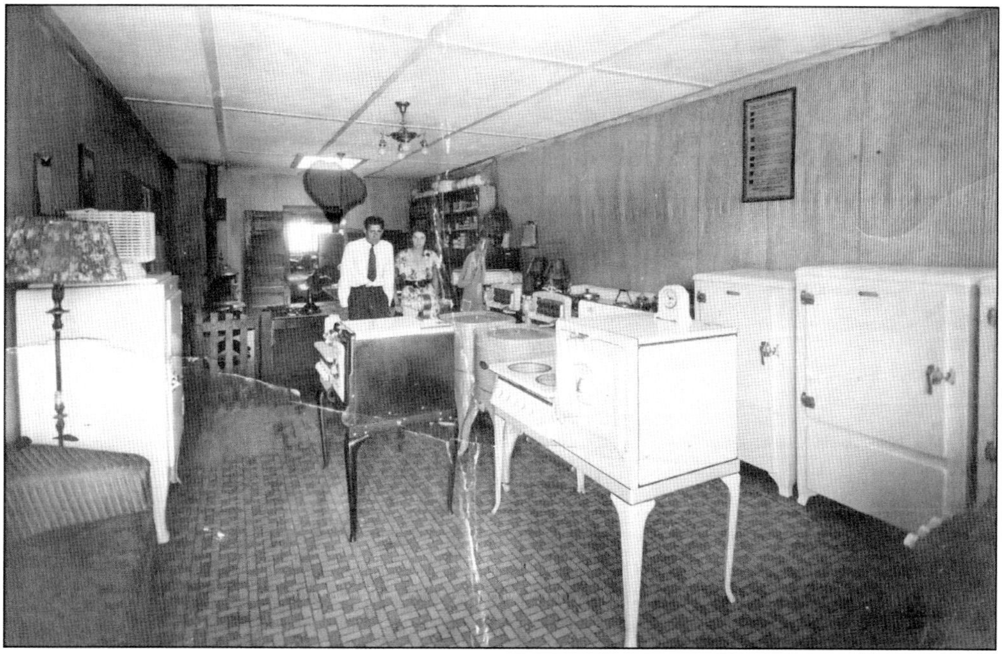

Electricity arrived in 1948 to most rural areas of the county. This early showroom at Highland Utilities on Main Street features a standing lamp, table lamps, a ceiling fixture, a fan, stoves, wringer washers, a clock, and refrigerators. Highland was purchased by Empire Electric Association in 1944. (Courtesy of Empire Electric Association.)

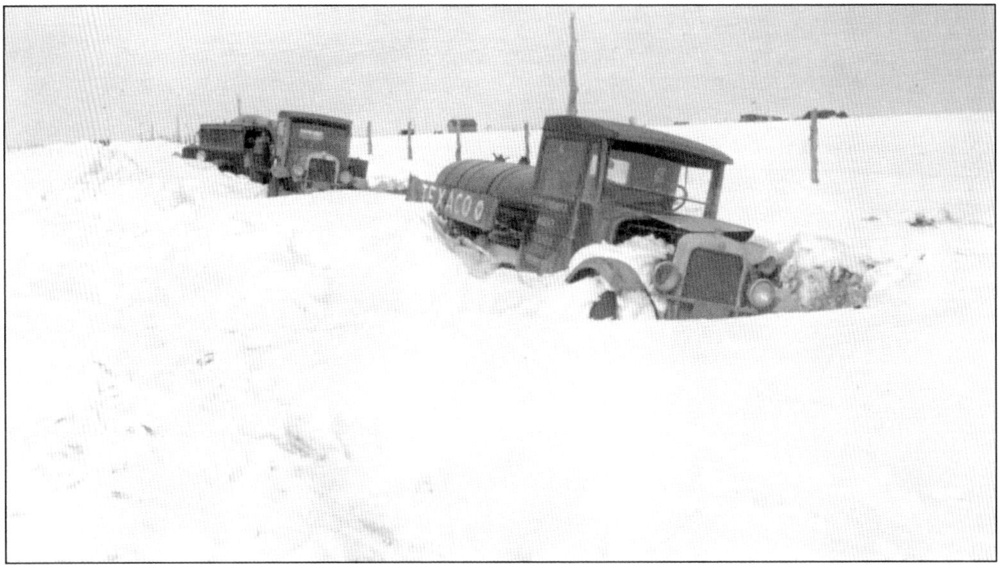

The winter of 1939 proved to be difficult, even if one had a sturdy vehicle. Fuel trucks were pushed off the road by ice, heavy snow, and winds. Eight feet of snow fell in Cortez and more on the ridges. People were lost in the blizzard and ended up in the hospital. Skis were touted as the best form of transportation in the drylands. (Courtesy of Larry Hauser.)

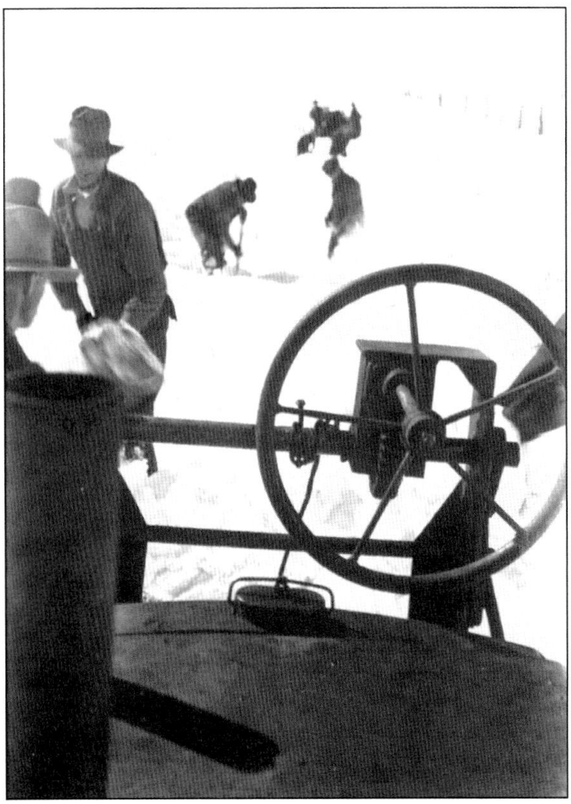

The blizzard conditions in 1939 left snowy roads that were cleared by men with hand shovels and an early mechanized snowplow. The newspaper reported at least three storms that stopped traffic and hampered mail delivery. Windblown drifts closed county roads for a week each time. (Courtesy of Larry Hauser.)

Six

A Wider View of the World

The 1940s were all about war. Men volunteered before drafting began. Women volunteered for Red Cross and other auxiliary services. The Boy and Girl Scouts started an aluminum drive.

The county and federal governments began directing local industries in the war effort. Local farmers planned a defense program. Approximately 1,400 men from Montezuma County registered for the draft in early 1943. Local newspapers reported that 205 men were inducted. Women were left to carry the burden of work.

Fears rose. Aliens were required to turn cameras, guns, and shortwave radios over to the sheriff. The newspaper expressed concern that Japanese-American citizens might be interned in the Cortez Civilian Conservation Corps (CCC) camp.

Gasoline rations were three gallons per week. Food production required more fuel, so rations were set so farmers could produce. Tires and trucks were hard for farmers to find. Retired teachers were called back to work because teachers were being drafted. Farm labor was scarce. And yet, Montezuma County received an award for outstanding performance of food and fiber in 1943. Only one county per state received this award. The sale of war bonds always exceeded quotas.

Germany surrendered in April 1945. When Japan signed accords in August, gas rationing ended. The newspaper listed 33 local citizens who were killed. Four were missing in action.

At home, the American Legion continued to coordinate the county fair and feature horse races. Cortez petitioned the state to help pave Main Street. The town council voted to pursue municipal ownership of the power system. When Cortez granted the franchise to Highland Utilities, Empire Electric bought Highland out.

State representative Elizabeth Pellet worked to get a local water conservation district. Bureau of Reclamation engineers explored a proposed dam site and completed a feasibility study. The county continued health education and nursing services. Cortez purchased low priority water for 10,000 people. The town voted for a $25,000 bond for water works improvements and to extend mains to the new hospital on South Broadway.

Cortez Flying Service opened. The new county airport was dedicated. Colorado Carbonics was incorporated in McElmo Canyon. Peace was looking good.

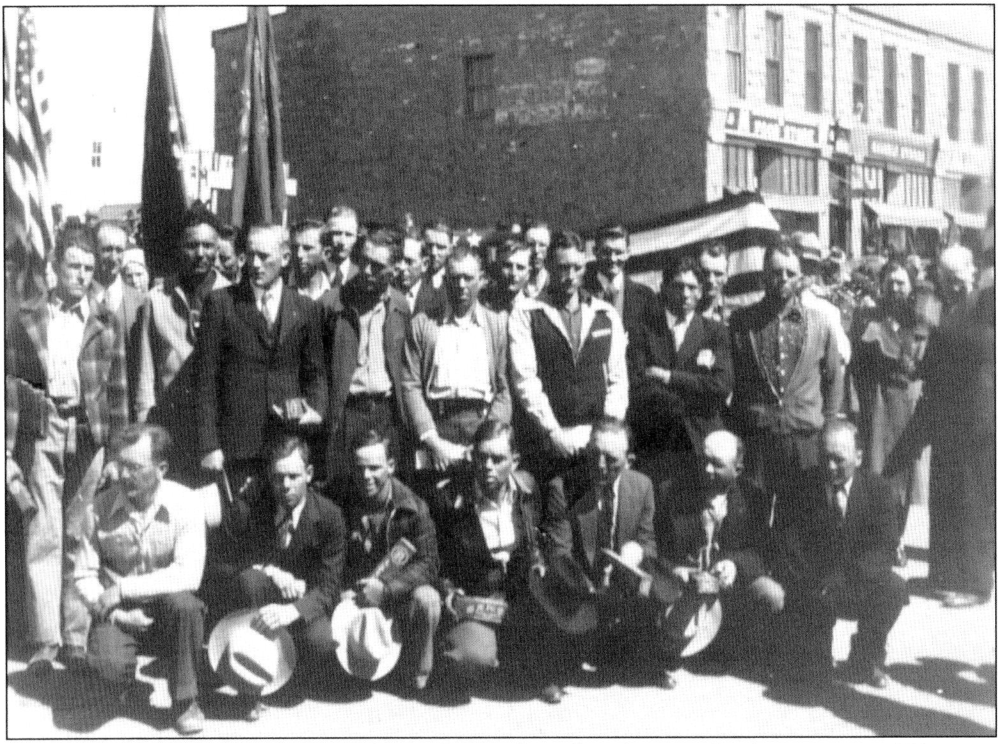

Somber-looking men gather for speeches and a parade in this photograph taken just east of Chestnut Street on Main Street. The Stone Block stands behind the men and several flags. On the back of the photograph is written, "WWII dedication, Lion's Memorial Board." (Courtesy of Larry Hauser.)

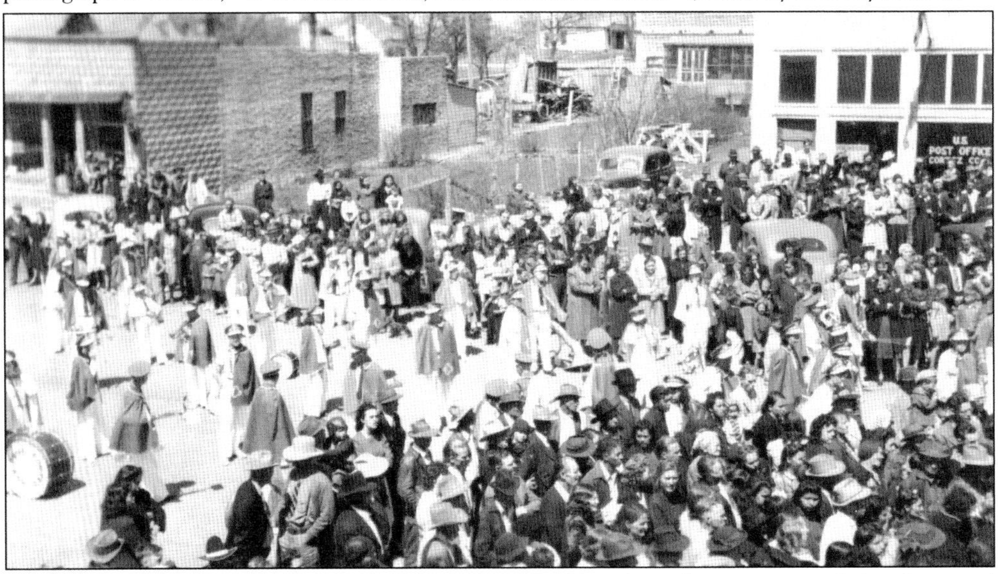

The Cortez High School marching band, in white slacks and purple capes, waits behind a crowd gathered to listen to speakers near the post office on Main Street. The clothing and hairstyles suggest the same crowd as the photograph above. In April 1941, Cortez organized a parade for draftees and enlistees headed to war. Farmers planned a war defense program, volunteers were enlisting, and war bonds were being sold. (Courtesy of Cortez Area Chamber of Commerce.)

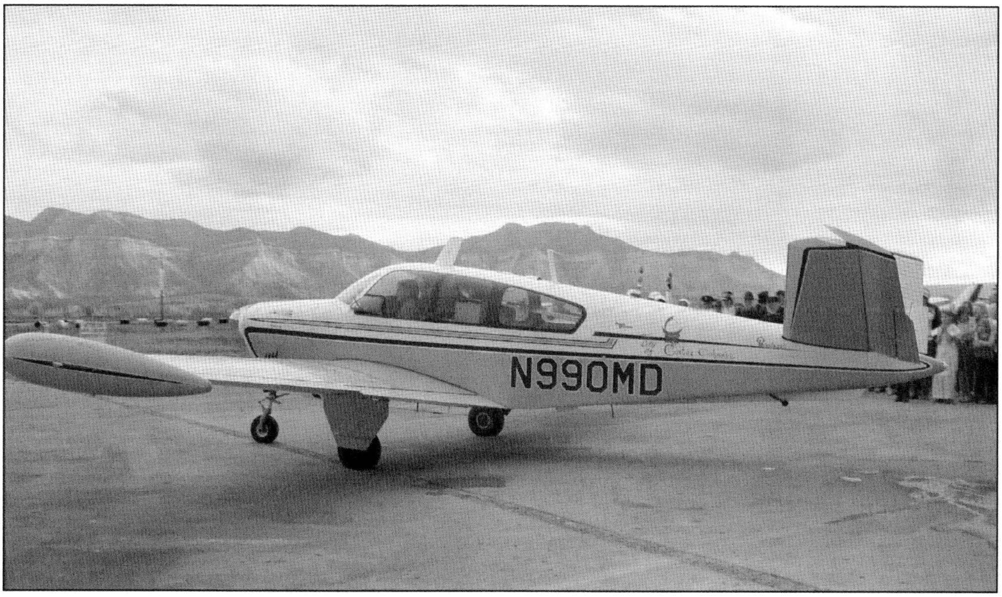

In 1934, Civil Works Administration (CWA) funds were available for an airport, and construction began east of town. A new Montezuma County Airport was dedicated in 1949 at a business park south of McElmo Creek. R.N. and Polly Usher opened Cortez Flying Service there the same year. In this 1977 photograph, Cortez residents Herman Benham and Jack Rudd have just landed after lopping 28.5 hours off the old world record for circumnavigation of the globe in their single-engine plane. (Courtesy of Mrs. Charles L. Luellen and Larry Hauser.)

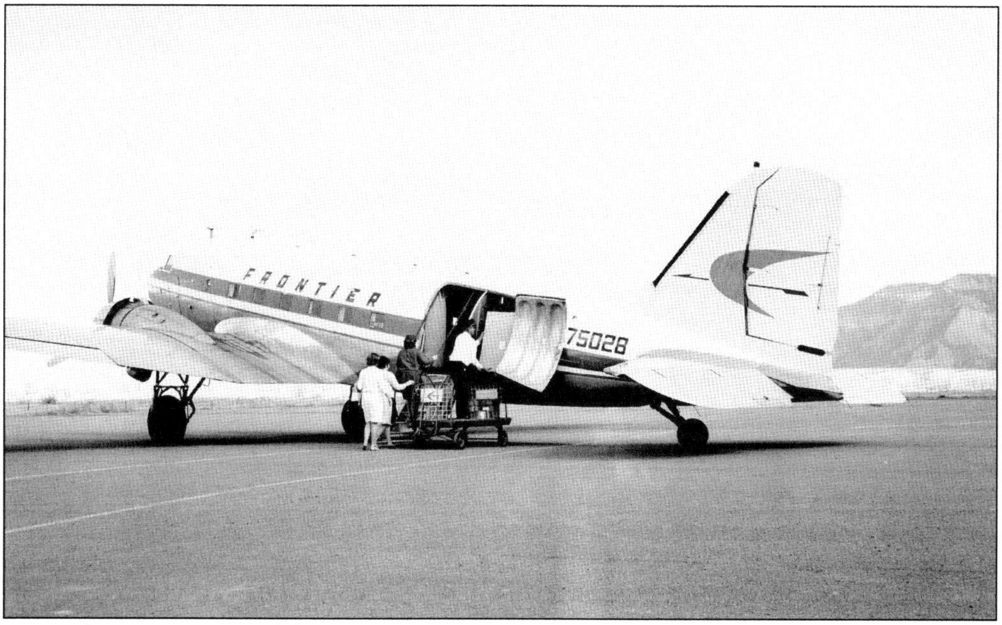

Monarch Air Lines served the Four Corners states starting in 1946. In 1950, Monarch merged with Challenger Airlines and Arizona Airways to form Frontier Airlines. The new airport south of town began receiving commercial planes in 1952. In 1958, the runway was paved, and a new terminal opened in 1960. Frontier's DC-3 (shown here) and Convair 580 aircraft served the Cortez public until the airline's bankruptcy in 1986. (Courtesy of Larry Hauser.)

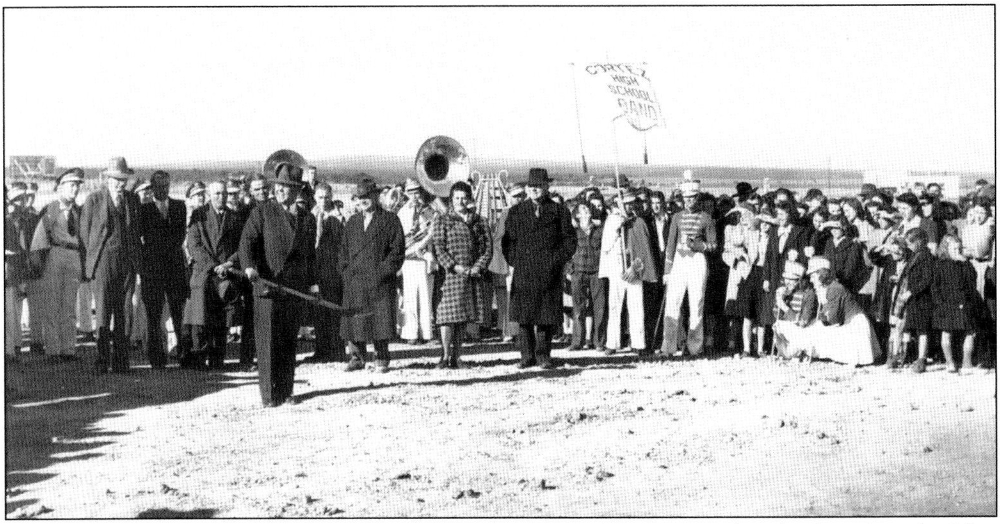

The whole town turned out when Colorado governor Ralph L. Carr dug the first shovel of dirt at the site of the new Montezuma County High School in 1941. Ahead of his time, Governor Carr spoke out for the constitutional rights of all Americans, regardless of the birthplace of their grandfathers. This stance ruined his political future. (Courtesy of Cortez Public Library.)

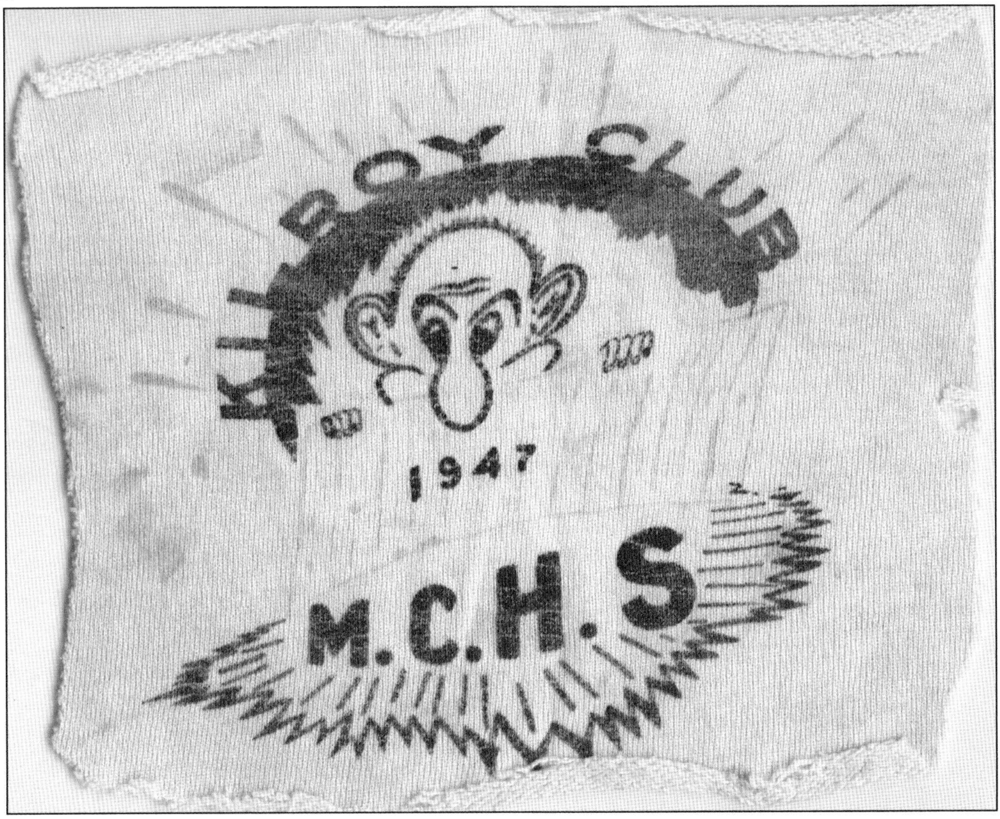

Kilroy Club was a Montezuma County High School–approved club whose members all served in World War II. "Kilroy Was Here" was known around the world during World War II. The 1947 graduates had Richard Lindsay's logo printed on sweatshirts. (Courtesy of Jack Winbourn.)

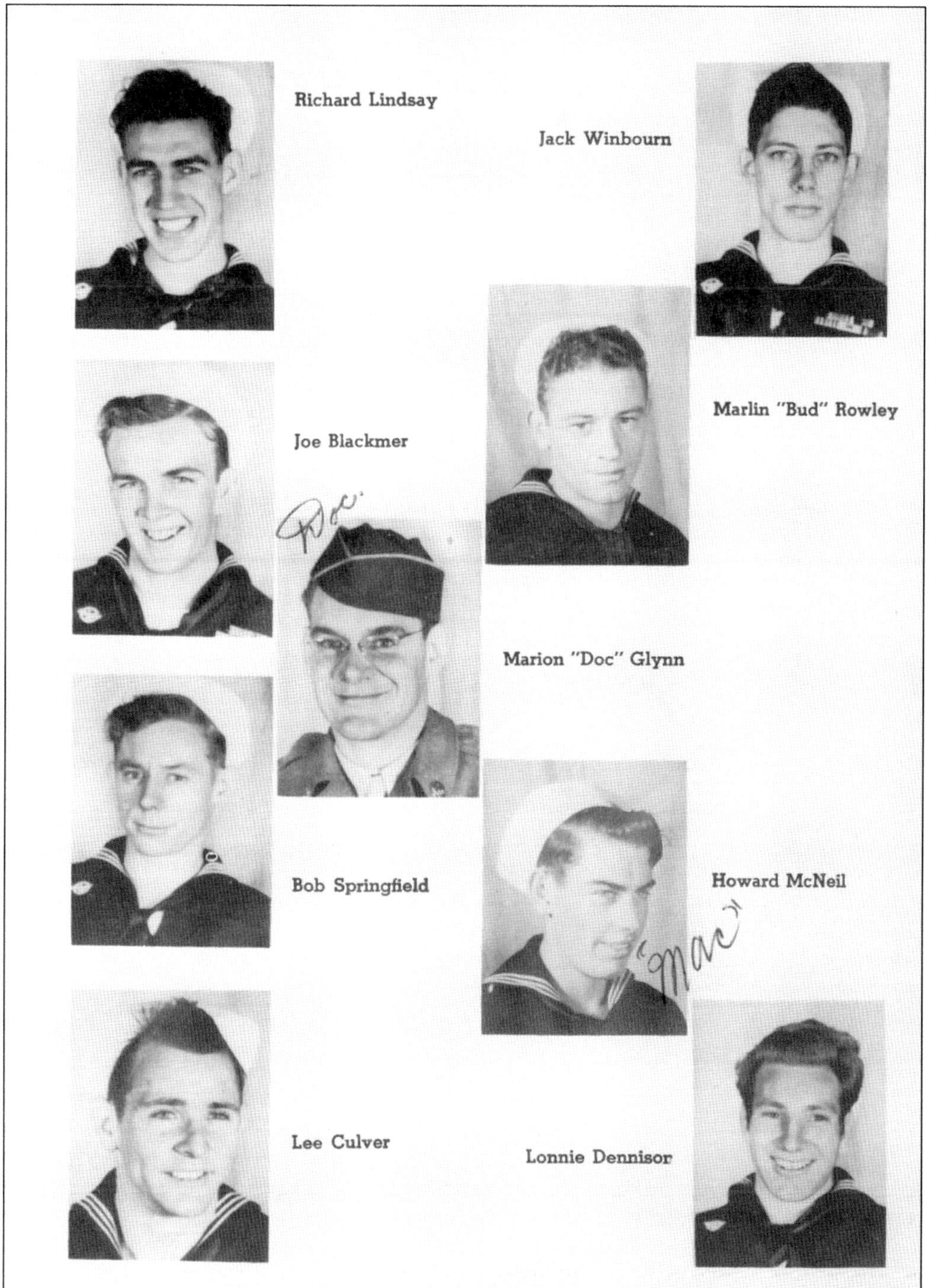

Returning GIs were featured on a page from the 1947 Montezuma County High School yearbook. Jack Winbourn, at top right, offered his yearbook, complete with signatures, for use in this book. In 1946, Winbourn asked the principal, Vencil Lester, if he could finish high school. Lester was delighted and asked Winbourn to talk to the other young veterans. (Courtesy of Jack Winbourn.)

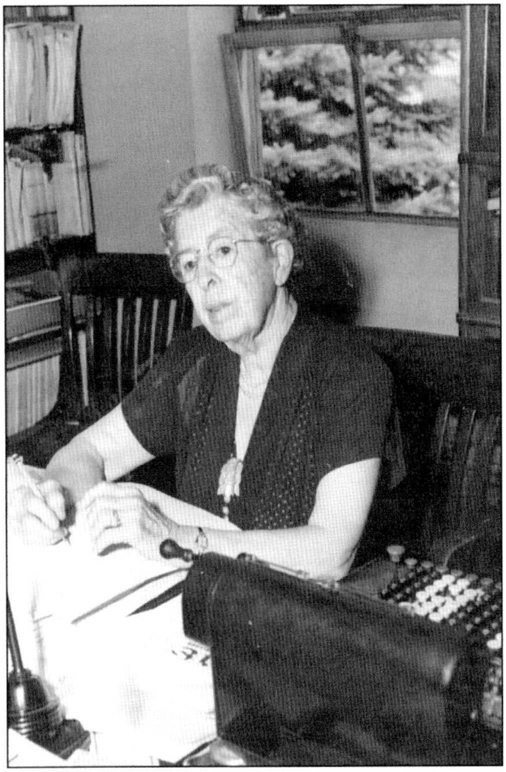

Lotta Manaugh was stalwart in insisting that the future of the county lay in the education of the youth. After teaching for many years, she was elected superintendent of schools. When two new elementary schools were built, the district honored Manaugh by naming one of the new schools after her. (Courtesy of Montezuma-Cortez School District Re-1.)

After World War II, Cortez experienced the same growth that was occurring across the nation. Soldiers returned from war theaters, and renewed domestic life helped create the baby boom. The country's economy was stimulated by war industries, and money was easier to find for burgeoning schools. Downey and Manaugh Elementary Schools were both built in the early 1950s. (Courtesy of Dale Davidson.)

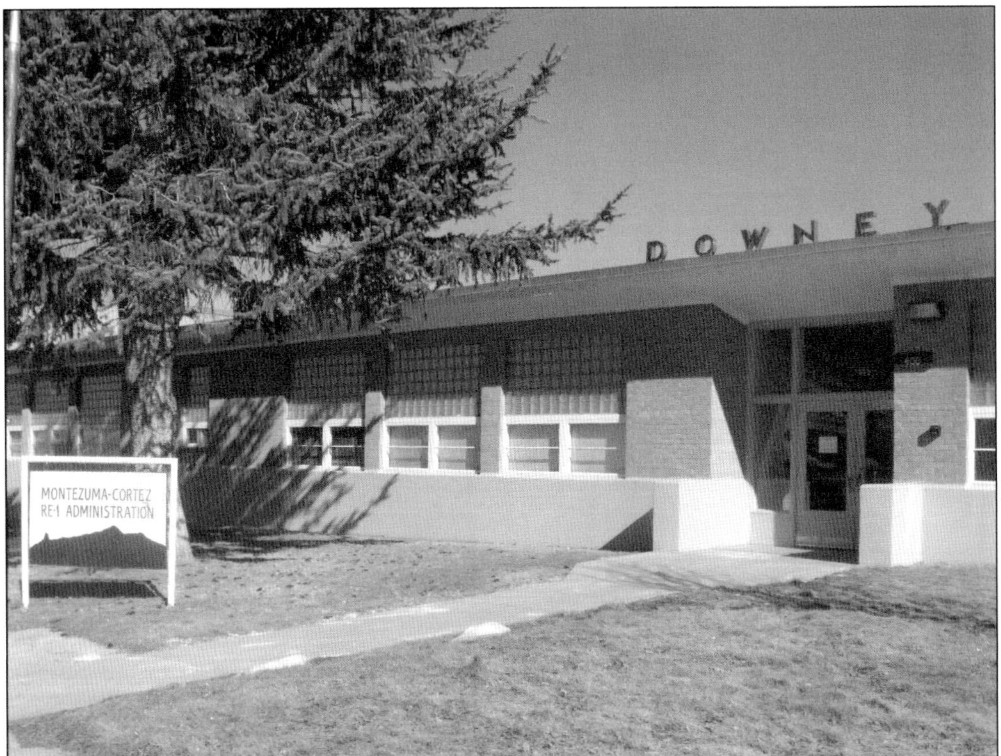

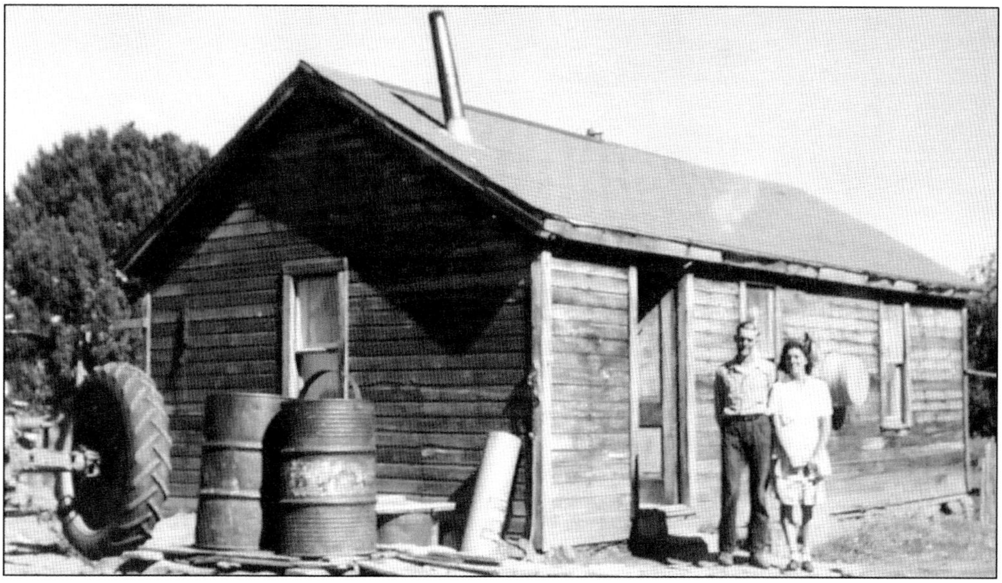

Identified as the White home, this young couple stands smiling beside their house near Pleasant View. The stovepipe indicates wood heat and cooking. No overhead wiring yet connects them to a local utility, but they value the tractor. It would help build a successful dryland enterprise to support their growing family. (Courtesy of Anasazi Heritage Center.)

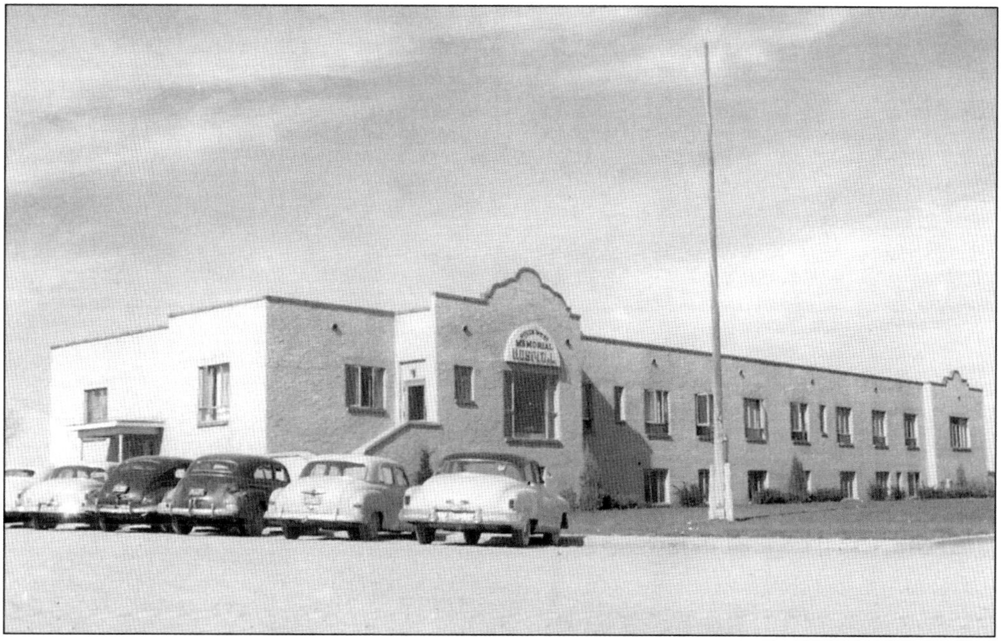

The new Southwest Memorial Hospital was dedicated at 927 South Broadway in 1948, five years after Dr. Johnson died. J.W. Ertel donated the land for the 30-bed facility. The original staff of six medical doctors included Dr. R.T. Speck, Dr. C.E. Parmley, Dr. I.E. Maxwell, Dr. E.G. Merritt, Dr. E.D. Kadlub, and Dr. V.E. Gardner. Its two dentists were Dr. W.J. Roper and Dr. T.W. Quinn. Dr. Royal Calkins was an honorary member. (Courtesy of Empire Electric Association.)

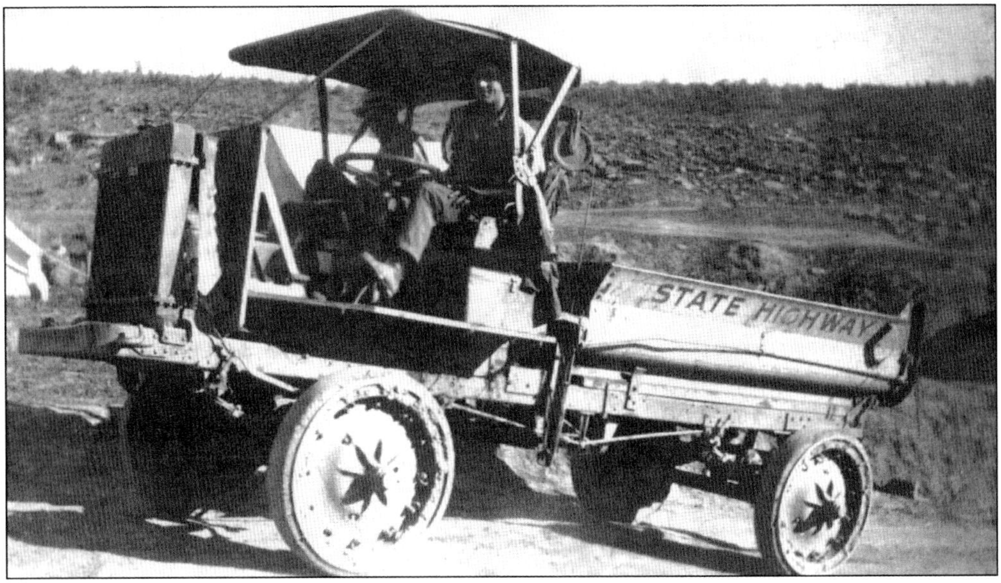

The state highway department began providing road-building trucks and equipment. Few safety and comfort features were included. But moving house-size boulders to carve safer highways through the canyons of the Southwest became manageable. In 1936, the first paving of US Highway 160 began in Cortez and started toward Mancos. In 1937, the county purchased equipment for heavy-duty roadwork. The Cortez to Dove Creek highway was graveled, and bids were let to oil pave 20 miles. A 27-mile section of the highway between Cortez and Shiprock was graveled and oil paved. A stretch of Highway 160 between Mancos and Cortez was oiled. Forty miles of road in Montezuma County were maintained by the state. (Courtesy of Cortez Newspapers.)

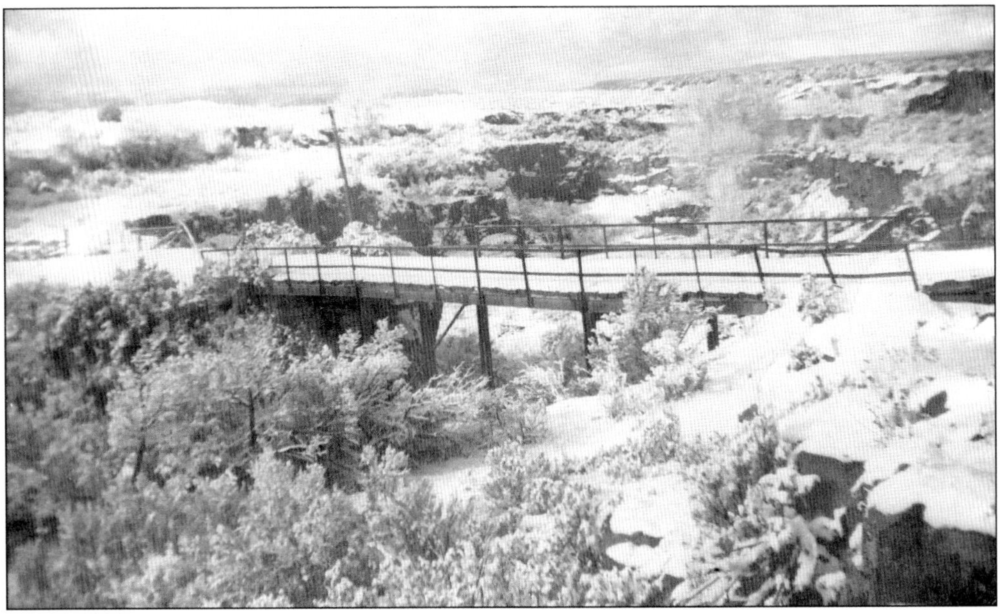

This photograph of the South Oak Street bridge across McElmo Canyon was taken in 1946. The slender guardrails did little to keep careless drivers from sliding off in snow and ice. However, the crossing was easier with the bridge than without. Compare this view of McElmo with the recent canyon photograph on page 11. (Courtesy of William R. Hartley.)

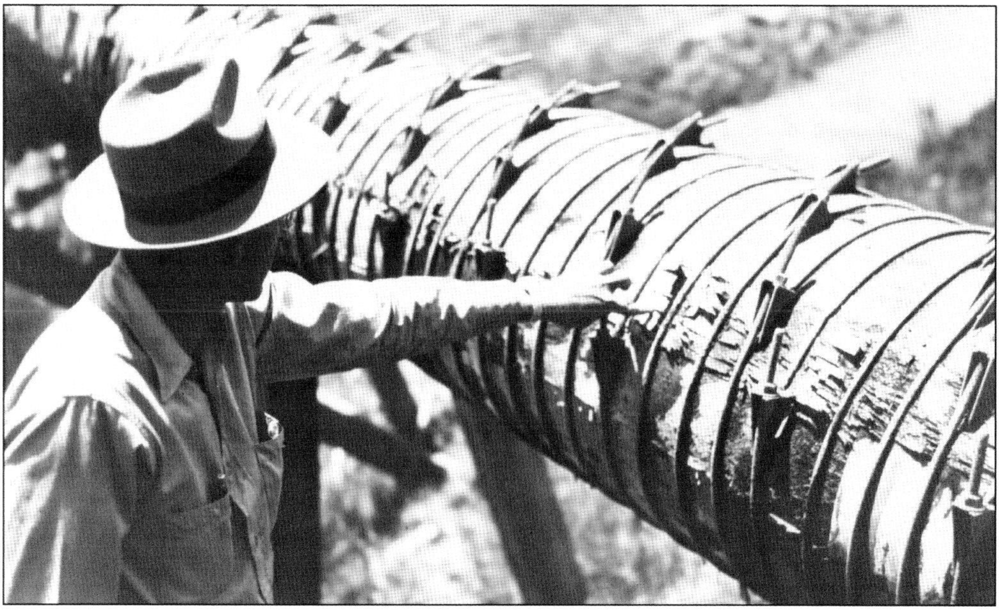

Wooden siphons, such as this one at Alkali Draw, were very expensive to maintain. The irrigation district faced ongoing financial stressors from equipment such as this. (Courtesy of Anasazi Heritage Center.)

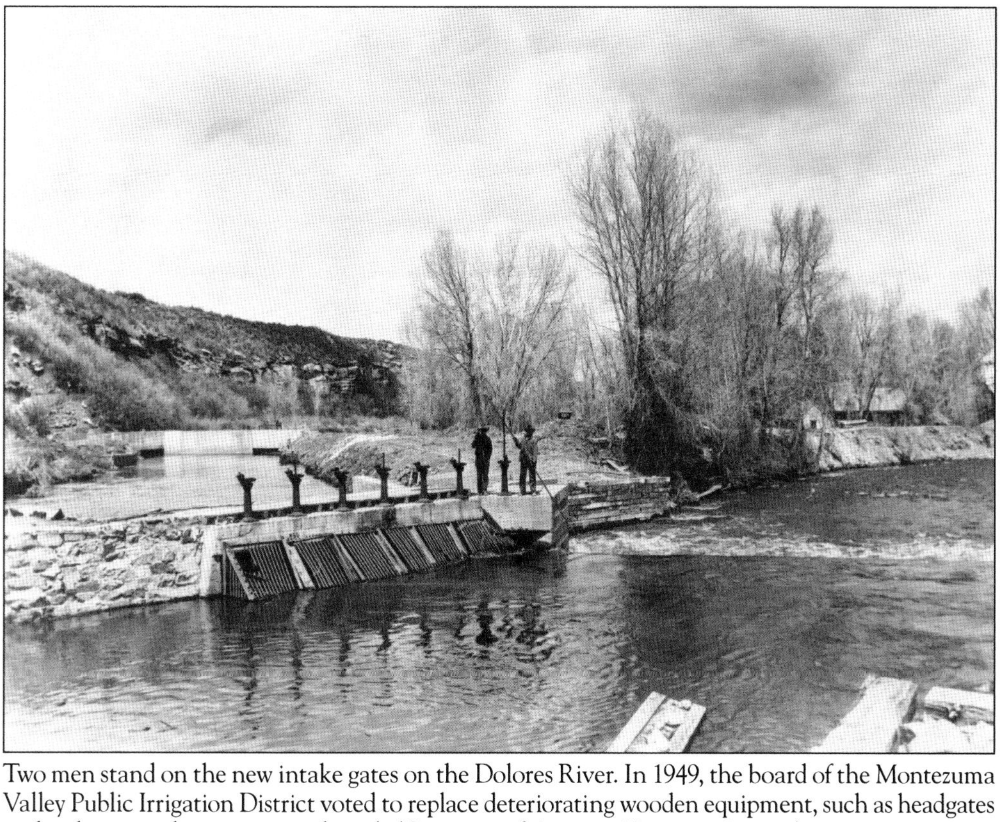

Two men stand on the new intake gates on the Dolores River. In 1949, the board of the Montezuma Valley Public Irrigation District voted to replace deteriorating wooden equipment, such as headgates and siphons, with concrete and steel. (Courtesy of Anasazi Heritage Center.)

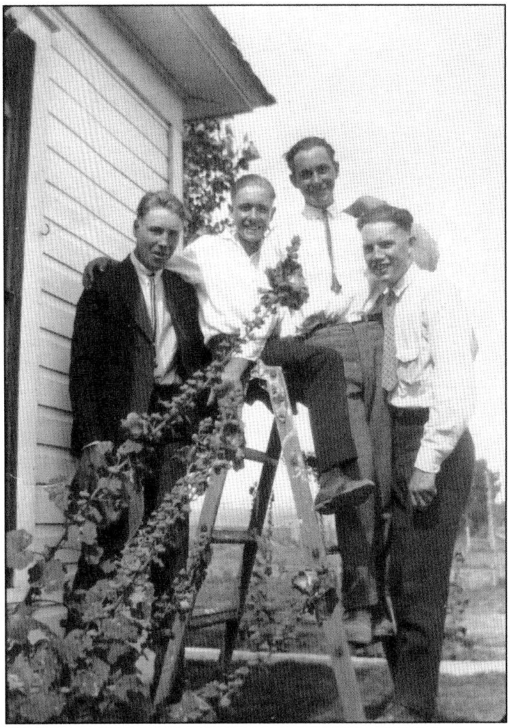

Pictured from left to right, George Clark, Dewey and Dwight Brown, and a friend fool around for the camera in this 1924 photograph. Dwight and Dewey's parents, John Ellsworth and Frances Dewey Brown, purchased the *Cortez Herald* in 1911. The Brown family either owned or managed the newspaper until they sold it to the Ballantine family of Durango in 1999. (Courtesy of Barbara Breternitz.)

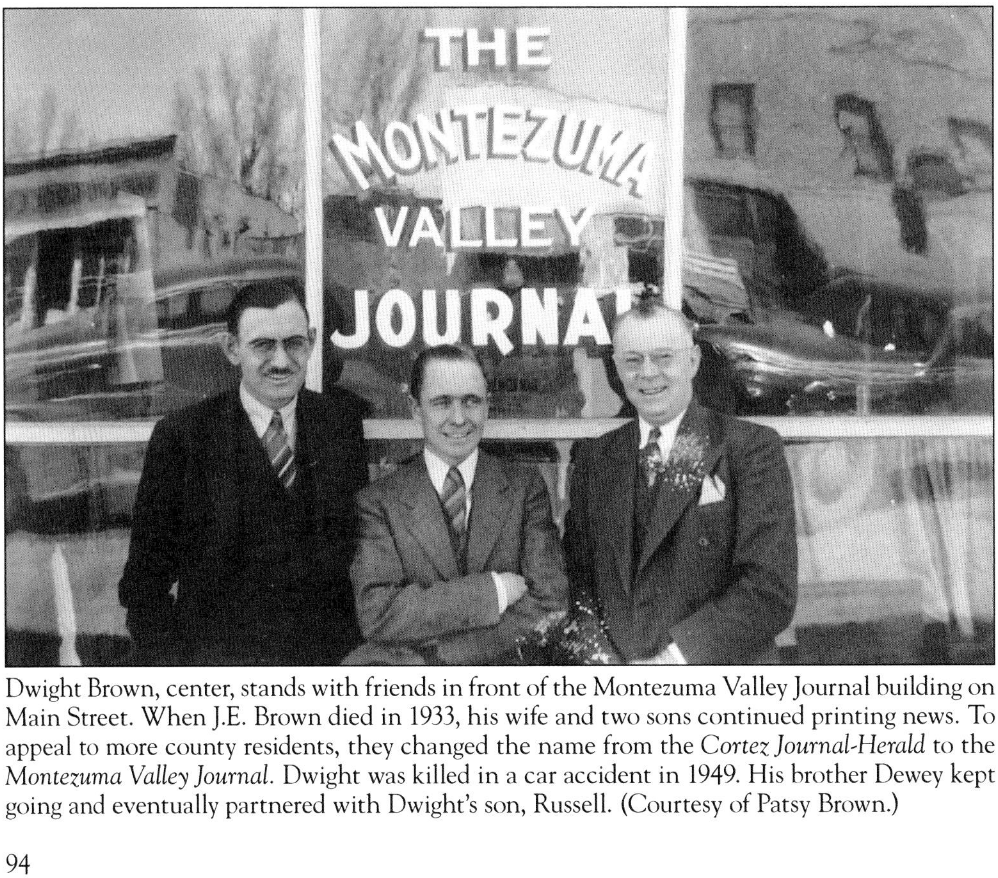

Dwight Brown, center, stands with friends in front of the Montezuma Valley Journal building on Main Street. When J.E. Brown died in 1933, his wife and two sons continued printing news. To appeal to more county residents, they changed the name from the *Cortez Journal-Herald* to the *Montezuma Valley Journal*. Dwight was killed in a car accident in 1949. His brother Dewey kept going and eventually partnered with Dwight's son, Russell. (Courtesy of Patsy Brown.)

Seven

THE LITTLE CITY THAT COULD

The discovery of the Aneth oil field in Utah put Cortez on the map for good. In the early 1950s, Cortez became the base of operations because it sat on the best road to Aneth. The biggest local player in oil development was Superior Oil. It operated out of Cortez offices while developing oil production from about 200 wells on the Navajo reservation.

Chief Jack House and the Ute Mountain Ute tribe negotiated sizable leases for uranium, oil, and gas development. The Pacific Northwest Pipeline Company constructed a cross-country pipeline through Montezuma County.

Oil field workers lived in Cortez and commuted to work, which created a housing and construction boom. Between 1955 and 1970, Cortez's population rose to nearly 10,000. The school district enlarged Manaugh and built two more elementary schools. The city paved the airport runway and built a new terminal to accommodate oil executives.

In 1955, KVFC radio station started broadcasting local news and events. The city constructed a new city hall that also housed the library, museum, and chamber of commerce. Local and state lawmakers and chambers of commerce worked to complete the Navajo Trail—a direct route from Los Angeles to Chicago.

Technological progress transformed Cortez from an agricultural to a trade center. Chain stores moved in, including J.C. Penney, Sears, Safeway, Ben Franklin, and City Market. Two drive-in and two indoor theaters opened. A National Guard unit was formed. In 1960, Cortez opened a new water filtration plant.

Archaeological research gained a more public face in the 1970s when Dr. Edward and Jo Berger established Crow Canyon School. Crow Canyon Archaeological Center has emerged as an internationally recognized research center for southwestern archaeology.

The controversial Colorado River Basin Act of 1968 passed. The financing from this legislation allowed construction of three water projects in Colorado. McPhee Dam on the Dolores River was completed in 1986. The Dolores Archaeological Project made an important contribution to the local economy and culture.

Traffic from American Indians on reservations in New Mexico, Arizona, and Utah continues to increase. Cortez's stores, its extensive parks, and its recreation center are major attractions.

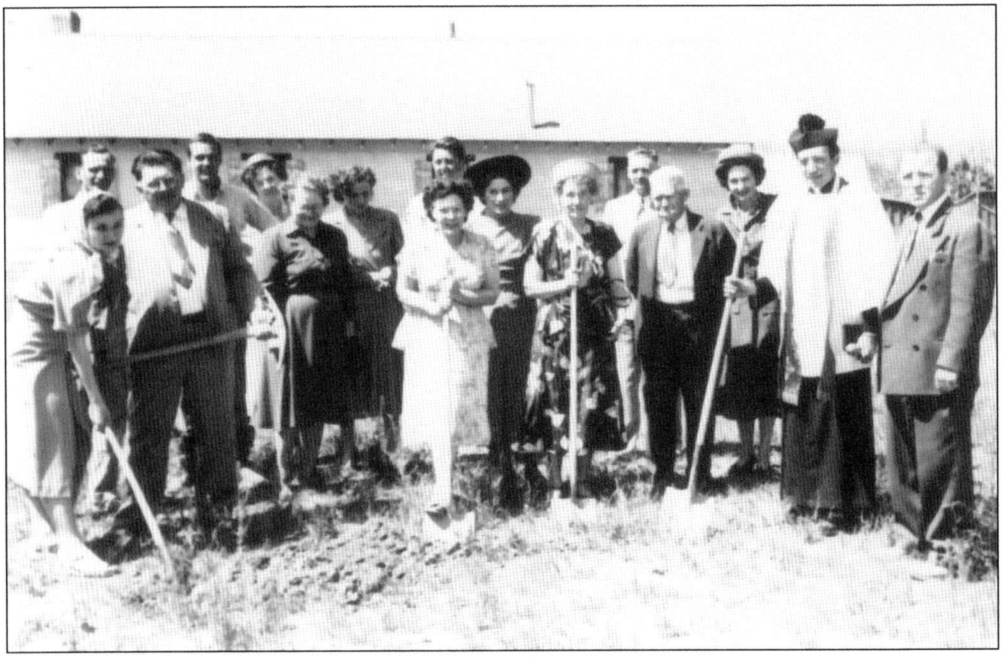

St. Margaret Mary Catholic Church of Cortez held ground breaking ceremonies in May 1949. Shovels and picks were wielded by parishioners (first row, from left to right) Agnes Havran, Frank Havran, Hattie Havran, June Kassel, Anna Johnson, Axel Johnson, Fr. Francis Papesh, and Ken Carmichael. Witnesses, pictured from left to right in the second row, included Joseph Kinsley, an unidentified contractor, Inez Walker, Jo Carmichael, Dick Peel, Aura Wark, Werner Helms, and Mary Helms. (Courtesy of St. Margaret Mary Catholic Church of Cortez.)

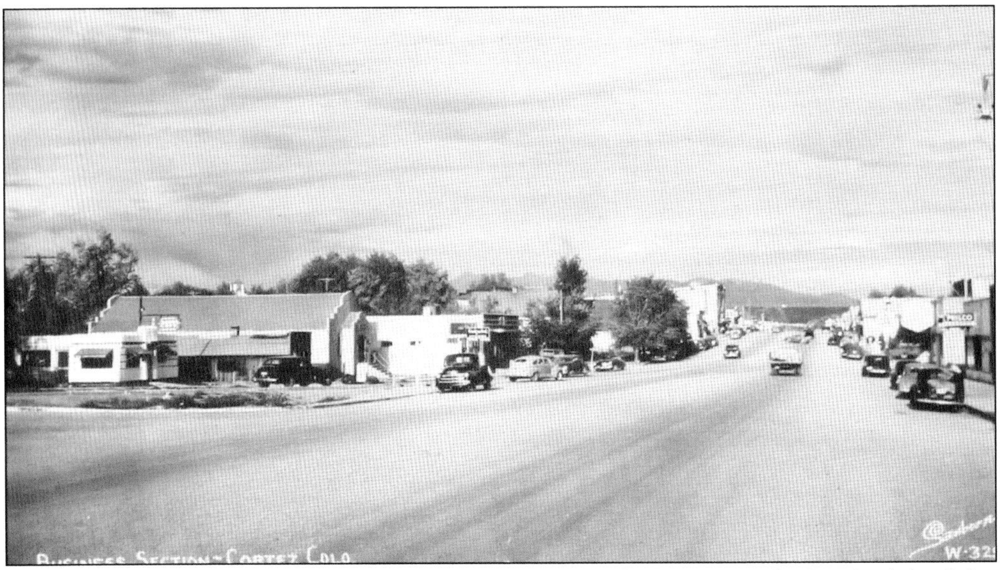

Hispanic Americans were a large and often quiet part of the city's growth. On the left of this late-1940s photograph sits the Assembly of God Church, built in Spanish style for its congregants. A café, the church, and Maxey Stephens's Hot Point Store are situated along Pinon Drive as it enters West Main Street. A Philco store is across the street. (Courtesy of Pauline Sleeper and Denise Carver and First National Bank of Cortez.)

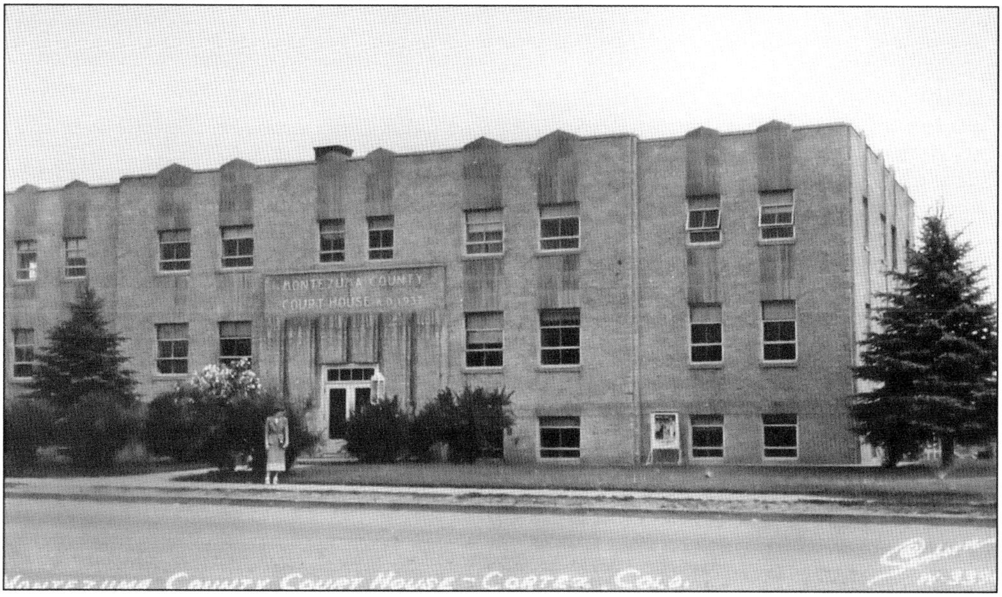

In July 1936, Montezuma County received $29,250 in Works Progress Administration (WPA) funds for a new courthouse, along with $28,000 to $30,000 for a building fund. In September, the contract was let for the courthouse construction. By October, work had begun on the new county courthouse. The county commissioners approved a memorial plaque for W.W. Dunlap in the new courthouse, finished in 1937. (Courtesy of Pauline Sleeper and Denise Carver and First National Bank of Cortez.)

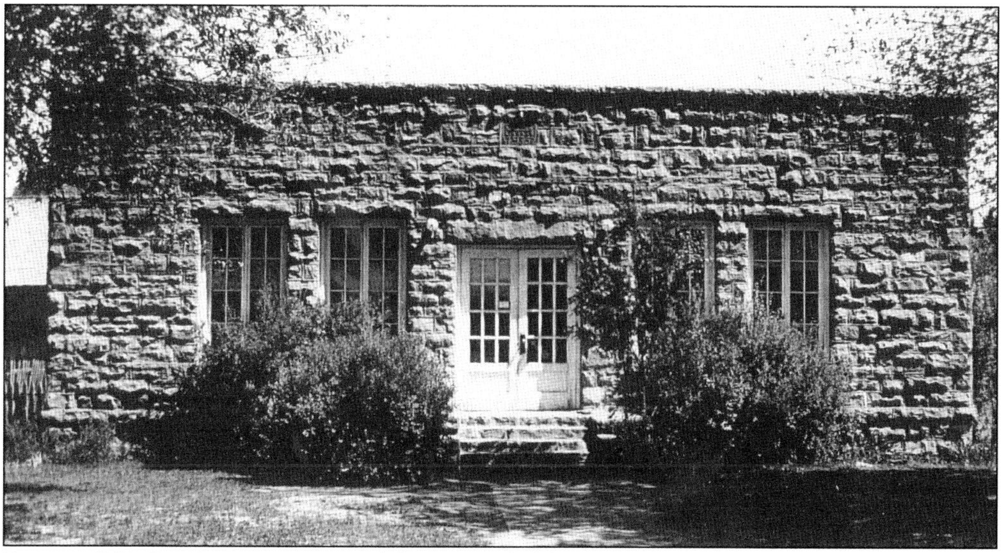

Prior to 1917, the Cortez Women's Club managed a library of donated books. The Ute Mountain Study Club was formed in 1927 and underwrote most library expenses. In 1935, Frederick Henry arranged for the WPA to build a library on East Main Street using donated sandstone. Tall French windows on the east and south let in sunshine, pooling warmth on hardwood floors. Cortez passed a mill levy in 1942 for staff salary and more books. A brick-faced remodel of city hall in the 1950s encased most of the rock. (Courtesy of Cortez Area Chamber of Commerce.)

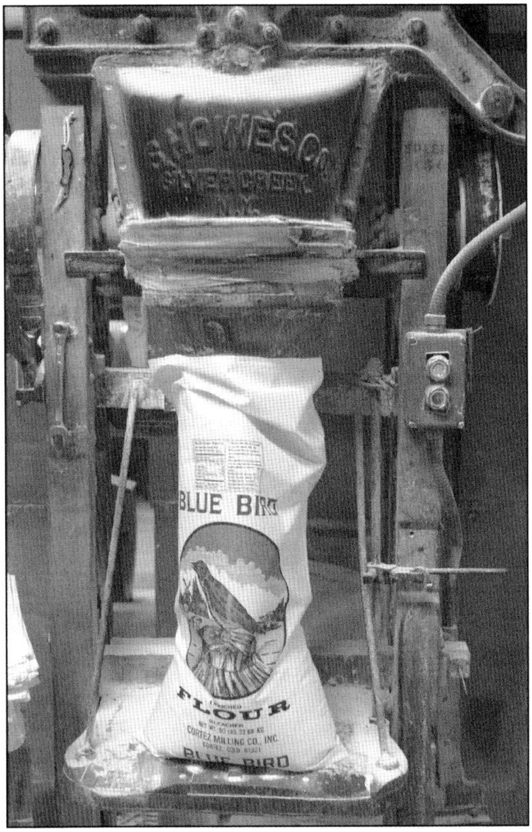

Blue Bird Flour is a well-known brand carried by Cortez Milling, which supplies two-thirds of its flour to Arizona and Navajo reservation customers. Many cooks use it for traditional Navajo fry bread and tortillas. Cortez Milling purchases hard, red winter wheat grown on dryland farms near Cortez and in eastern Utah. The company produces 12 to 13 million pounds of flour annually, processing about 65,000 pounds of wheat daily. The mill also grinds and sells blue corn. (Courtesy of Cortez Journal.)

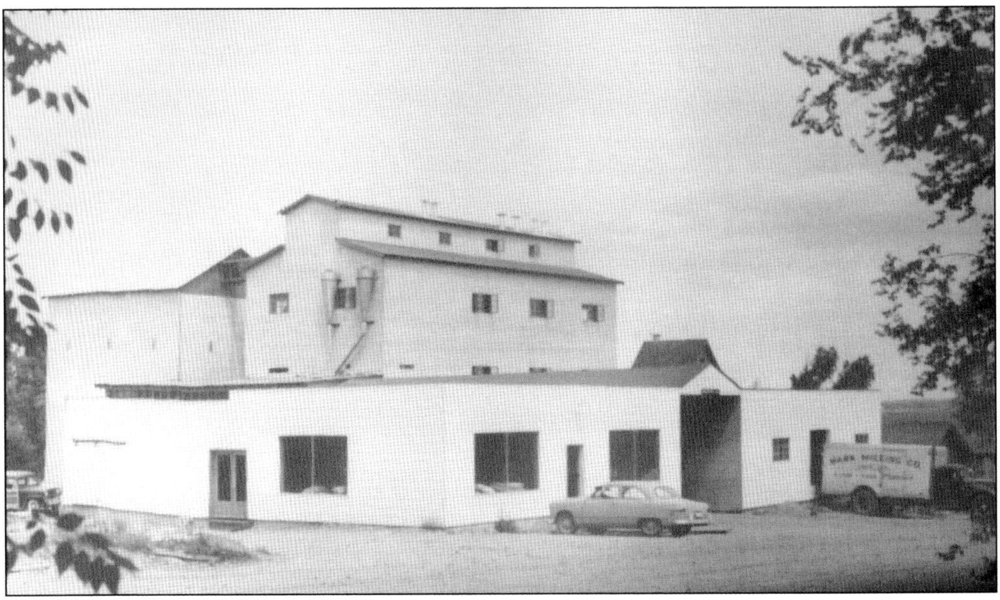

Wark's flour mill opened more than 80 years ago. A.W. Wark and his son W.C. Wark bought a flour mill at Marvel, moved it to 309 North Market Street in Cortez, and Wark Milling Company opened for business in 1928. The mill ran successfully until it burned in 1949. It was rebuilt immediately at the same site with increased capacity. (Courtesy of Sue Wark Patterson.)

P.W. Wark and his granddaughter Judy Clever enjoy the sun near the loading area at the flour mill that his son W.C. "Bill" built. Bill's son Tommy managed the finances, and his son Billy managed the trucking fleet. The mill has always been a family business, even after the Warks sold it to the Tanner and Palmer families in 1965. (Courtesy of Sue Wark Patterson.)

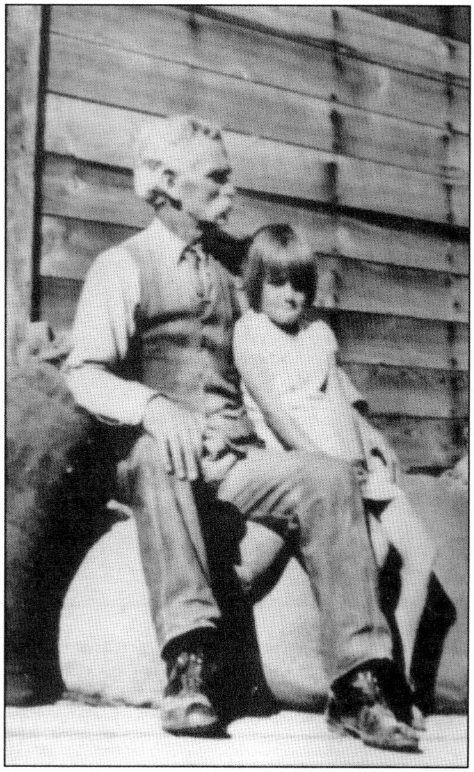

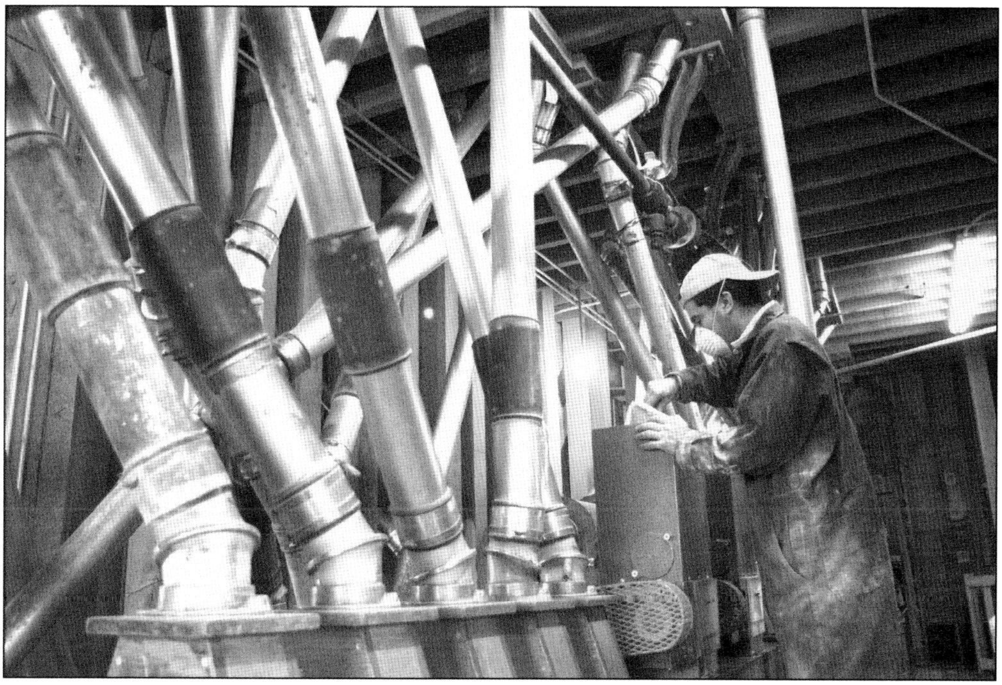

Jesus Lopez, employee at Cortez Milling Company, adds enrichment to the flour as it flows from the sifting level to the bagging floor. Much of their machinery is a half-century old and uses gravity-flow and conveyor belts to move product. (Courtesy of Cortez Journal.)

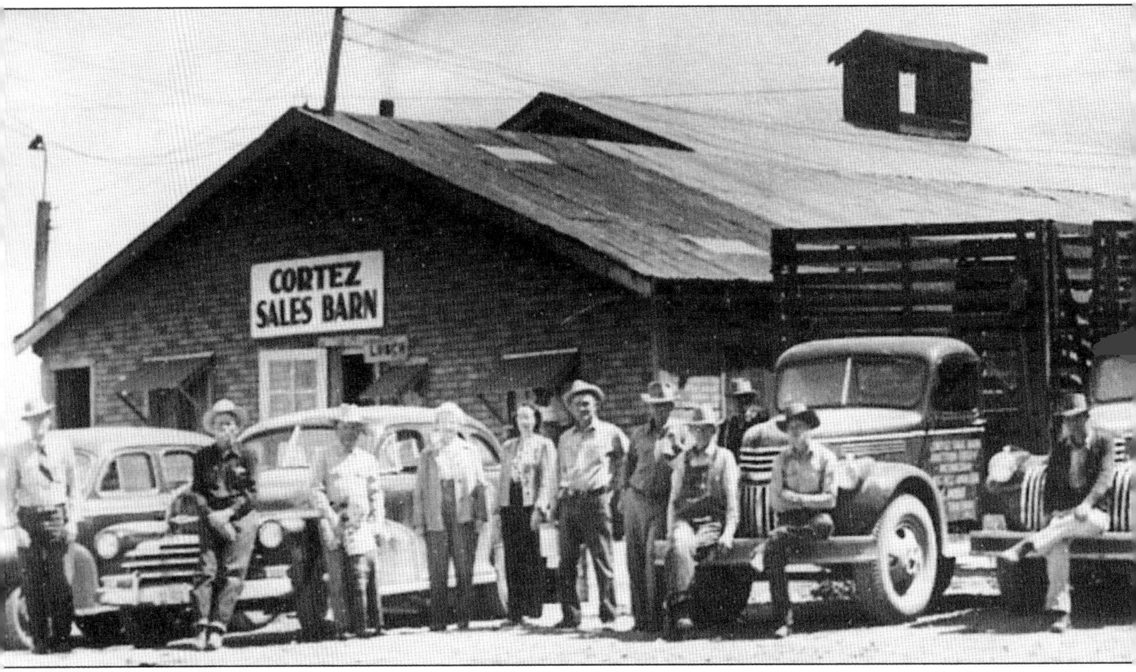

From left, Art Lichliter, Bill Lichliter, Jimmy Barrett, Larry Lichliter (child), Minnie Jones, Clara Higman, Mose Jones, Henry "Hank" Hickey, Frank Olson, Joe Cornett (behind truck), Ernie Boren, Roy Lichliter, Babe Haller, Earl Haller, and Bob Heel pose in front of the Cortez Sale Barn. Bill Lichliter purchased the business in 1951. Lawrence Nichols was yard manager

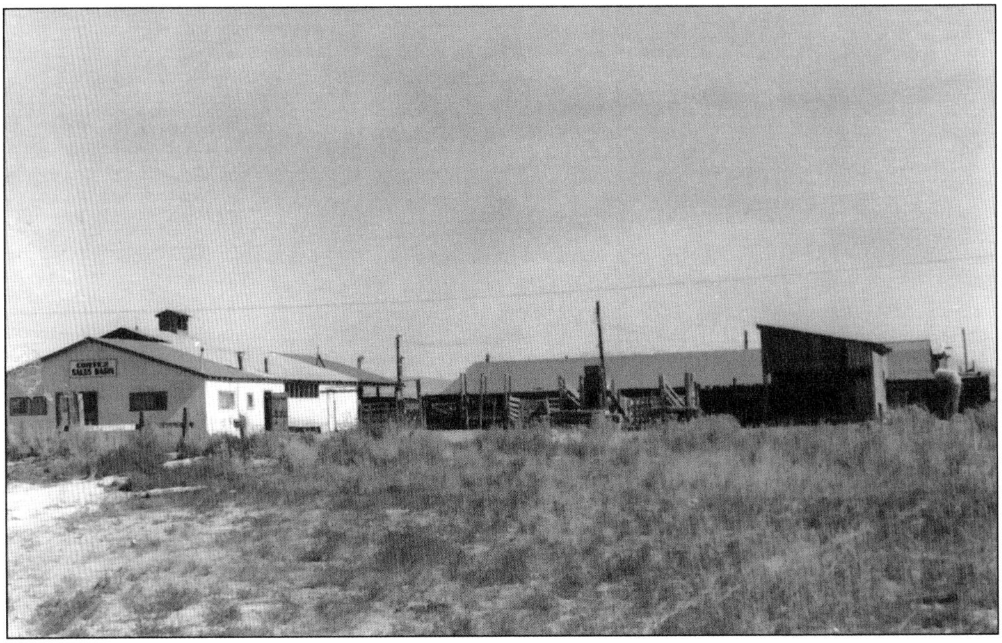

Lichliter's sale barn was located between Park Street and Mildred Road at what was then the end of Montezuma Avenue. At the time this photograph was taken, the auction's yard was showing some disuse. The Suckla family may have already moved the business to its present location four miles north of town. (Courtesy of Larry Hauser.)

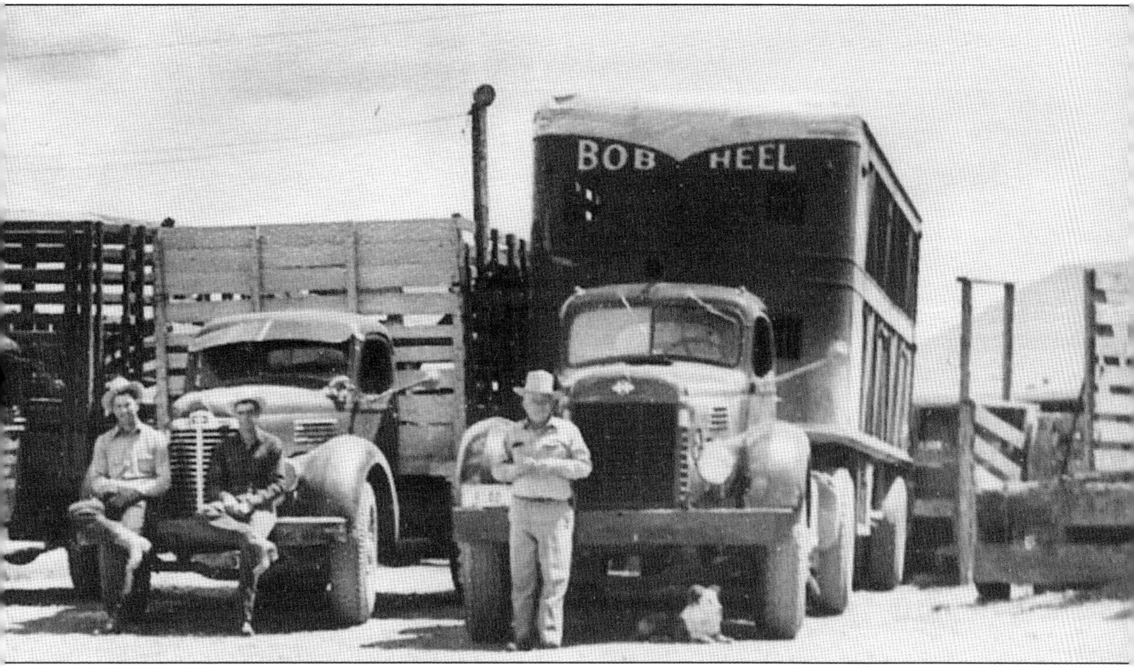

for Lichliter and James Suckla, who purchased the auction in 1953. In 1959, Suckla moved the Cortez Sale Barn three miles north of town. Troy Lichliter worked for Bill, his uncle, and is the current yard manager for the Suckla family. (Courtesy of Troy Lichliter.)

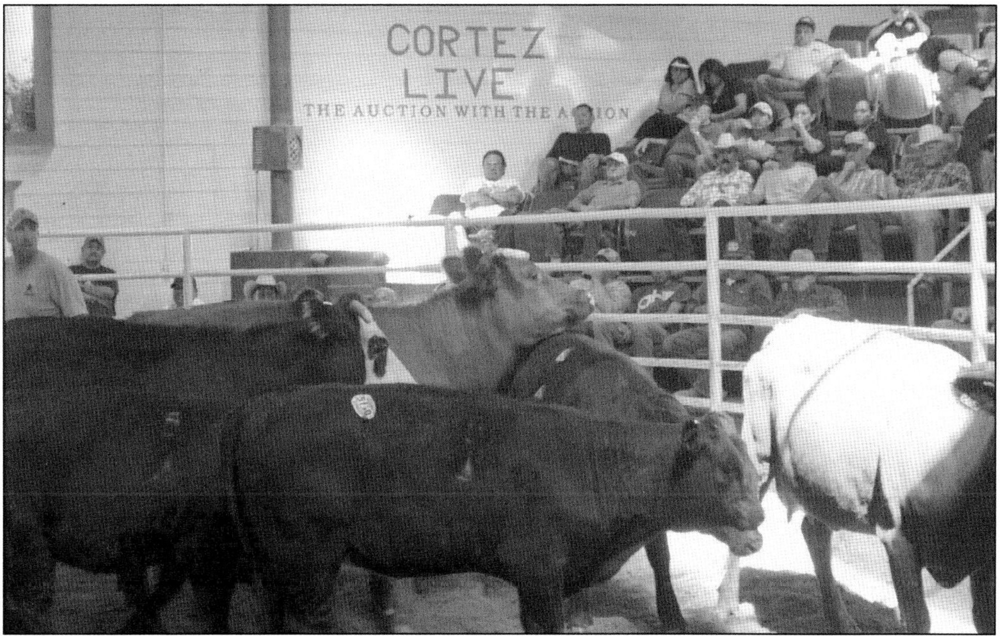

The Suckla-owned Cortez Livestock Auction, Inc., continues to provide a vital service to area ranchers. The Wednesday livestock auction is a popular event for people of both genders and of various ages and ethnic backgrounds, who drive in from all four states. (Photograph by Barbara Grist Photography.)

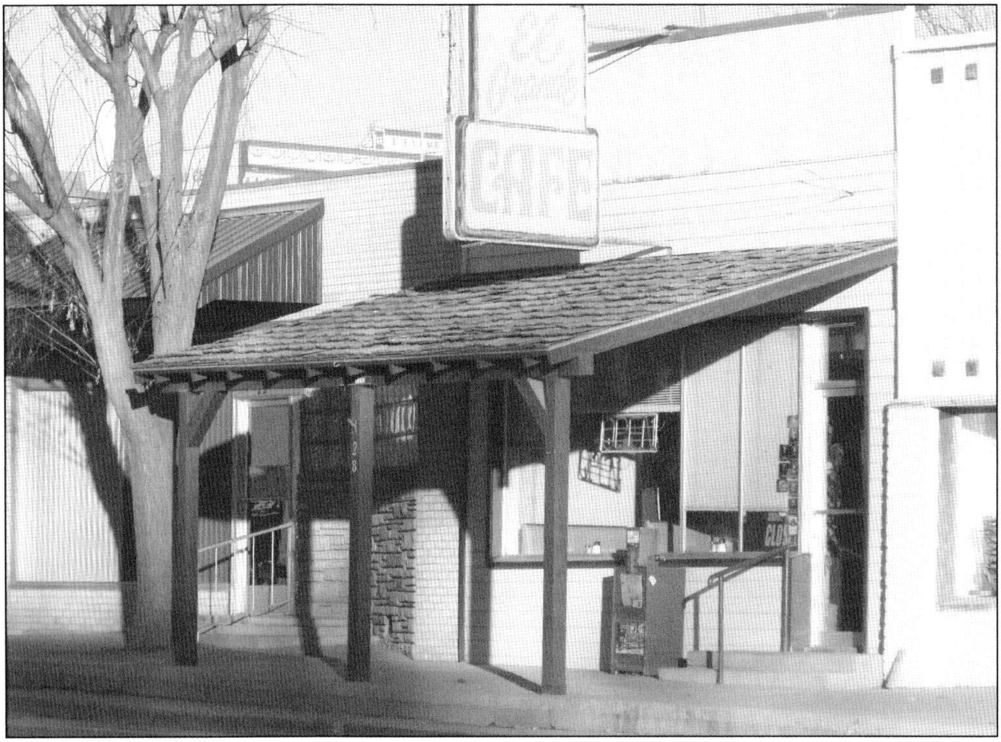

The restaurant at 28 East Main Street has been a key meeting place for downtown businessmen since 1894. For 42 years, Jimmie and Beulah King owned and ran El Grande Café. Before that, Beulah worked there for Bud McCormick. Beulah's daughter and son-in-law Sharon and Kent Lindsay purchased the café in 1980. The Lindsays say a lot of important discussions about real estate and law are shared across the tables. (Courtesy of Dale Davidson.)

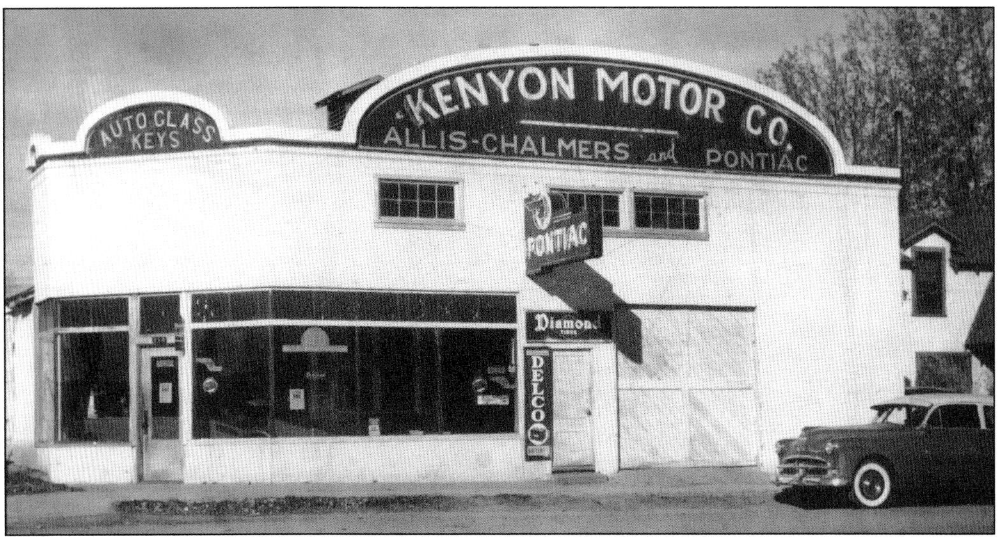

Automobiles continued to rule commerce. Local residents were able to start businesses that would help their neighbors. Bill Kenyon supported his family by selling and maintaining automobiles, tractors, other farm equipment, and parts with this tidy business on East Main Street. (Courtesy of Cortez Area Chamber of Commerce.)

Arnie Haak checks the uniform inventory at the National Guard Armory, which was located on the east side of Cortez. The National Guard in Cortez was formed in the 1950s. (Courtesy of Larry Hauser.)

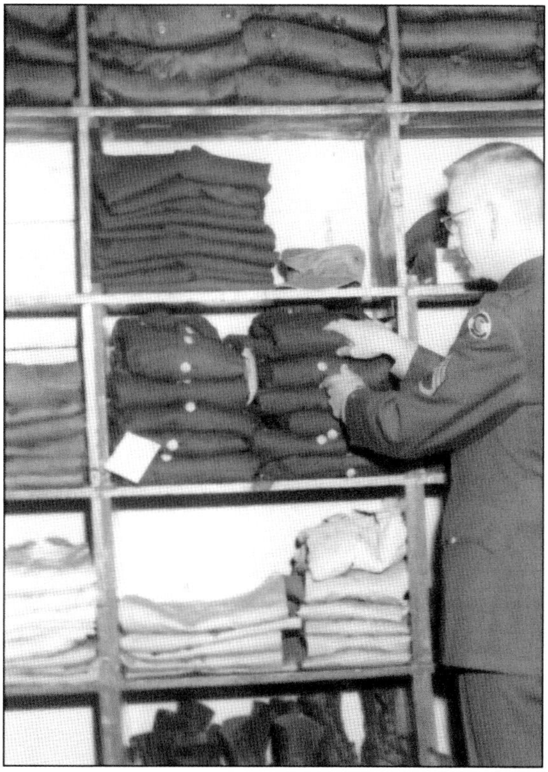

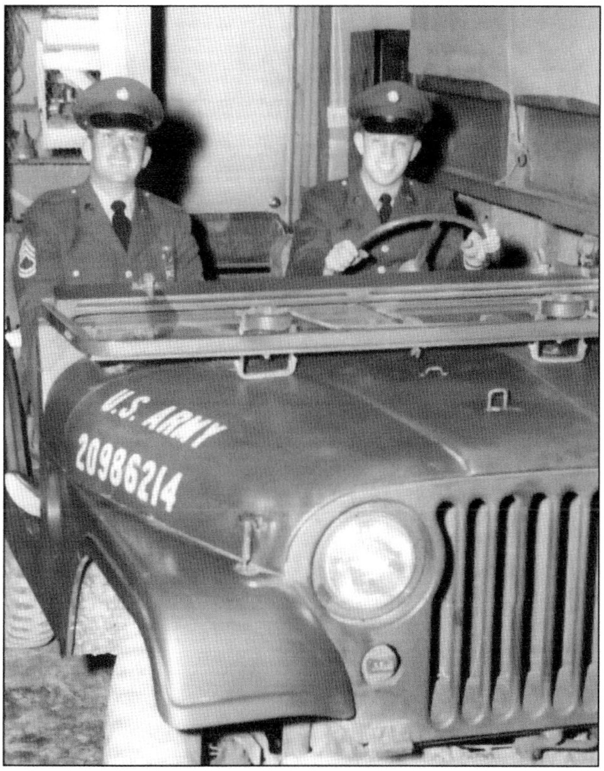

Two unidentified National Guardsmen are obviously looking forward to getting out of the armory in an open-air vehicle. Some Colorado Guards were recalled for federal service in 1950 for the Korean conflict, in 1961 during the Berlin crisis, and again for the 1962 Cuban missile crisis. More recently, National Guard units have been called to assist with armed conflict in Iraq and Afghanistan along with disasters such as Hurricane Katrina. (Courtesy of Larry Hauser.)

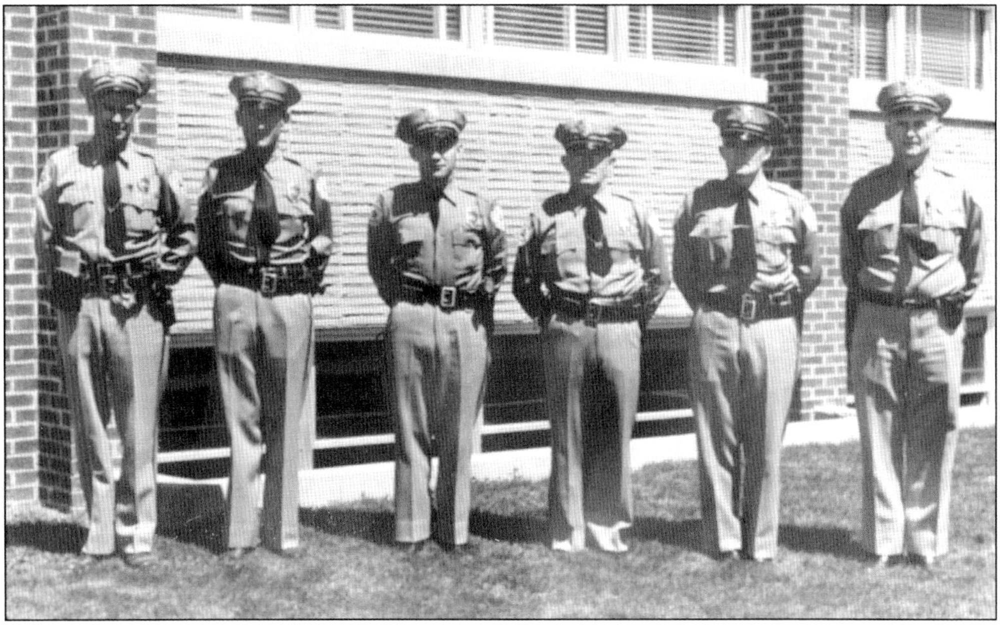

From left to right, patrol officers Bill Thomas, Ralph Bird, Floyd Morris, Ralph Fowler, Bill Rutledge, and Ralph Seelig stand outside Cortez City Hall, which housed the police department in 1956. Rutledge said when he was hired in 1952, a patrolman's salary was $300 a month. He had to furnish his own weapon, and he worked six days per week on eight-hour shifts. He also worked additional time for court appearances and on weekend nights. (Courtesy of City of Cortez.)

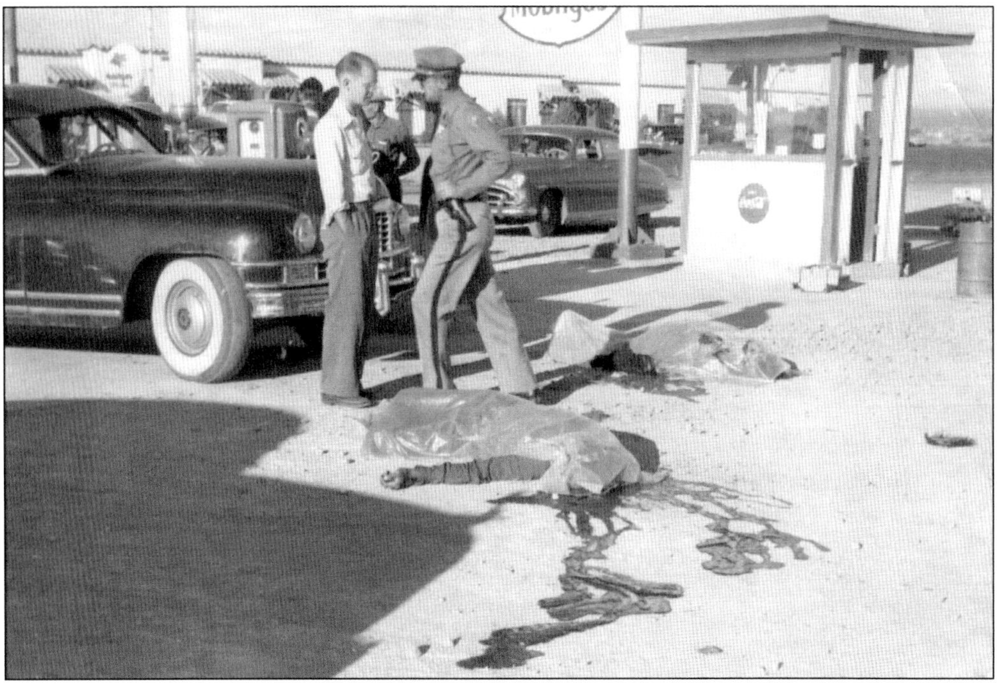

Life was not always placid in Cortez. Two officials discuss possible circumstances around the violent deaths at their feet. The apparent disagreement occurred at a Mobil gas station on the east side of Cortez. A motel for Mesa Verde tourists is across the highway. (Courtesy of Larry Hauser.)

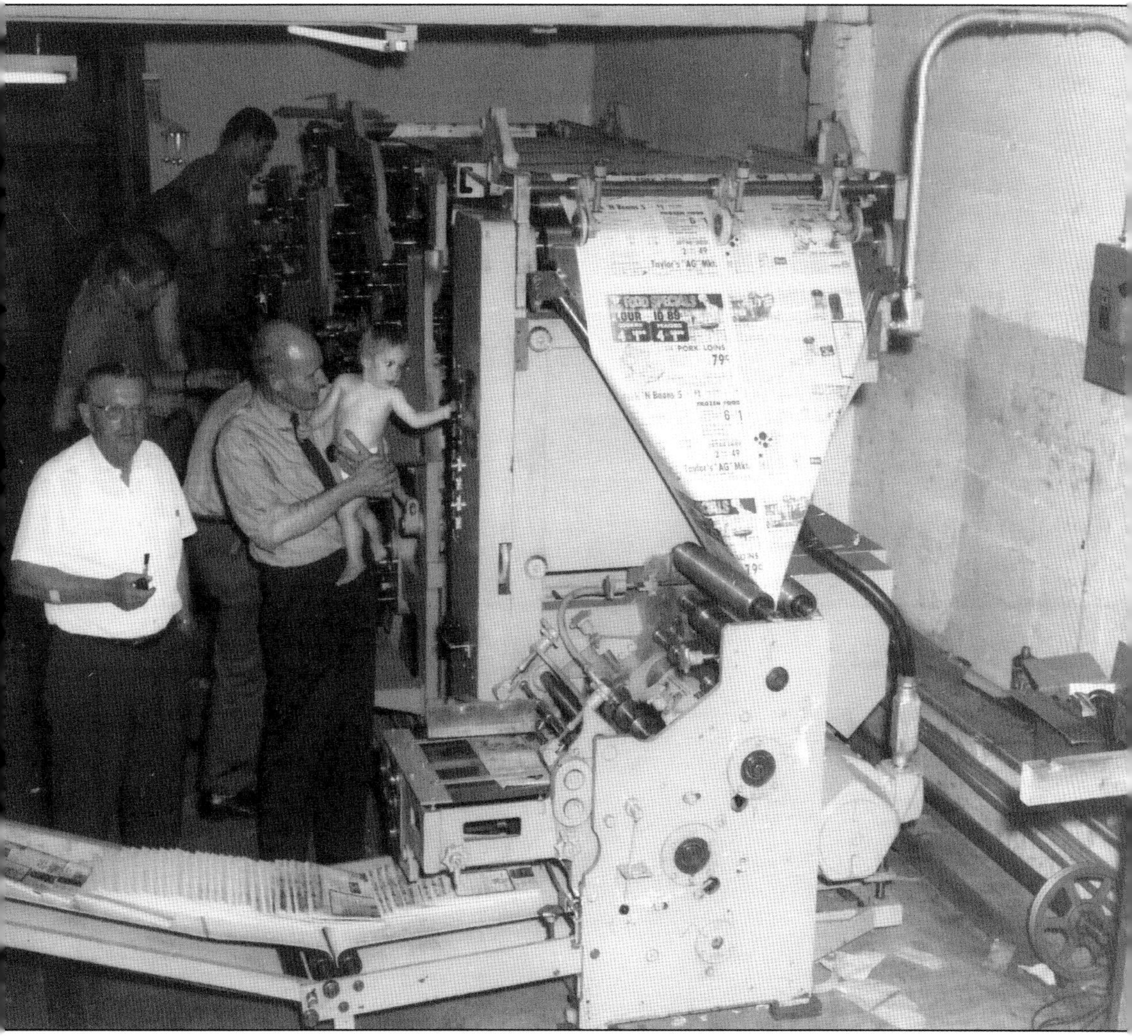

A new web press gets up and running at the *Montezuma Valley Journal* in the mid-1960s. Publisher Dewey Brown holds his grandniece Tammy to oversee the press run as friend Giff Pruner looks on. Russell Brown, Dewey's nephew, graduated with a degree in journalism from the University of Missouri in 1955. Over the next 44 years, the two men partnered in the newspaper production. Between 1911 and 1999, the Brown family updated printing technologies from linotype to flatbed to web press to electronic equipment. (Courtesy of Patsy Brown.)

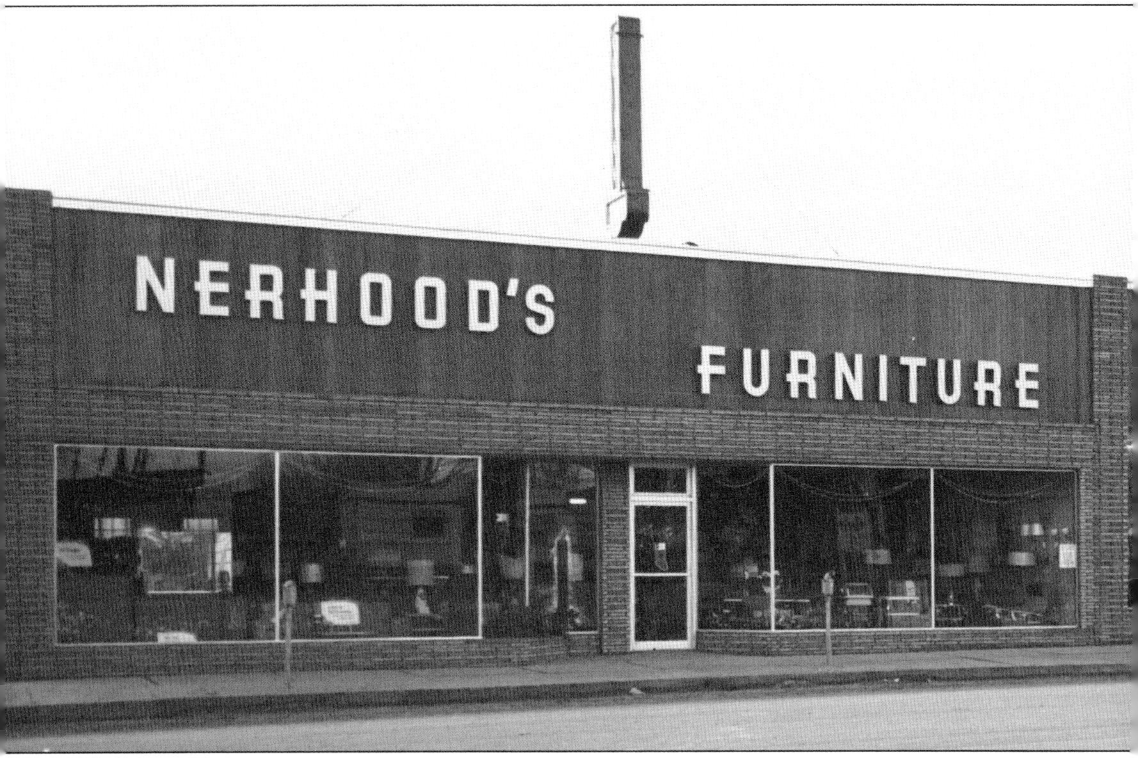

Three businesses anchored West Main Street in 1958—Nerhood's Furniture, Slavens Hardware, and Campbell's Appliances. The third generation of the Slavens family continues to strengthen

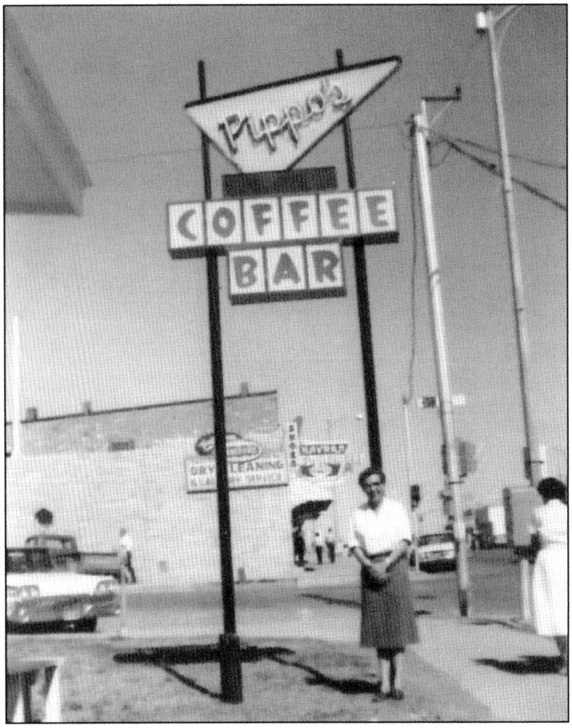

Local real estate and business maven Marge Gai was the daughter of T. and Anna Gai. In this photograph, she stands in front of Pippo's Coffee Bar, which she named after her uncle Pippo from Switzerland. This still-popular downtown café is one of the businesses Gai owned and managed in the 1950s and 1960s. (Courtesy of Pennie Sanford.)

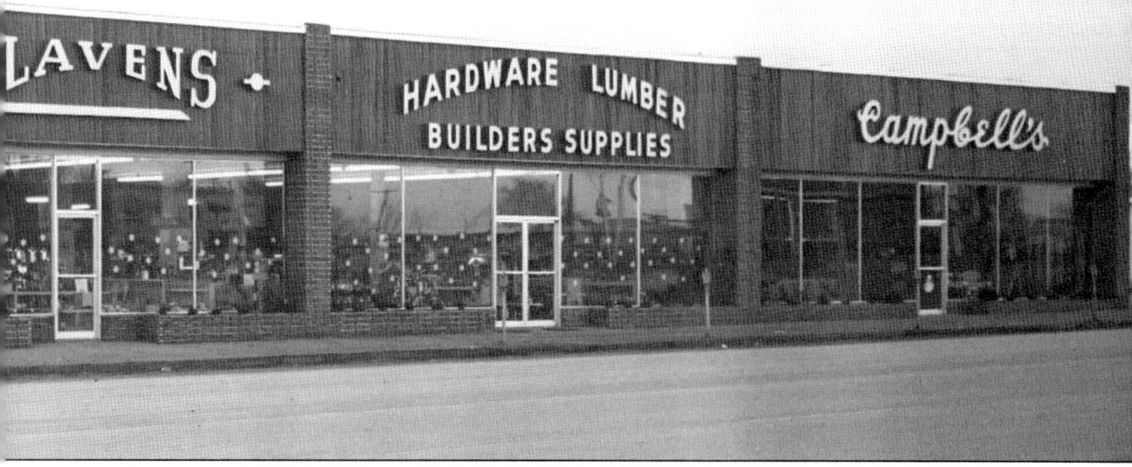

the local economy at the same site. (Courtesy of City of Cortez.)

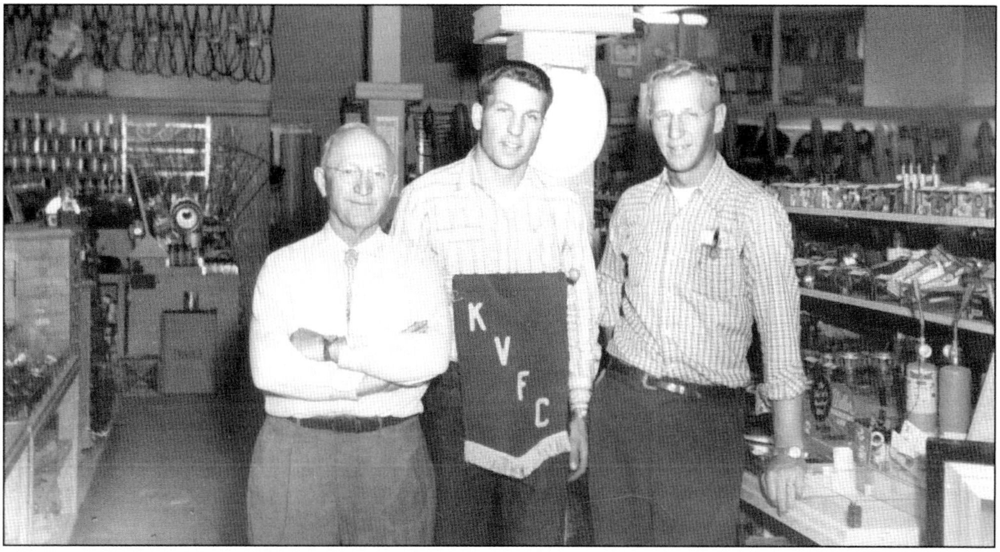

Basil Slavens and his wife, Estie, bought Jett Hardware in 1953. Basil had managed the store since 1943, and Estie also worked there. In this June 13, 1959, photograph, Basil (left) and son Dale (right) stand with a local radio station representative (center) to broadcast the newly named Slavens Hardware. Dale bought the store in 1971, retired in 1991, and his sons Les and Gary stepped in. The business has grown to include a rental department and roof truss plant. (Courtesy of the Slavens family and Slavens Hardware.)

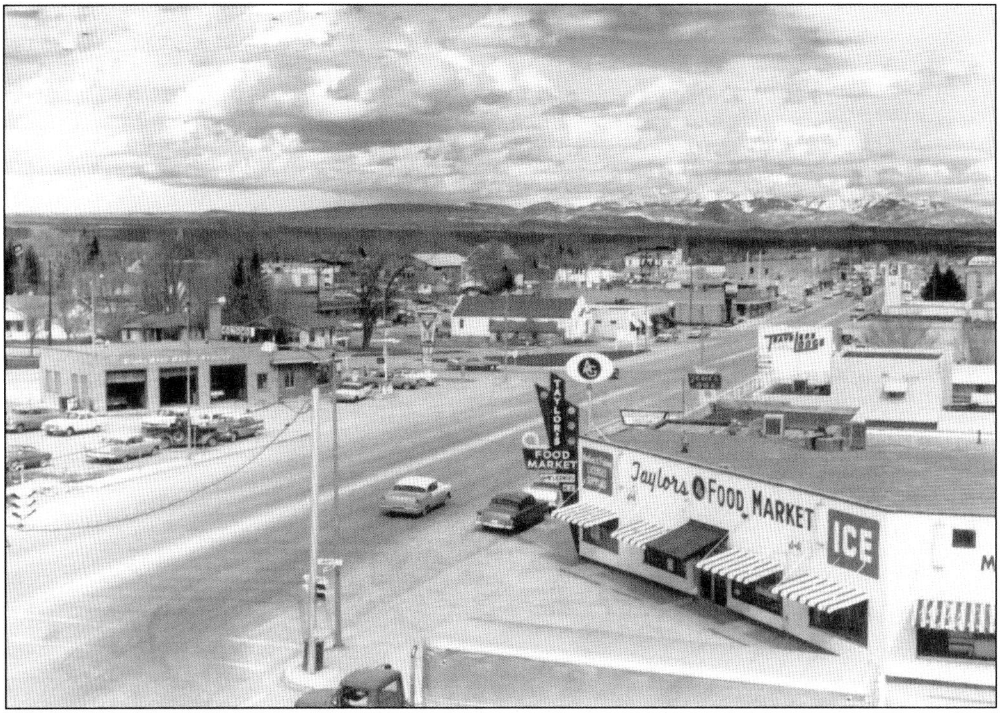

In the early 1960s, Taylors Food Market sat at the corner of Maple and Main Streets. They catered to residents with a wide selection of groceries but also to hunters by providing meat lockers and butcher services. The corner looks much the same in 2011, although business names are different. This photograph was taken from the Macorado bean elevator and feed store that stood on the southwest corner, which is now a parking lot. (Courtesy of City of Cortez.)

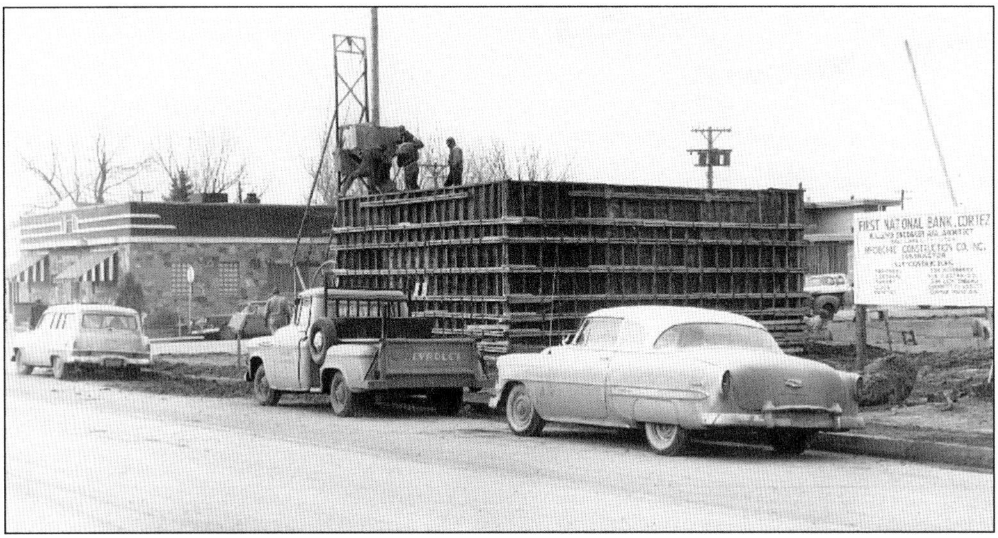

In the 1950s, Cortez felt the positive growth impact of energy development, both in the oil fields in Utah and the Colorado uranium mines to the north. Strong prices for cattle also helped. In 1957, the local McGechie Construction Company built a new First National Bank of Cortez on a prominent corner downtown. In early 2011, the bank opened a brand-new building at the east end of Cortez. (Courtesy of Cortez Area Chamber of Commerce.)

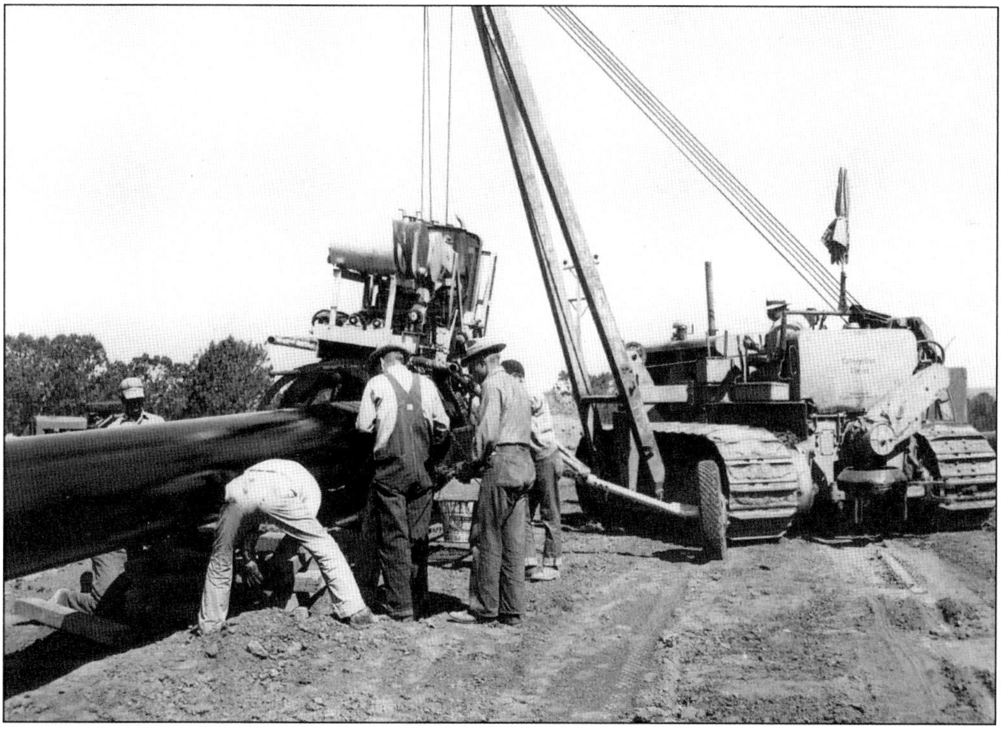

Engineers designed newer and more efficient machinery to lay pipelines for transporting raw materials from mines to processing centers. In this July 1955 photograph, agricultural lands north of Cortez were methodically and diligently dissected for new commercial resources. (Courtesy of Montezuma County Historical Society.)

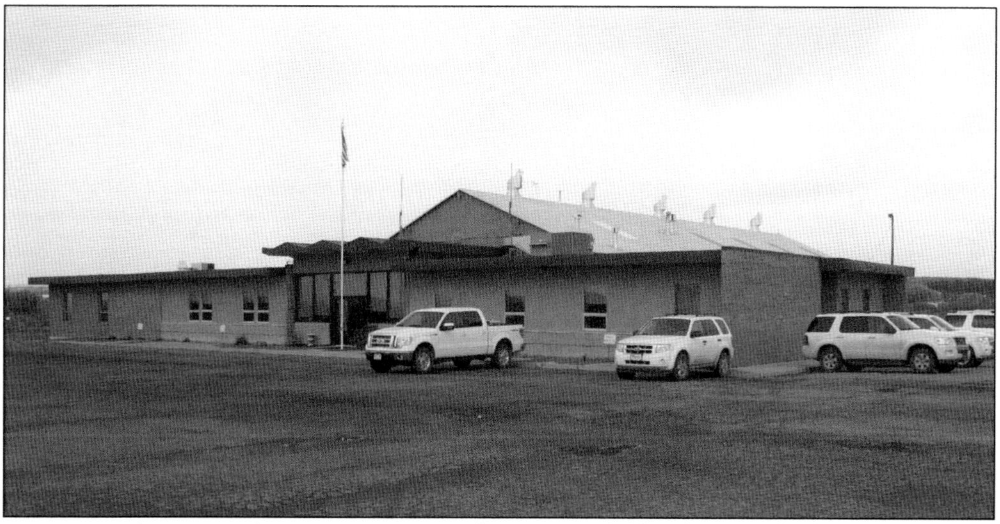

In 2011, Resolute Natural Resources occupies the Superior Oil headquarters built in 1959 near the airport. Oil was first discovered west of Cortez in 1908. County commissioners prudently provided $1,000 to improve the McElmo Canyon road to the San Juan oil fields. In 1910, Montezuma Oil and Development Company was organized, secured leases, and brought in a standard rig to drill down to the 5,000-foot level. The Four Corners–area oil and gas reserves continue to be exploited in the 21st century. (Photograph by Barbara Grist Photography.)

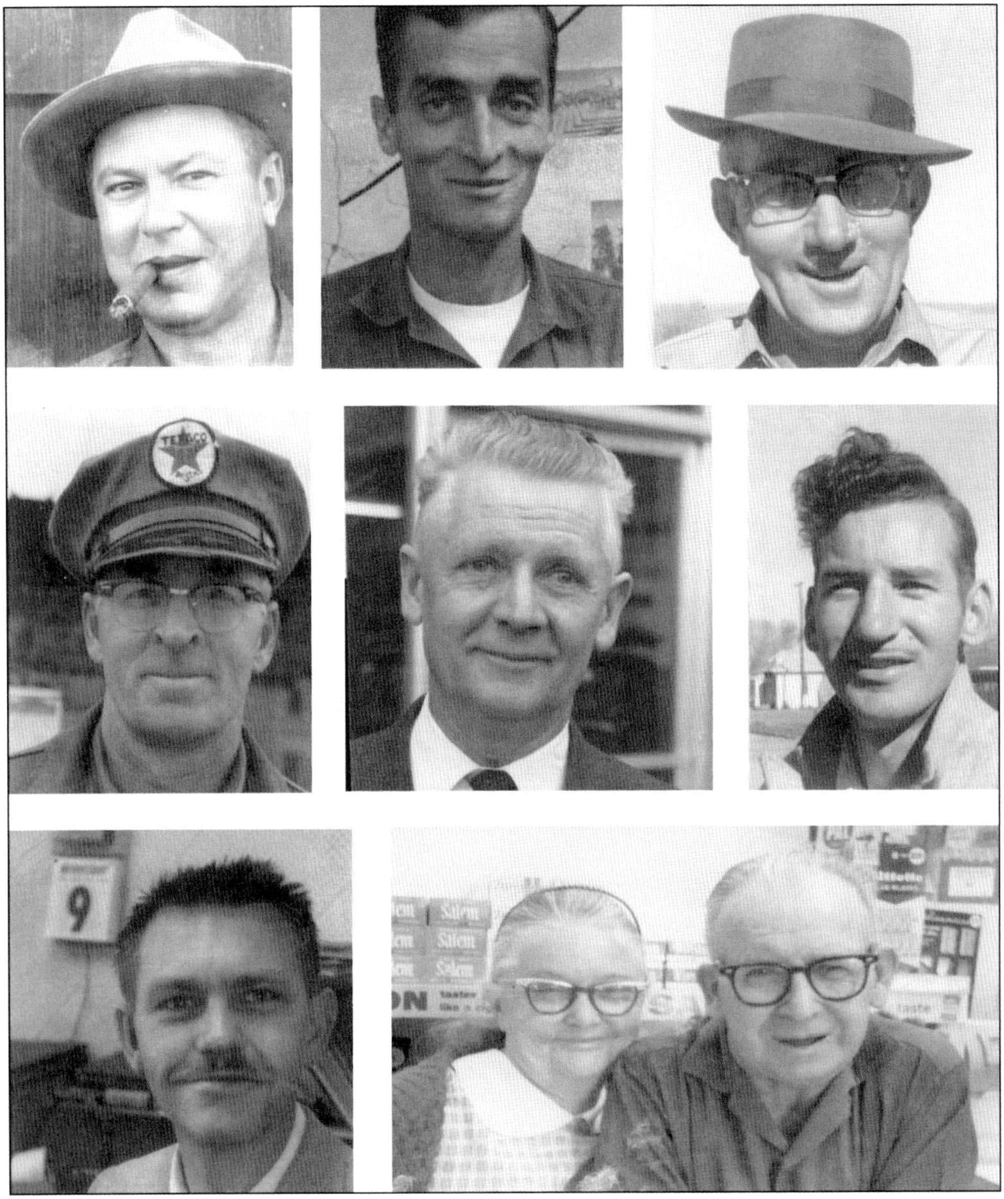

These are a few of the faces Cortez shoppers would greet as neighbors in the 1960s. The photographs were gleaned from several taken by the Cortez newspaper for an article about local merchants. Included are, from left to right, (top row) George Kemnitz, Walt Frazer, and Bill Powell, lead man for Rio Grande Motorway; (middle row) Cleo Hicks, owner of Hicks Texaco Station, Werner Helms, owner of The Toggery, and Jim Delaney; (bottom row) Val Kruse, and Mr. and Mrs. B.L. Hamlin, managers of Speedy's Grocery. (Courtesy of Larry Hauser and Vince Conti.)

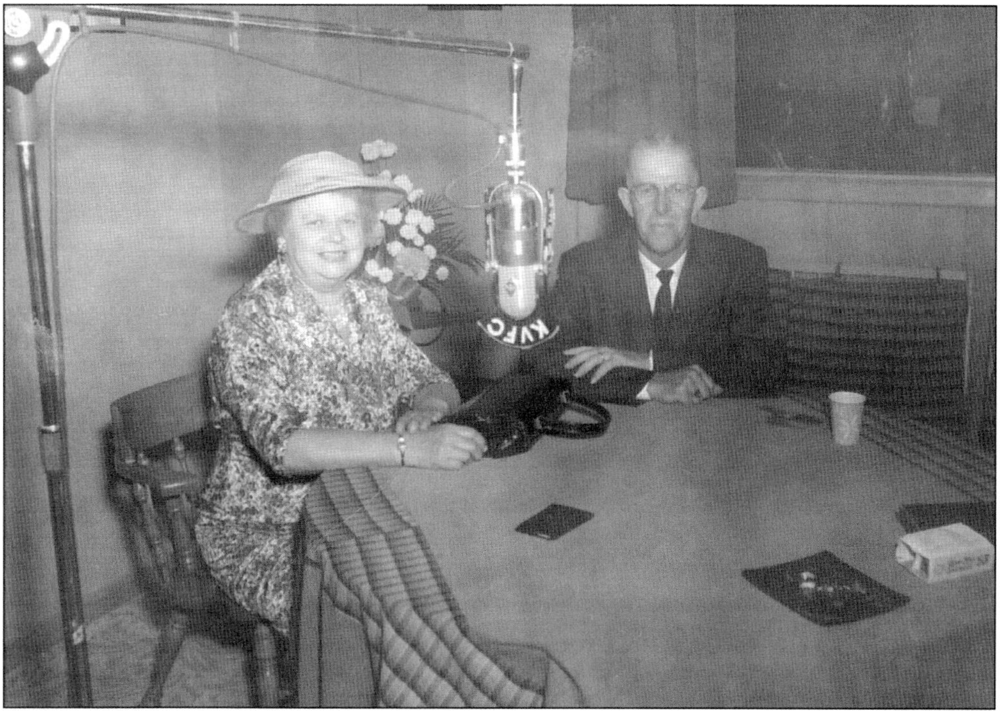

Elizabeth Pellet, a longtime Rico resident, was elected to serve in the Colorado legislature in 1941. Instrumental in procuring a water conservation district for the area, Pellet also petitioned and won a loan from Washington, DC, to keep the Galloping Goose railroad running. Charles Porter, an area agriculturalist, was county commissioner for eight years and state senator from 1956 to 1962. Porter worked with county employee Jack Allum to lay gravel on many miles of county roads. The local radio station made sure residents knew their elected officials and how they represented the public. (Courtesy of Dotty Wayt.)

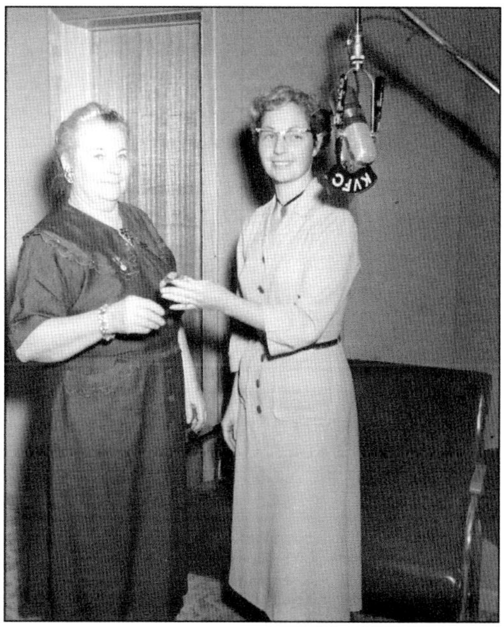

Nurse Uvah M. Brown (left) was honored by reporter and announcer Dotty Wayt (right) from the local radio station for all the dolls she made and donated to children on the Navajo and Ute reservations. Jack Hawkins and Barney Hubbs started KVFC, the popular local radio station, in 1955. (Courtesy of Dotty Wayt.)

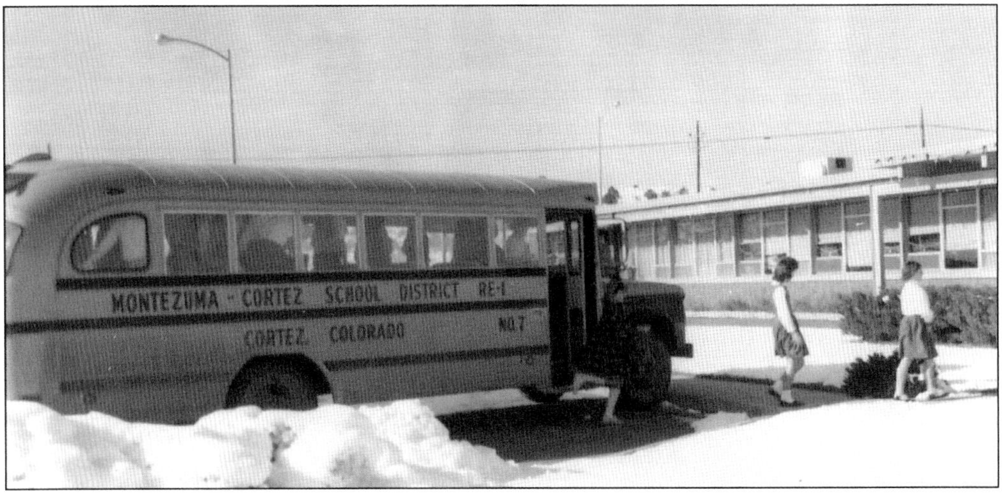

Early residents recall walking five miles to school in all kinds of weather. Orpha Adams Koppenhafer said her brother made her walk first to break through the snowdrifts. By mid-century, the big yellow buses helped rural children get to consolidated schools in Cortez. (Courtesy of Empire Electric Association.)

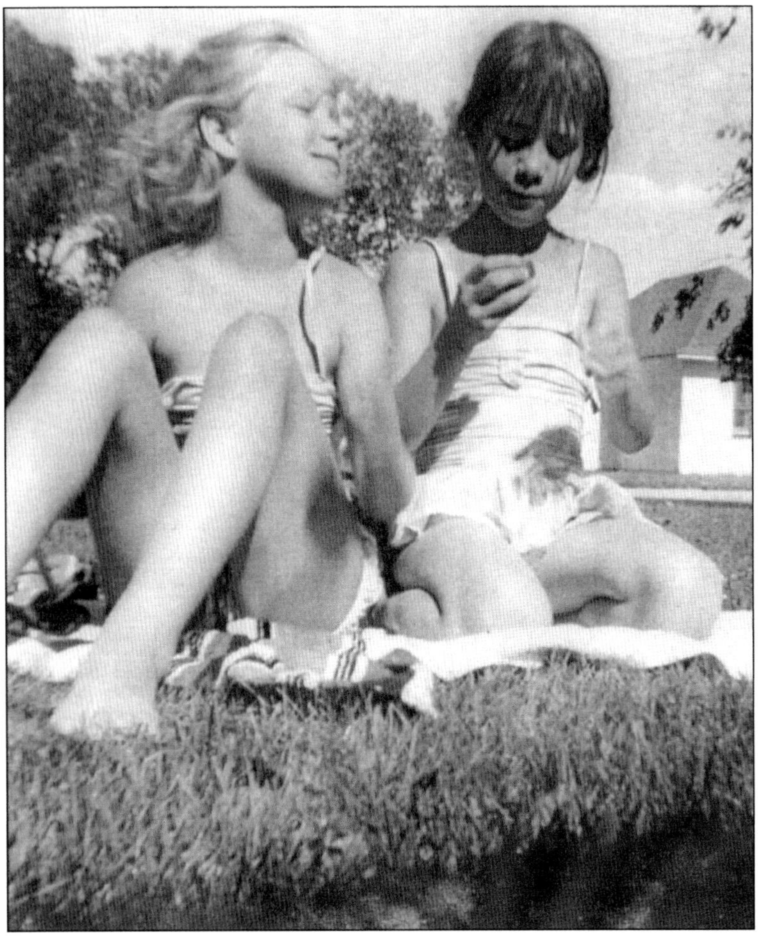

Karen Bradley (left), daughter of Richard Bradley who worked for Superior Oil in its Cortez heyday, and Vila Schwindt, daughter of Methodist minister J. Wayne Schwindt, and one of the authors of this title, enjoy the sun and search for four-leaf clovers in this 1960 photograph. (Courtesy of Vila Schwindt.)

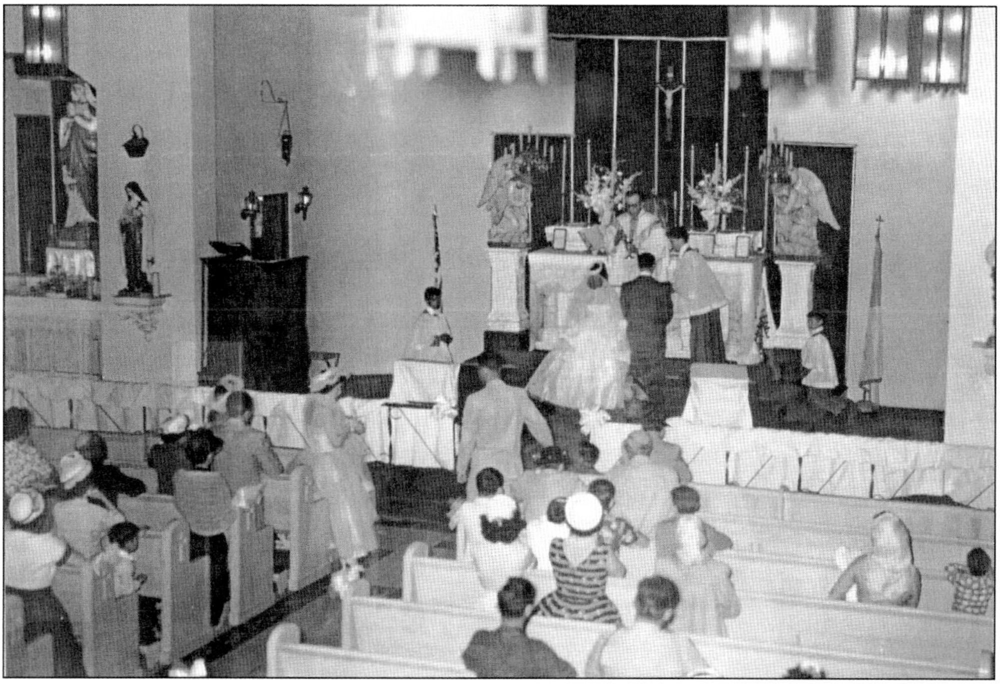

A June 1955 wedding in St. Margaret Mary Catholic Church in Cortez was a formal affair. Fred and Louise (Gomez) Torres were married by Fr. Francis Papesh. Fred later became a city councilman to support his hometown and neighbors. (Courtesy of St. Margaret Mary Catholic Church.)

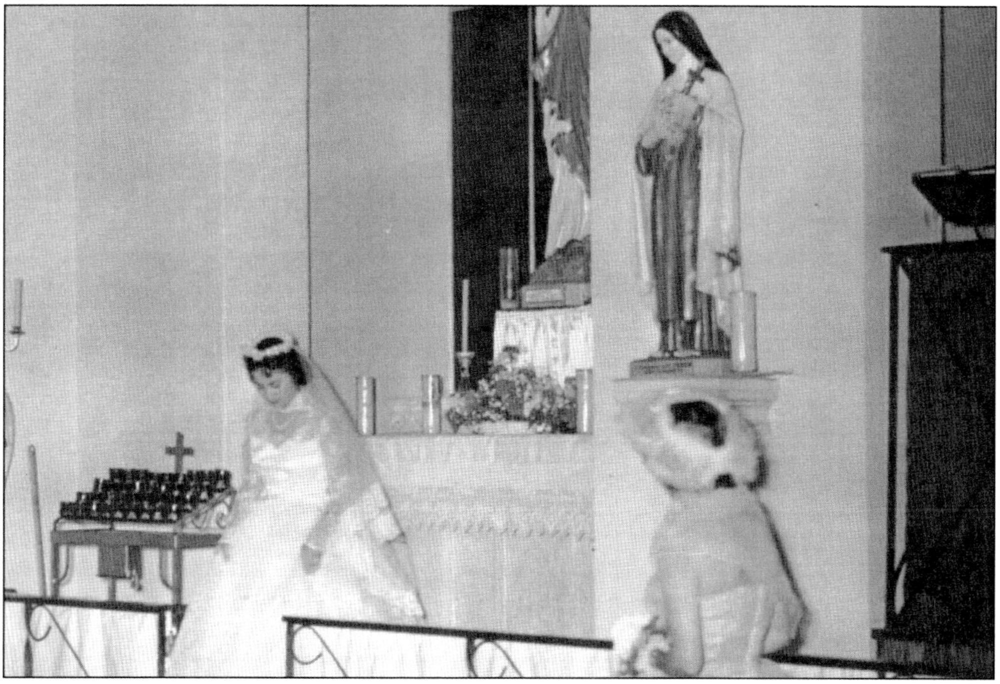

The new Mrs. Fred Torres (Louise) has presented her bouquet to the Virgin Mary and descends the altar steps as her bridesmaid waits to accompany her return to the groom. (Courtesy of St. Margaret Mary Catholic Church.)

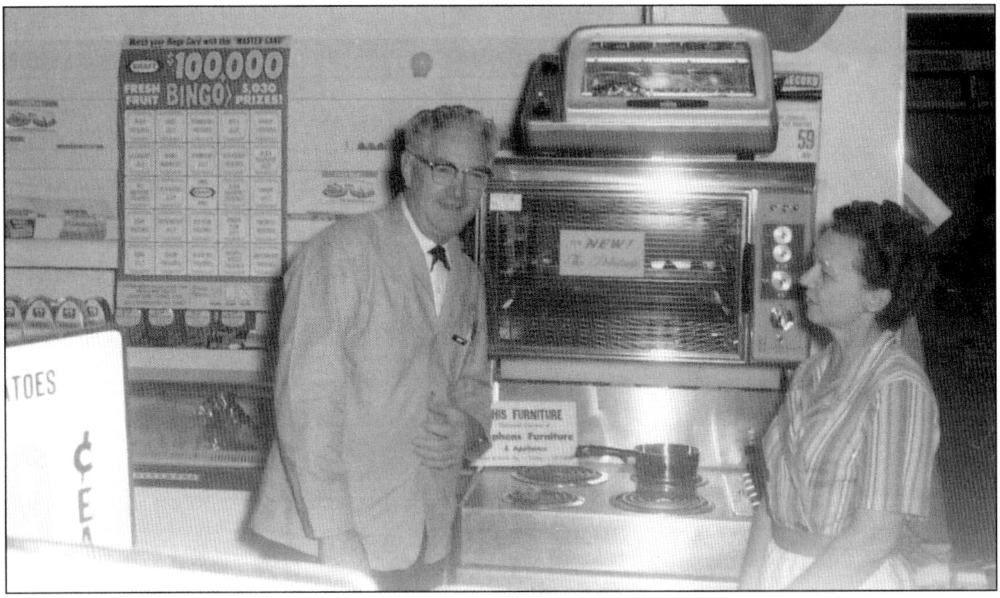

Roy Wells, manager, and Maxine Hodges pose for the promotion of an electric appliance giveaway sponsored by City Market, at that time a Western Slope grocery chain. Wells was active outside the Cortez store and served the community as state representative. (Courtesy of Empire Electric Association.)

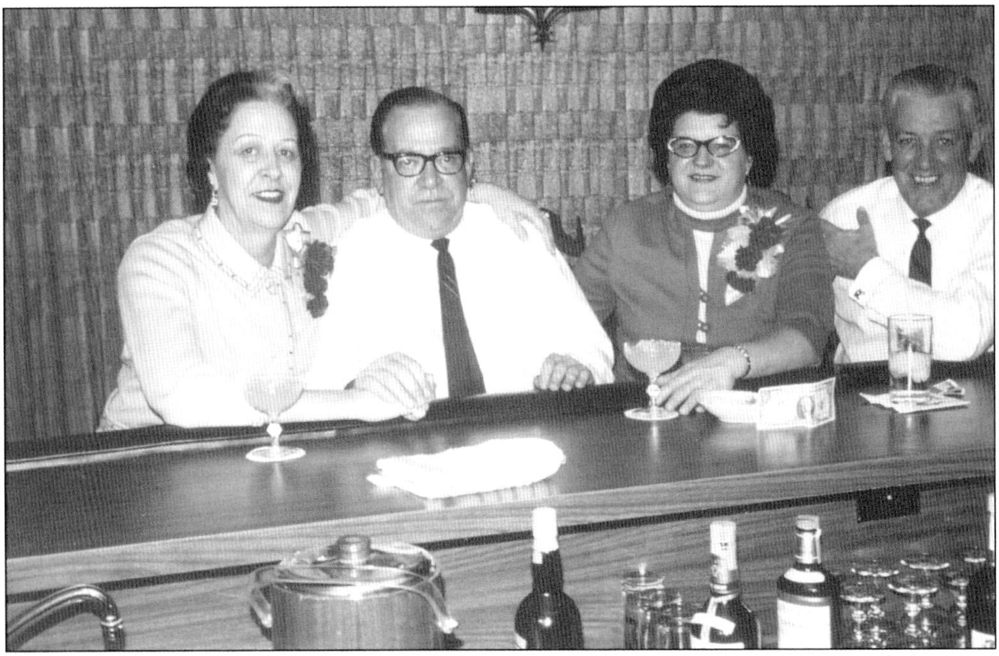

Pictured second from left, John Vogel, owner of the Pony Express Restaurant, sits with his sister Margaret Jeffrey (left), wife Lorraine, and brother-in-law Robert Jeffrey. The "Pony" was the uptown restaurant and watering hole through the oil boom years. Governors, members of Congress, locals who wanted a special dinner out, and tourists kept the place humming. The Vogels were successful, as was F.M. Goodykoontz, who opened the first boardinghouse and restaurant in Cortez. Goodykoontz served up to 90 meals a day in a 12- by 14-foot tent. (Courtesy of Lorraine Vogel.)

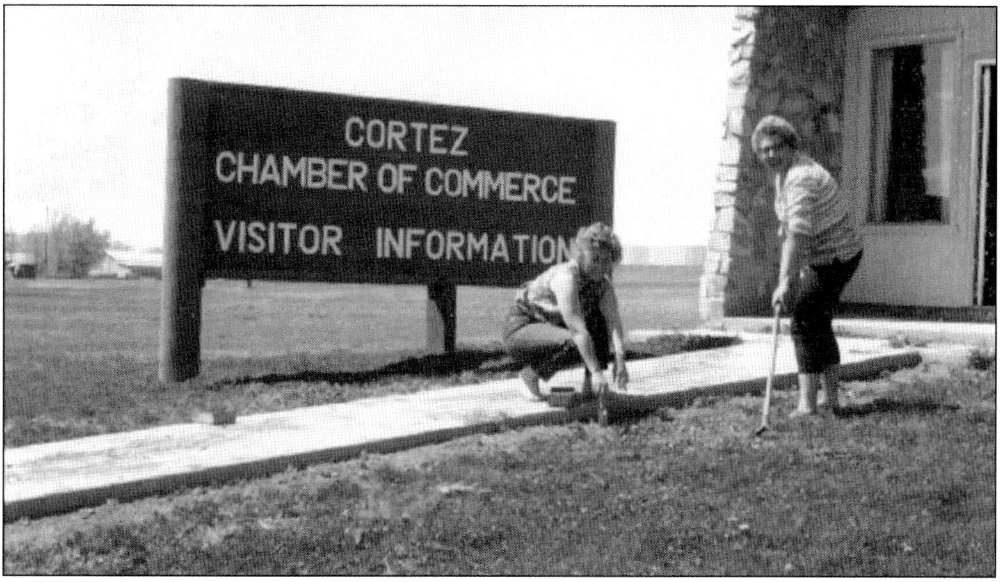

Two women prepare flower beds to greet visitors to the new chamber of commerce on East Main Street. Clayton Melby and Marshall Denton instigated its construction in the mid-1960s. Beyond the building stretches the new, open City Park, which was later planted to specifications developed by landscape designer and author George W. Kelly. (Courtesy of Cortez Area Chamber of Commerce.)

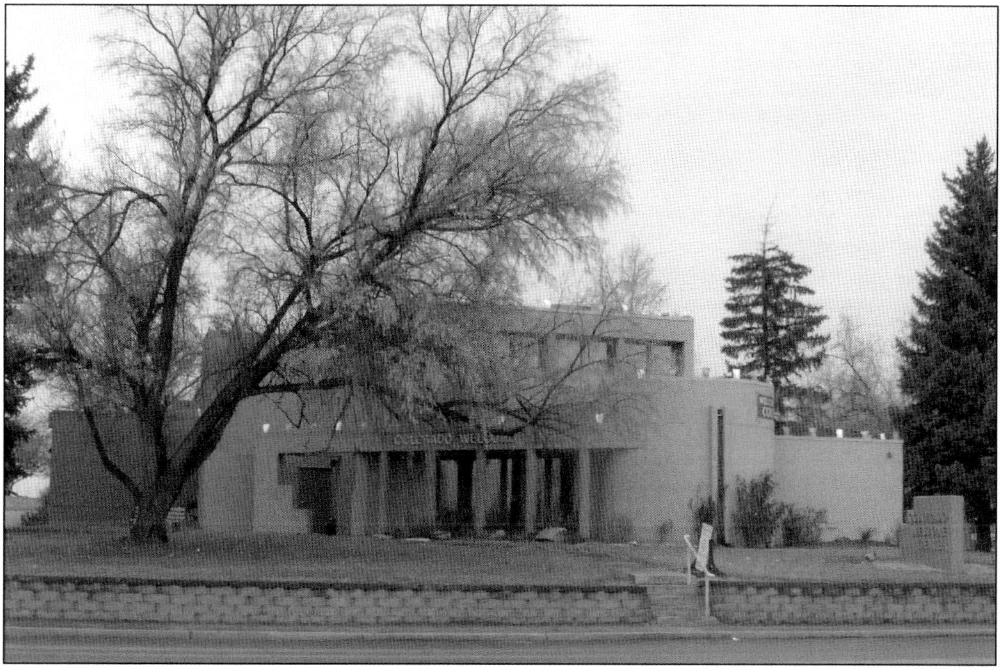

In 1986, a new Colorado Welcome Center was built with funds from the state to replace the chamber of commerce building. The center hosts several community support organizations, including the Cortez Area Chamber of Commerce, Mesa Verde Country, Cortez Retail Enhancement, City of Cortez IT, and Mesa Verde Museum Association. (Courtesy of Dale Davidson.)

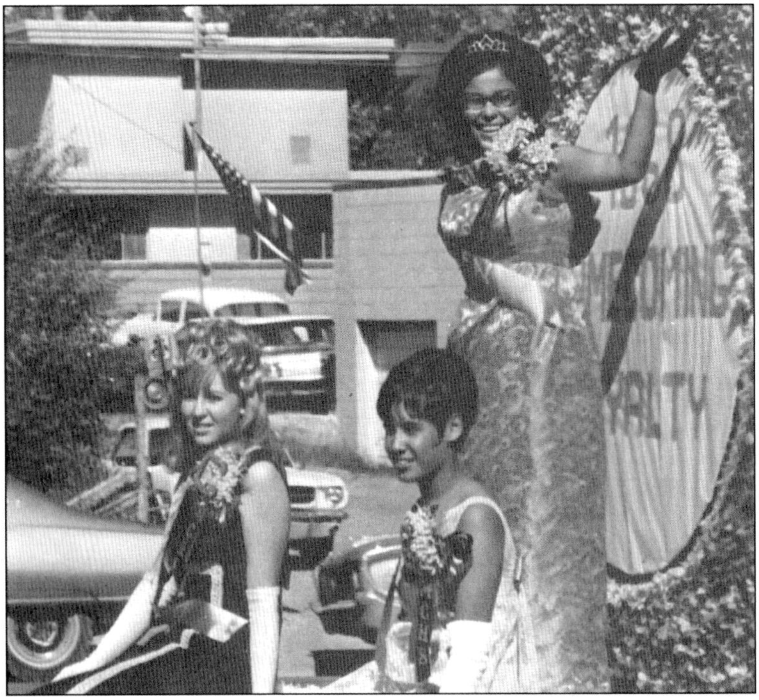

Homecoming royalty for Montezuma County High School in the fall of 1968 reflected the civil rights changes the nation was undergoing. Cheryl Neskahi, a Navajo, was elected queen. Zenda Ruiz, a Hispanic-Filipina, and Rolana Adams, an Anglo American, were runners-up. (Photograph from 1969 MCHS yearbook.)

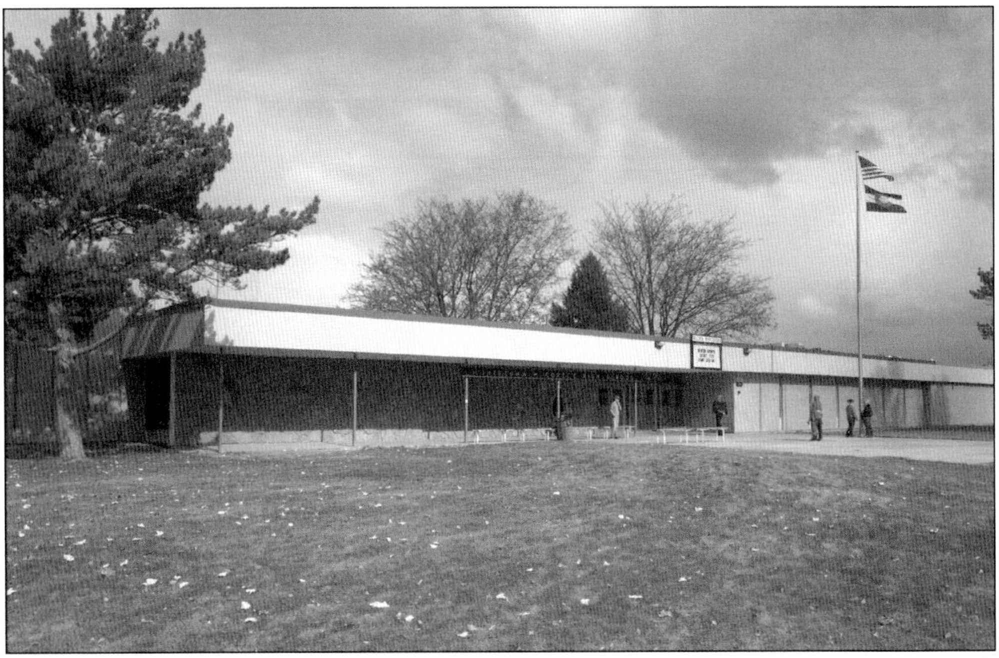

Montezuma County and Cortez built a new high school for their students on West Seventh Street. Its first senior class graduated in 1968. This current photograph shows the school much as it looked then, less the landscaping. With Cortez's growth in economy and population, the school's name was eventually changed to Montezuma-Cortez High School. In 2010, the district opened discussions to determine if another new school is needed, as demographics and populations continue to change. (Photograph by Barbara Grist Photography.)

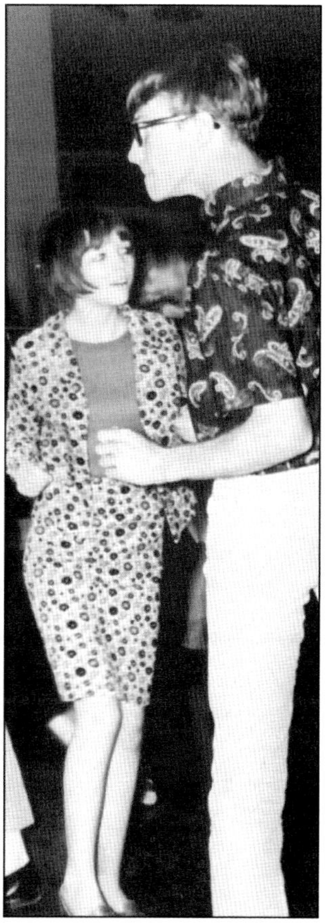

Seniors David Cantrell and Karen Bunde rock to the music at a school dance. Paisley and "flower power" prints were popular with youth because of the British invasion. (Photograph from 1968 MCHS yearbook.)

The Cortez area's music departments have always been strong. In 1974, the choral group Colorado's Children performed popular music around the larger community. Members included, from left to right, (first row) Stanley McNeil and Corey Brubaker; (second row) Terry Bessy, Carol Cromar, Jim McRae, Carolyn Hindmarsh, Kathie Allmon, Teresa Craig, Debbie Diffendaffer, and Cindy Gray; (third row) David Snair, Mike Stockdale, Bonnie McGettrick, Judy Wilson, Cindy Fowler, Laureen Fene, Sandy Fene, and Brad Stauffer; (fourth row) Jody Randol. (Photograph from 1975 MCHS yearbook.)

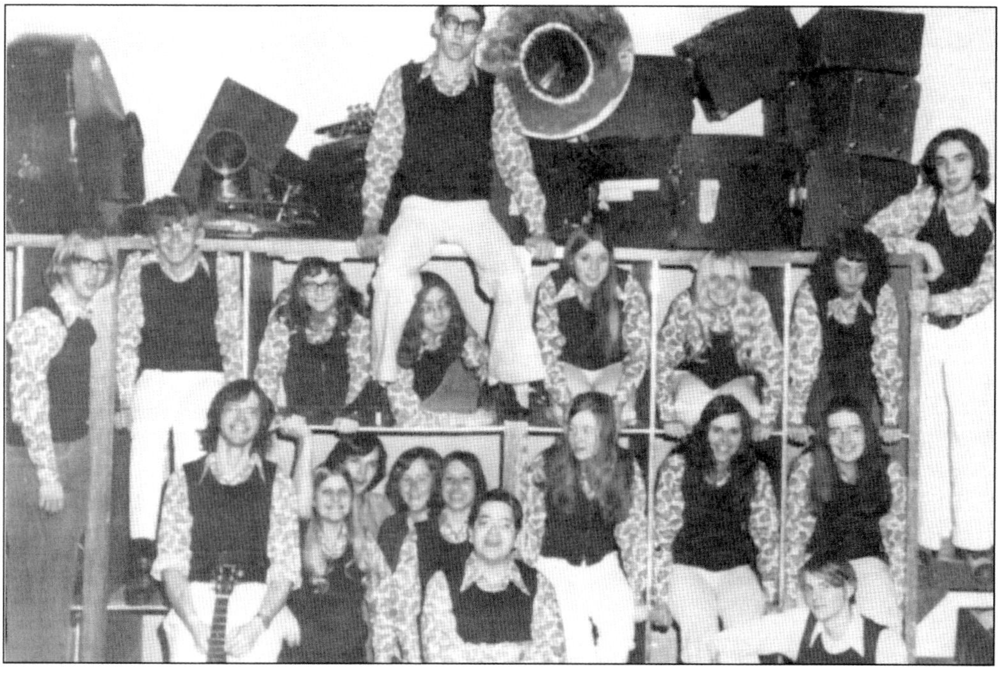

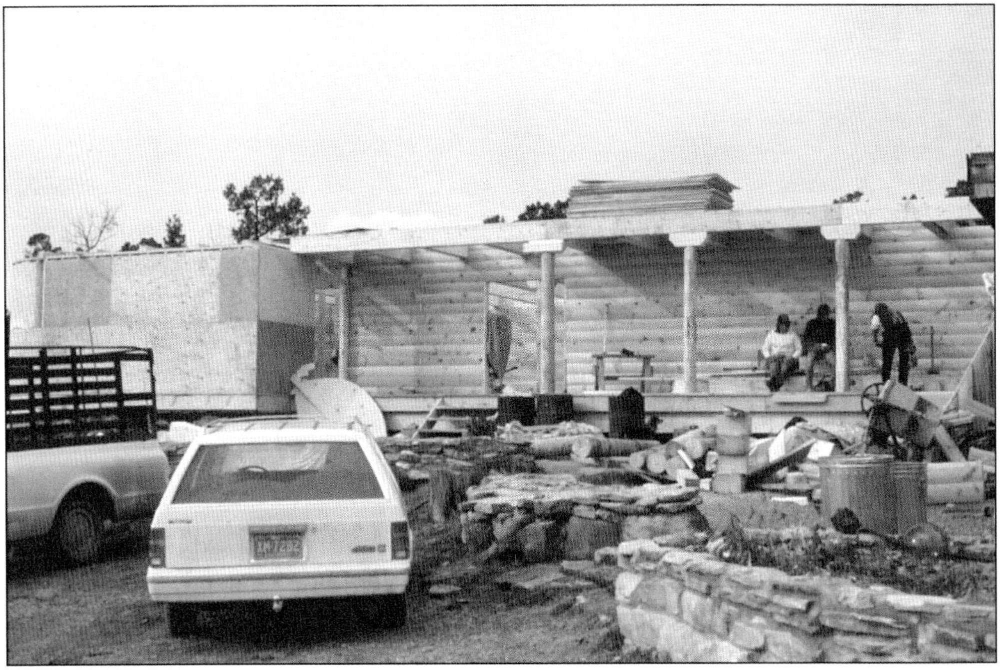

In the 1970s, Dr. Edward and Jo Berger created Crow Canyon School on a low budget but a big idea. They wanted students to find excitement in learning by working alongside professional archaeologists in the field and laboratory. (Courtesy of Crow Canyon Archaeological Center.)

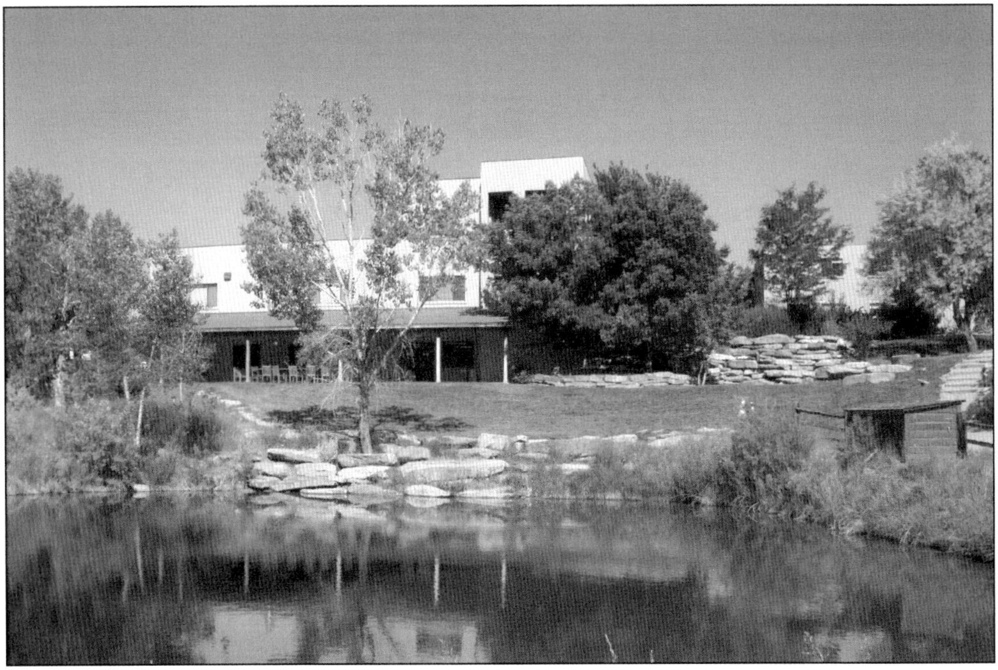

In 1985, Crow Canyon Archaeological Center emerged as a nonprofit, focusing on research and education. The center's programs, for students of all ages, matured through a decade-long study of the archaeology of the nearby Sand Canyon Anasazi site, the development of computerized databases, and the creation of a publications division. (Courtesy of Crow Canyon Archaeological Center.)

As principal investigator, Dr. David A. Breternitz spearheaded the University of Colorado's efforts to survey archaeological sites that would be covered by McPhee reservoir waters. The Dolores Archaeological Program was funded by the Bureau of Reclamation, Department of the Interior. Breternitz has since retired and lives north of Cortez. (Courtesy of Anasazi Heritage Center.)

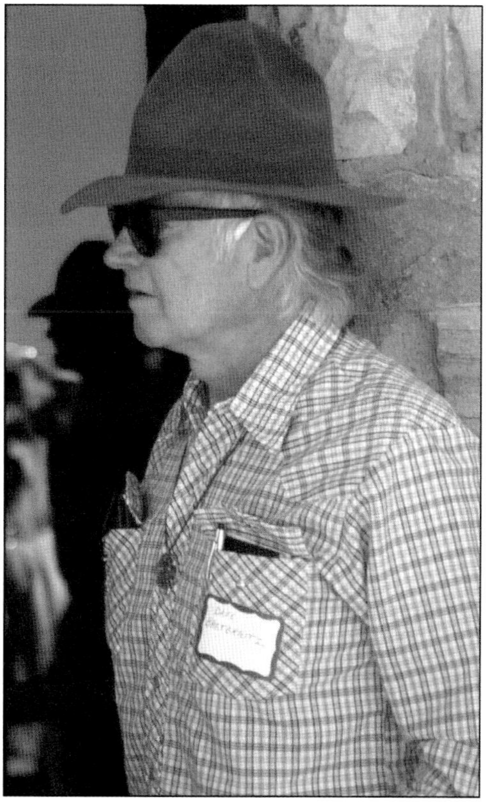

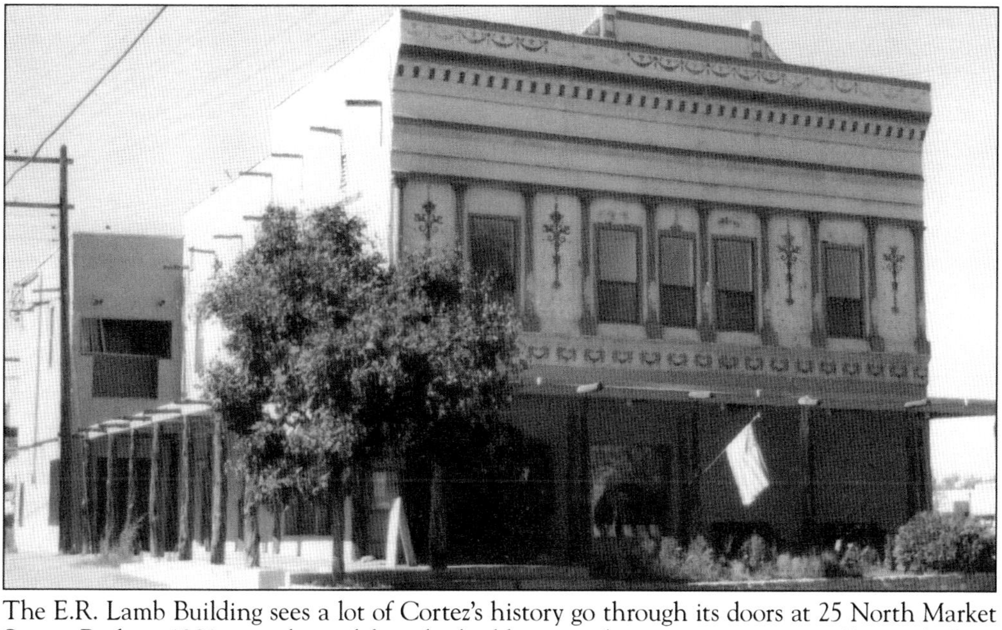

The E.R. Lamb Building sees a lot of Cortez's history go through its doors at 25 North Market Street. Built in 1908 to withstand fire, the building now houses a museum, a gallery, gift shop, classrooms, a library, and Cortez Cultural Center offices. In the 1980s, the building was known as the CU Center and held archaeological research offices as well as being a cultural center. (Courtesy of Cortez Cultural Center.)

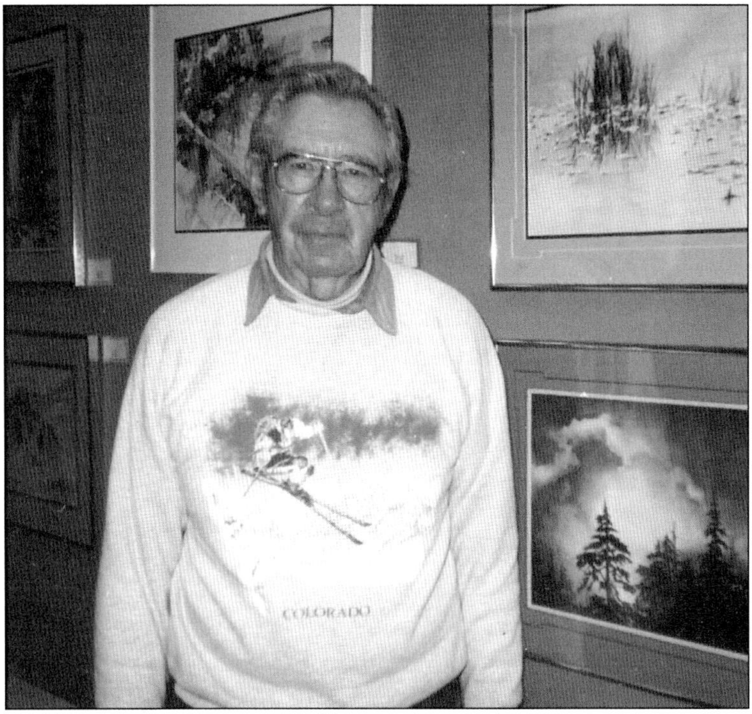

Buford Wayt encouraged music, art, and cultural pursuits his whole life in Cortez. He designed and led the team that painted the mural on the north side of the Cortez Cultural Center, led the high school band and choir for years, and directed a community choral group, among many other leadership activities. (Courtesy of Cortez Cultural Center.)

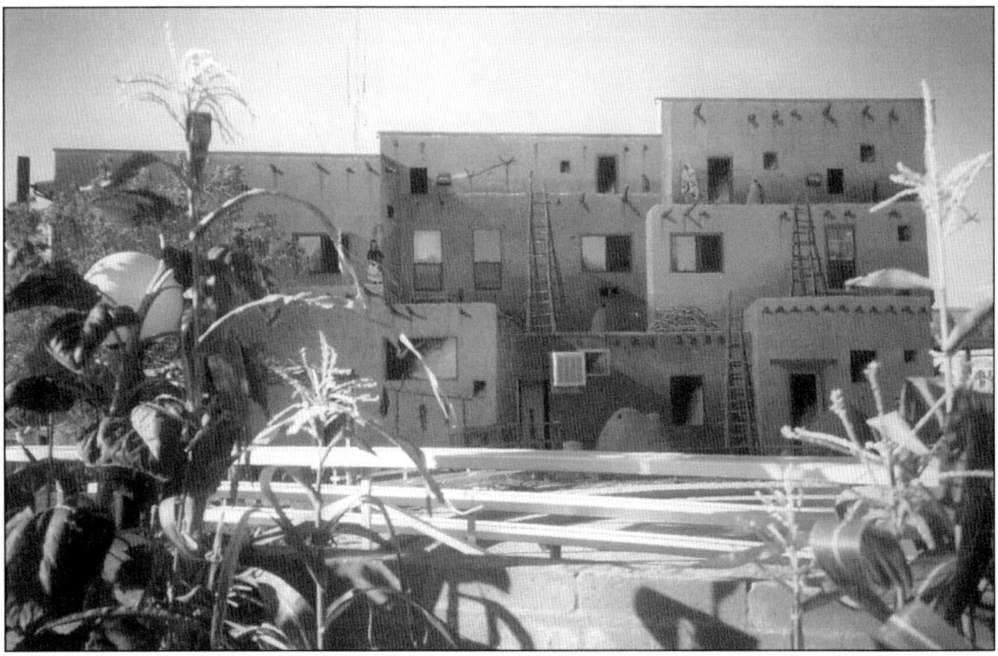

From a distance, the Cultural Center's mural appears to be an actual pueblo. The Cortez Cultural Center's dance plaza, where American Indian dances are held most evenings during the summer tourist season, stands in front. (Courtesy of Cortez Cultural Center.)

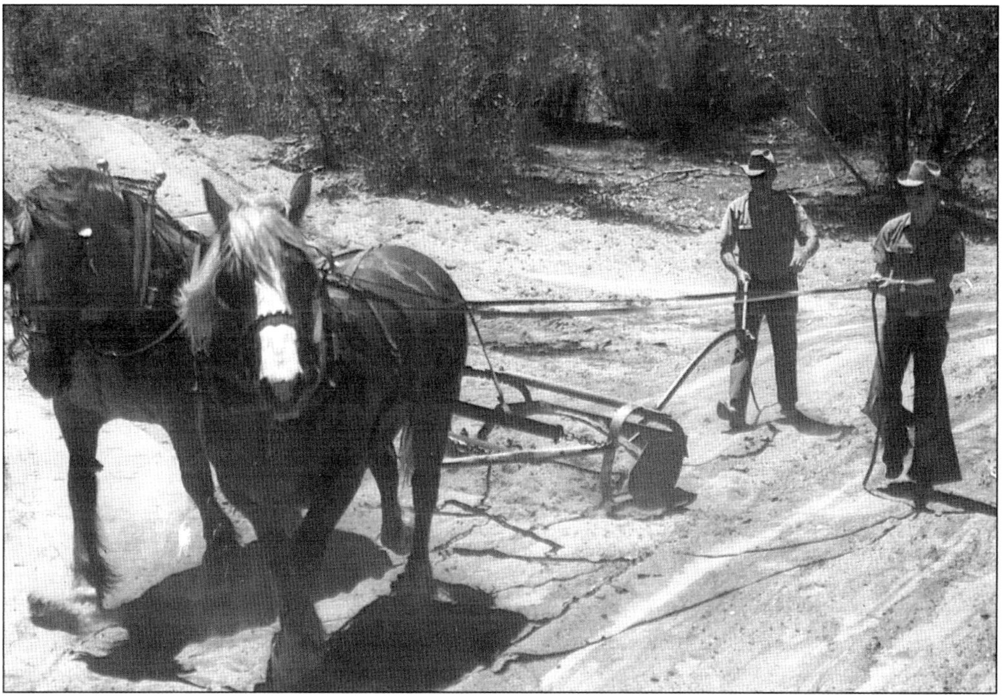

This modern photograph of a horse-drawn Fresno illustrates how Narraguinnep and Groundhog reservoirs were dredged out of natural terrain to hold water for the incoming human population. (Courtesy of William B. Finley.)

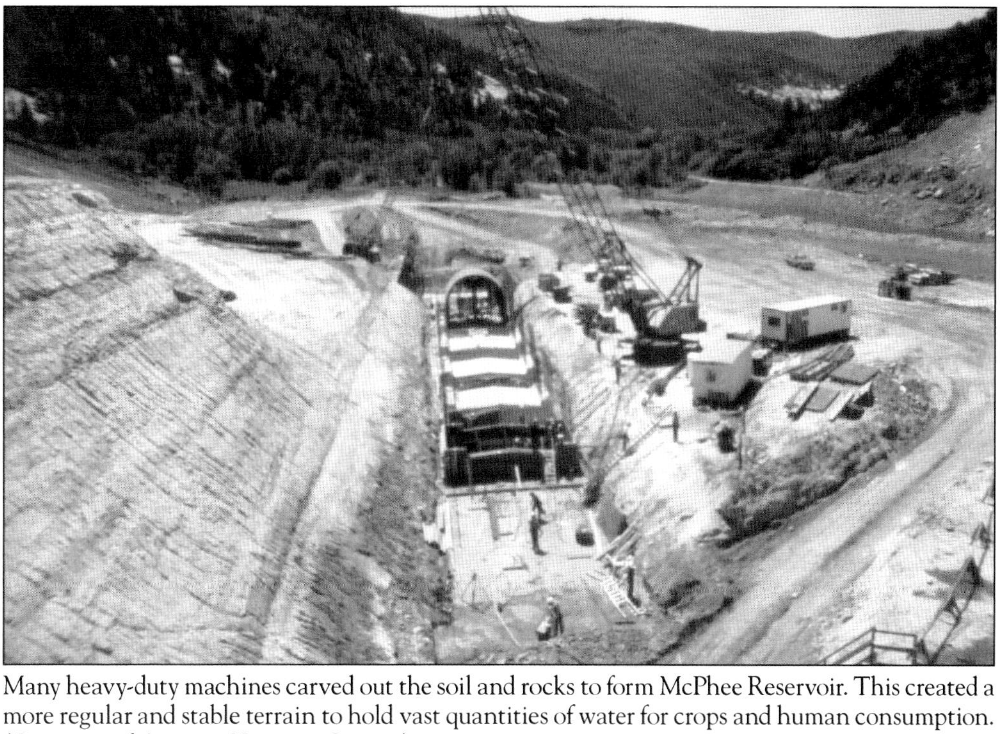

Many heavy-duty machines carved out the soil and rocks to form McPhee Reservoir. This created a more regular and stable terrain to hold vast quantities of water for crops and human consumption. (Courtesy of Anasazi Heritage Center.)

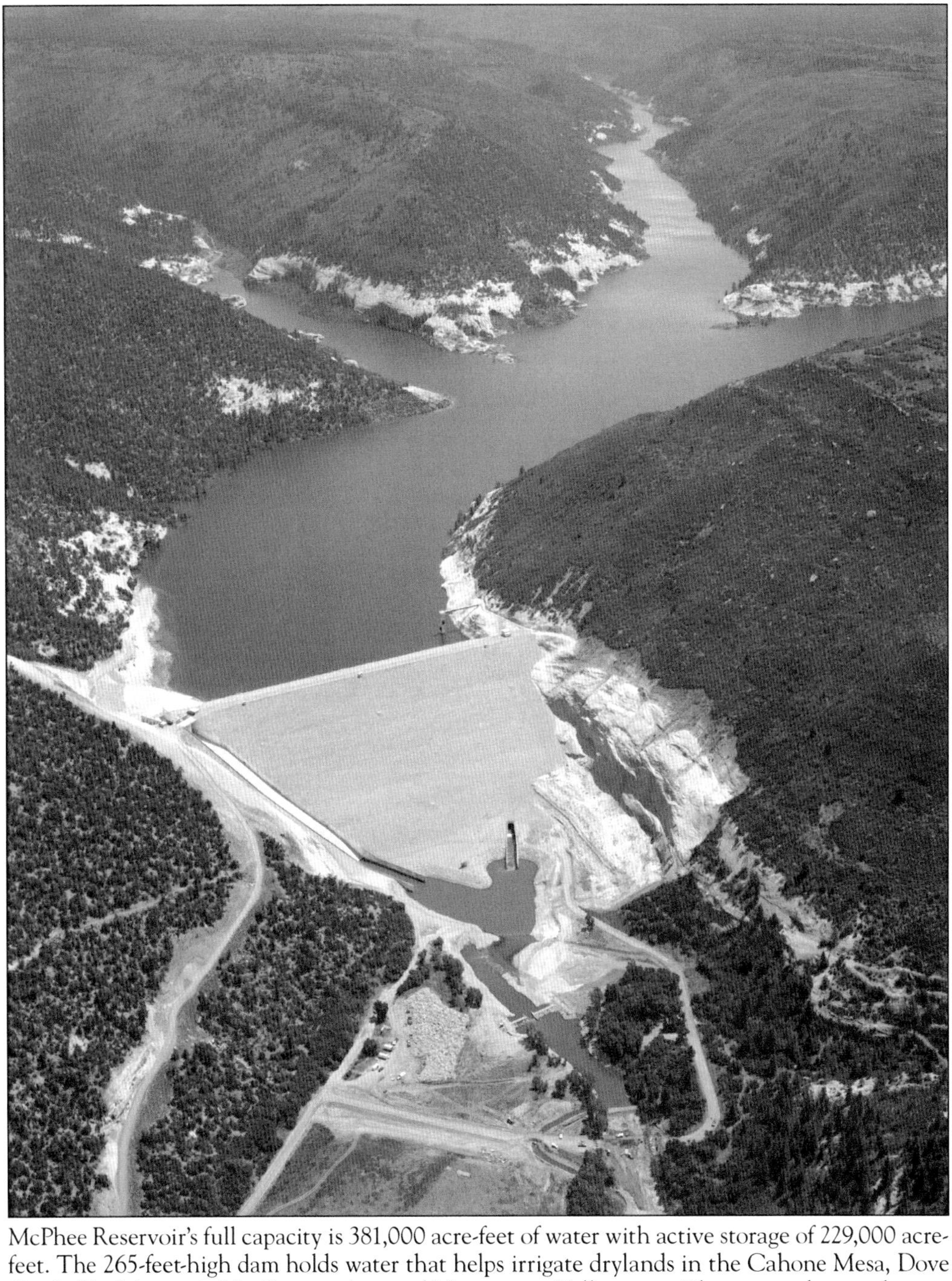

McPhee Reservoir's full capacity is 381,000 acre-feet of water with active storage of 229,000 acre-feet. The 265-feet-high dam holds water that helps irrigate drylands in the Cahone Mesa, Dove Creek, Ute Mountain Ute Reservation, and Montezuma Valley areas. The waters also supplement irrigated lands and provide municipal water to Cortez, Cahone, Pleasant View, and Dove Creek. Water for recreation is an additional benefit. McPhee Reservoir is located 10 miles north of Cortez, off State Highway 184. (Courtesy of Anasazi Heritage Center.)

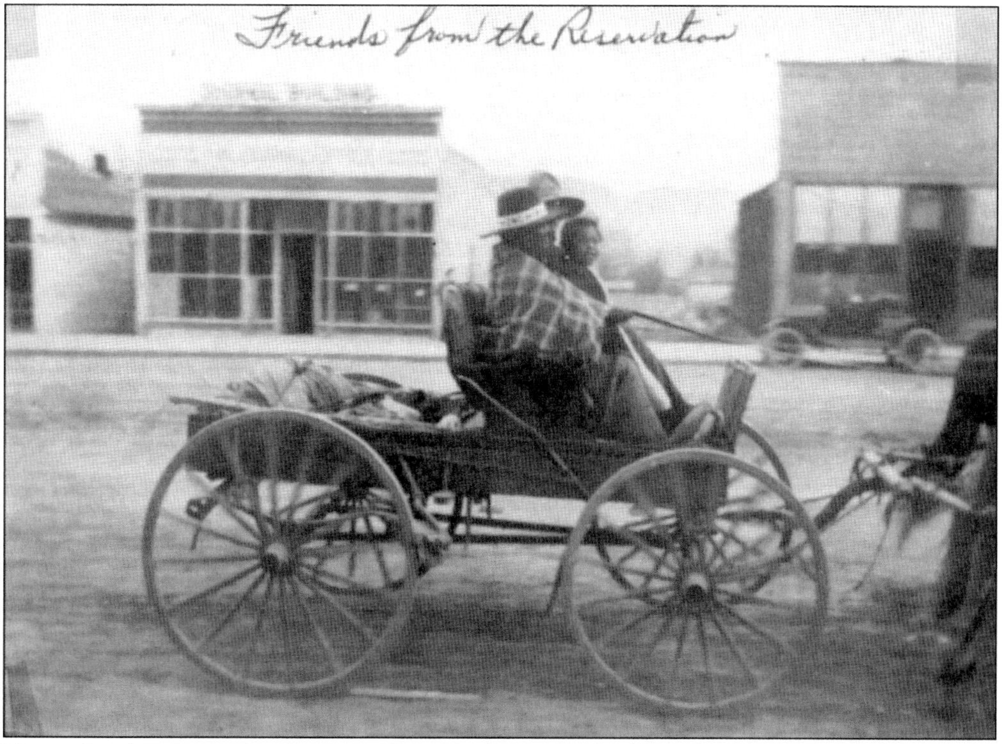

Navajo families shopped in Cortez in the early days, using buckboards to transport trade items and their purchases. They drove many miles from their homes in the Four Corners states, on what were often dirt tracks through sagebrush and canyons, to trade. (Courtesy of Cortez Newspapers.)

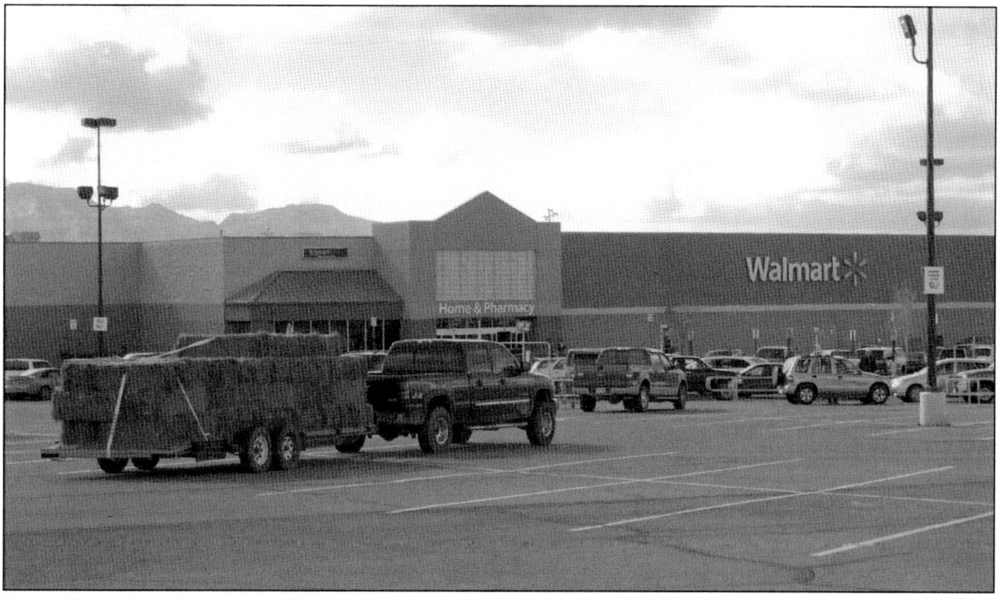

Nowadays, the Navajo people drive large pickup trucks from homes faraway to shop in Cortez for food and supplies for themselves and their livestock. Shelves in big-box stores provide the goods instead of shelves in stores such as Sam Walker's mercantile (pictured on page 60). (Photograph by Barbara Grist Photography.)

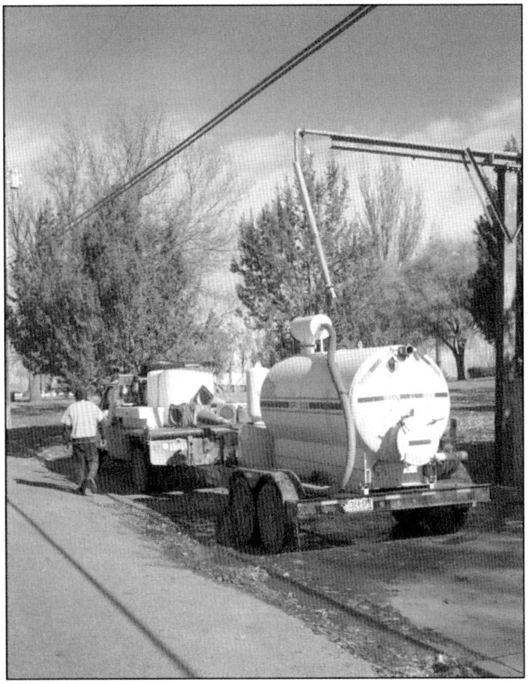

Water distribution is still an issue in the arid and sparsely populated Southwest. Most towns in the area provide an industrial-size outlet so families and households can haul tanks of water to their homes in areas where it is still too expensive to pipe water. (Photograph by Barbara Grist Photography.)

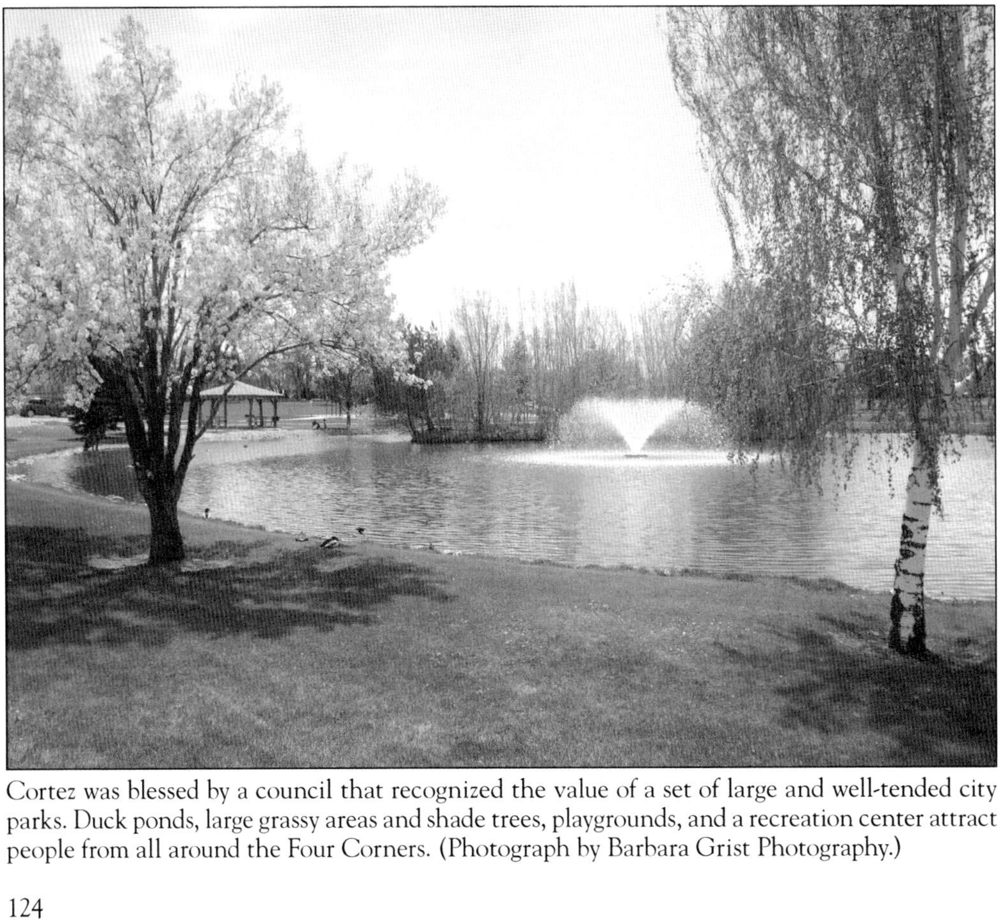

Cortez was blessed by a council that recognized the value of a set of large and well-tended city parks. Duck ponds, large grassy areas and shade trees, playgrounds, and a recreation center attract people from all around the Four Corners. (Photograph by Barbara Grist Photography.)

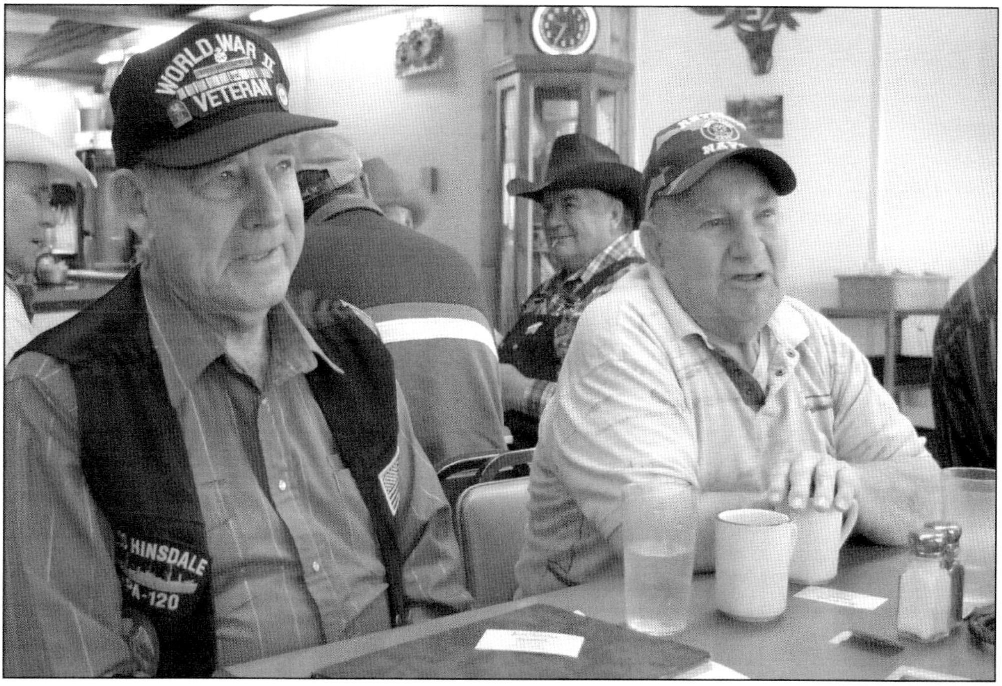

Members of the 1940s Kilroy Club, Jack Winbourn and Lonnie Dennison, discuss their common history at the Ute Café in Cortez. Winbourn is a member of the Montezuma County Historical Society and is descended from one of the earliest families to settle Montezuma Valley. Dennison has passed on since the photograph was taken. (Courtesy of Cortez Journal.)

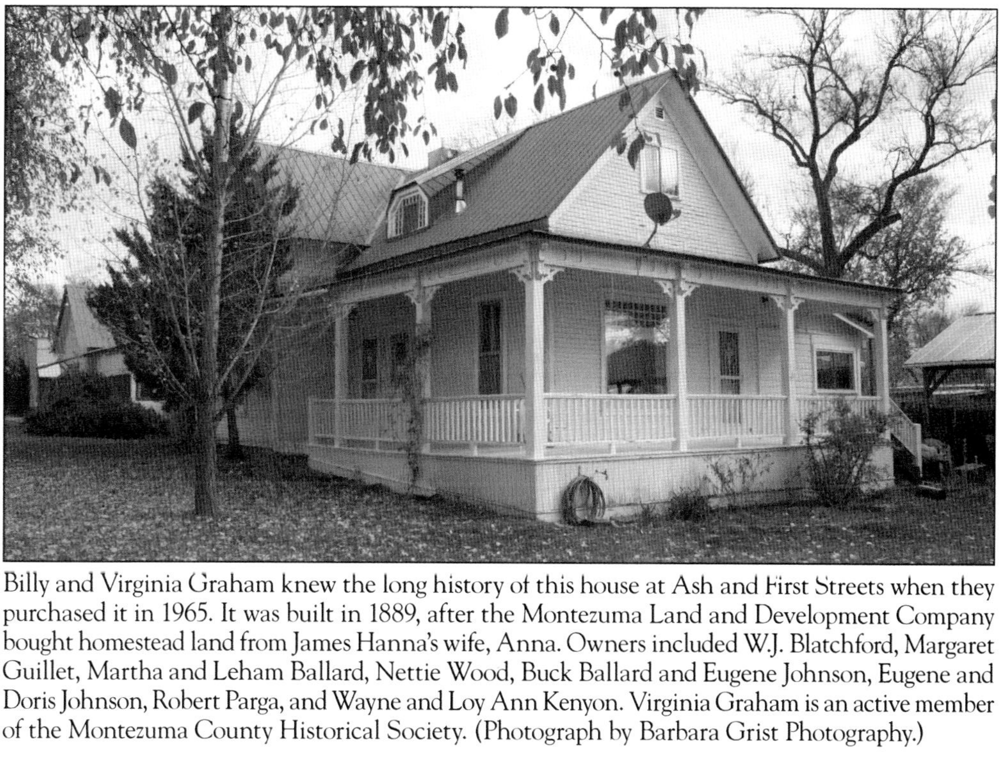

Billy and Virginia Graham knew the long history of this house at Ash and First Streets when they purchased it in 1965. It was built in 1889, after the Montezuma Land and Development Company bought homestead land from James Hanna's wife, Anna. Owners included W.J. Blatchford, Margaret Guillet, Martha and Leham Ballard, Nettie Wood, Buck Ballard and Eugene Johnson, Eugene and Doris Johnson, Robert Parga, and Wayne and Loy Ann Kenyon. Virginia Graham is an active member of the Montezuma County Historical Society. (Photograph by Barbara Grist Photography.)

Bibliography

Amundson, Michael A. *Yellow Towns: Uranium Mining Communities in the American West.* University of Colorado Press: Boulder, CO, 2002.

Bankston, Wilma Crisp. *Where Eagles Winter: History and Legends of the Disappointment Country.* Mesa Verde Press, Inc.: Cortez, CO, 1987.

Blackburn, Fred M. *The Wetherills: Friends of Mesa Verde.* Durango Herald Small Press: Durango, CO, 2006.

Burton, Lloyd. *American Indian Water Rights and the Limits of the Law.* University of Kansas Press: Lawrence, KS, 1991.

Byrne, Bernard J., M.D. *A Frontier Army Surgeon: Life in Colorado in the Eighties.* Exposition Press, New York, New York, 1935.

———. "*Cortez: The Town That Wanted to Be.*" Supplement to the *Cortez Sentinel:* Cortez, CO, 1986.

Delaney, Robert W. *The Ute Mountain Utes.* University of New Mexico Press: Albuquerque, NM, 1989.

Ellis, Fern. *Come Back to My Valley: Historical Remembrances of Mancos, Colorado.* Cortez Printers: Cortez, CO, 1976.

Freeman, Ira S. *A History of Montezuma County Colorado: Land of Promise and Fulfillment.* Johnson Publishing Company: Boulder CO, 1958.

Head, June and Virginia Graham, eds. *Great Sage to Timberline "Our Pioneer History" Vol. 1.* Montezuma County Historical Society: Cortez, CO, November 2009.

———. *Great Sage to Timberline "Our Pioneer History" Vol. 2.* Montezuma County Historical Society: Cortez, CO, May 2010.

K., Molly. *Montezuma's Trails of Time.* M.K. Wardrip: Cortez, CO, 1993.

Kendrick, Gregory D., ed. *The River of Sorrows: The History of the Lower Dolores River Valley.* US Department of the Interior, National Park Service: Rocky Mountain Regional Office, N.D.

McNitt, Frank. *The Indian Traders.* University of Oklahoma Press: Norman, OK, 1962.

McPherson, Robert S. *A History of San Juan County.* Utah State Historical Society: Salt Lake City, UT, 1995.

O'Rourke, Paul M. *Frontier in Transition: A History of Southwestern Colorado.* US Department of Interior, Bureau of Land Management, Cultural Resource Series No. 10, Government Printing Office: Washington, DC, 1992.

———. "*Plane Flames Out Over Cortez: Jet Pilot Can Thank His Lucky Stars.*" *Montezuma Valley Journal,* August 6, 1959, Vol. 72, No. 39, p. 1A.

Robison, Anna Florence, Taped Interviews. Dolores, CO, 1934.

Skovlin, Jon M. and Donna McDaniel Skovlin. *In Pursuit of the McCartys.* Reflections Publishing Company: Cove, OR, 2001.

Southwestern Cowbelles. *'Pert Near Never Got Nowhere: A Collection of History Compiled by the Southwestern Cowbelles, Mostly True.* Southwestern Cowbelles: Cortez, CO, 1979.

———. *'Pert Near #2: Compiled by the Southwestern Cowbelles, Mostly True.* Southwestern Cowbelles: Cortez, CO, 2004.
Sturtevant, William C., Gen. Ed., Ortiz, Alfonso, Vol. Ed. *Handbook of North American Indians, Vol. 9: Southwest.* Smithsonian Institution: Washington DC, 1979.
——— *Handbook of North American Indians, Vol. 10: Southwest.* Smithsonian Institution: Washington, DC, 1983.
Sturtevant, William C., Gen. Ed., Warren L. d'Azevedo, Vol. Ed. *Handbook of North American Indians, Vol. 11: Great Basin.* Smithsonian Institution: Washington, DC, 1986.
Ubbelohde, Carl, Maxine Benson, and Duane Smith. *A Colorado History.* Pruett Press, Inc.: Boulder, CO, 1976.
Warner, Pat, with updates by Joyce Warner and Dr. Steve Lacy. *Last of the Bandit Riders . . . Revisited.* Big Moon Traders: Salt Lake City, UT, 2000.
Wilkenson, Charles F. *Crossing the Next Meridian: Land, Water, and the Future of the West. Island Press:* Washington, DC, 1992.
Young, Richard Keith. *The Ute Indians of Colorado in the Twentieth Century.* University of Oklahoma Press: Norman, 1977.

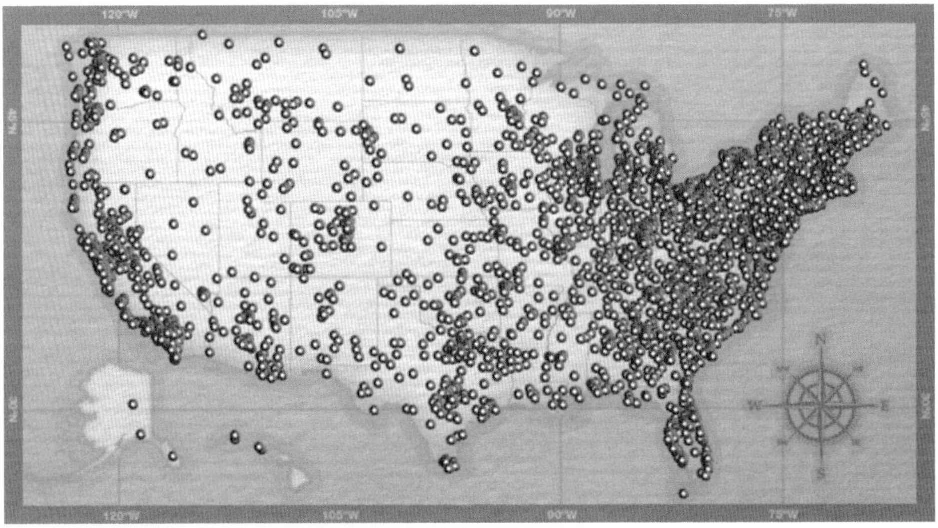